Pan American Women

Pan American Women

U.S. Internationalists and Revolutionary Mexico

Megan Threlkeld

PENN

UNIVERSITY OF PENNSYLVANIA PRESS

PHILADELPHIA

POLITICS AND CULTURE IN MODERN AMERICA

Series Editors
Margot Canaday, Glenda Gilmore, Michael Kazin, Thomas J. Sugrue, and Stephen Pitti

Volumes in the series narrate and analyze political and social change in the broadest dimensions
from 1865 to the present, including ideas about the ways people have sought and wielded power
in the public sphere and the language and institutions of politics at all levels—local, national,
and transnational. The series is motivated by a desire to reverse the fragmentation of modern
U.S. history and to encourage synthetic perspectives on social movements and the state, on
gender, race, and labor, and on intellectual history and popular culture.

Copyright © 2014 University of Pennsylvania Press

Published by
University of Pennsylvania Press
Philadelphia, Pennsylvania 19104-4112
www.upenn.edu/pennpress

Printed in the United States of America on acid-free paper
2 4 6 8 10 9 7 5 3 1

A Cataloging-in-Publication Record is available from the Library of Congress
ISBN 978-0-8122-4633-9

Frontispiece: Pan American Unity Mural: *The Marriage of the Artistic Expression of the North and
of the South on this Continent*, Diego Rivera. Courtesy of City College of San Francisco,
©2013 Banco de México Diego Rivera Frida Kahlo Museums Trust, Mexico, D.F. /
Artists Rights Society (ARS), New York.

For Trey

Contents

Introduction

In the summer of 1931, Ellen Starr Brinton, a pacifist from Pennsylvania, traveled to Mexico City as a representative of the Women's International League for Peace and Freedom (WILPF), which had been founded during World War I by activists in the United States and Europe. Part of Brinton's mission was to solicit topics on U.S.-Latin American relations for study and discussion by the U.S. section of WILPF. To that end she met with several groups of women students in Mexico City, who provided her with what she called "irritating suggestions." Their list of potential topics included Mexicans' hatred of the United States, discriminatory attitudes toward Mexican students in the United States, and "appropriation by residents of the U.S. of the term 'Americans, or North Americans.'" All U.S. Americans had an "irritating superiority attitude," the students told Brinton. "Your manners in this country suggest that you feel yourselves above us, and make us conscious that the United States is a powerful nation. You 'high hat' everyone you meet. Naturally we do not like it." They compared the segregation of Mexican students in the United States to that of African Americans, arguing it was done not with regard to "intelligence or language, but entirely as a matter of *race*." Finally, they resented what they saw as misuse of a key term. "We are Americans as well," the students informed Brinton. "You should call yourselves E---- U---- (using the Spanish equivalent of 'United Statesians')." When Brinton, bewildered, replied that there was no such word in English, "the serene answer was that we should get one."[1]

Brinton's bewilderment and irritation—and the Mexican students' frustration—capture the tensions between U.S. women's internationalist ideals and Mexican women's nationalist aspirations that lie at the heart of this book. Brinton and her colleagues in WILPF and in other U.S. organizations saw themselves as leaders of a globalizing women's movement that originated in the United States and Europe but had reached most of Latin America only recently. They believed they had much to teach women throughout the Americas about their campaigns for international peace, women's rights, and other causes. As Brinton's attempt at information gathering suggests, they also believed they had something to learn from Latin American women. But Brinton's irritation indicates she did not get the kinds of responses to her questions that she expected. The young women with whom she met demanded that Brinton recognize her own subject position as a "United Statesian," and that she acknowledge the larger relationship between the United States and Mexico that framed this encounter between women of the two nations. They further demanded that Brinton confront her own implicit presumption that the United States was representative of all "America." Like many U.S. women involved in activism across nations and cultures at this time, Brinton believed that her identity as a woman would allow her to forge bonds with women in Mexico and other Latin American countries. She assumed that even amid differences of race and nationality, gender would provide common ground on which all American women could build hemispheric connections. When the Mexican students continued to draw attention to her nationality, Brinton floundered.

What follows is an investigation of how women like Ellen Starr Brinton negotiated challenges to their internationalist ambitions like the ones posed by these Mexican students. *Pan American Women* examines U.S. women's efforts to advance inter-American cooperation among women and to further hemispheric peace between the world wars. I focus on U.S. women's work in Mexico, where diplomatic tensions and the ongoing Mexican Revolution heightened the significance of their enterprise. With different and sometimes competing agendas, groups like WILPF, the Young Women's Christian Association (YWCA), the League of Women Voters (LWV), and the Inter-American Commission of Women (IACW) tried to organize Mexican women and to influence U.S. foreign policy toward Mexico. They convened conferences, established in Mexico City new associations and new branches of existing ones, and rallied popular support in the United States for peaceful relations. On several occasions during the 1920s and 1930s they congratulated themselves on having propelled policy makers toward peace. They also grew more sophisticated in their methods, abandoning gendered arguments and appeals to womanhood in favor of more modern, politically savvy tactics.

But by the outbreak of World War II, many of their efforts among Mexican women had collapsed. Scarce resources and the growing threats in Europe and Asia contributed to this decline, but circumstantial explanations are insufficient. Even with their authority on the issues and their years of experience, U.S. women struggled to effect change in Mexico, to convince women living within a very different political and social context of the efficacy of U.S. methods and goals. The absence of a stable democracy in Mexico, for instance, gave women there a different perspective on suffrage and the significance of the vote. U.S. women's appeals to peace and nonviolence, meanwhile, felt to some Mexican women like a thinly veiled directive to abandon their Revolution.

U.S. women internationalists overestimated the viability of their agendas in Mexico because they assumed their ideals were universal enough to apply readily. They often brushed aside or ignored input from Mexican women that reflected the specific issues and challenges they faced. At the very moment that U.S. women were seeking to engage Mexican women and incorporate them into international networks, Mexican women were trying to negotiate the social and political upheaval of the Mexican Revolution—a fiercely nationalist revolution fueled in part by a reaction against decades of exploitative U.S. economic and foreign policies. As a result, U.S. women found themselves in a difficult position as they tried to forge gendered bonds in Mexico. At the same time that these U.S. internationalists were looking beyond their own borders and promoting global cooperation, Mexican women were becoming politicized in ways that tied them more closely to their own nation. U.S. internationalists envisioned "worlds of women" beyond the borders of nation-states, and beyond the nationalism that they argued had led to a world war.[2] Mexican women saw in the Revolution an opportunity to claim their national citizenship in previously unavailable ways. For U.S. women, nationalism was an ethos to be overcome; for Mexican women it was an identity and a strategy to be embraced. To U.S. women, internationalism represented the path to a more peaceful and equitable future. To Mexican women, internationalist rhetoric often seemed like old patterns of U.S. hegemony in a new guise. Even as many U.S. women protested U.S. imperialism in Latin America, they replicated imperialist patterns in their own organizations. Even as they abandoned an idealized, "spiritual" internationalism in favor of more politically sophisticated approaches, they failed to adapt their movement to the particular needs of Mexican women. They grew skilled at using international platforms to advance their agendas, but still could not forge lasting bonds. These were the tensions that underlay Ellen Starr Brinton's experience in Mexico City.

Defining Women's Internationalism

Both in terms of their ideology and their activism, Brinton and her WILPF colleagues adhered to what I term "women's internationalism." This concept has received increasing attention from historians over the last twenty years, though not all of them label it as such. What began in the 1990s with historian Leila Rupp's exploration of the communities and collective identities of the International Council of Women, the International Woman Suffrage Alliance (later the International Alliance of Women), and WILPF has grown slowly but surely into a field richly populated with studies of other organizations and other dimensions of the global interactions among women between the mid-nineteenth and early twentieth centuries.[3] I will address the thorny question of "internationalism" before I attempt to define the concept as a whole. For Rupp's subjects, internationalism was a "spirit rather than a formal ideology." Words such as "feeling" and "force" conveyed "the almost mystical quality of internationalism as an imagined community."[4] The term also had particular significance in the early twentieth century apart from its practice by women. As an ideal for cooperation among nation-states and for the creation of supranational systems of law and governance, it drew followers even as the great powers expanded their empires and careened toward World War I. Internationalism found its ultimate expression in the ideology of U.S. President Woodrow Wilson, who envisioned the League of Nations (led by the United States) as the center of a just, peaceful world order.[5] These visions of a world without war, characterized by the spread of democracy and human rights, significantly informed the ethos of women internationalists during this period.

I find most useful diplomatic historian Akira Iriye's broad definition of internationalism as a "global consciousness," the "idea that nations and peoples should cooperate instead of preoccupying themselves with their respective national interests or pursuing uncoordinated approaches to promote them."[6] Many of the women with whom I am concerned held this idea very dear; they argued that women had both an opportunity and a duty to take part in internationalist work. With one exception, the organizations to which they belonged are best characterized as nongovernmental organizations. These organizations began to emerge over the course of the nineteenth century, born from an awareness that "they shared certain interests and objectives across national boundaries" and "could best solve their many problems by pooling their resources and effecting transnational cooperation."[7] Beginning as early as the 1840s, educated women in the United States sought to participate in and began to form their own such organizations.

Not all scholars agree on the differences between "internationalism" and "transnationalism." Historians of U.S. foreign relations, among others, have used the former to denote formal relations among nation-states, and the latter to describe the movement of people, goods, and ideas across national boundaries.[8] Among women's historians, by contrast, "internationalism" has generally been used to characterize activism across borders before 1945, and "transnationalism" to describe the period after World War II and especially since the 1970s. As historians Ellen Carol DuBois and Katie Oliviero have observed, "The distinction was meant to pose an opposition between the multiple, diverse, worldwide voices speaking on behalf of women's needs and rights in our own era, and the allegedly hegemonic, falsely monolithic, Eurocentric leadership of an earlier period." These and other scholars have challenged the rigidity of that distinction, arguing that the transnationalist feminism of the later twentieth century had important precursors that deserve to be labeled as such, but they acknowledge that differences remain between the organizations of the earlier period and the "less formal networks of interactions" of the later one.[9]

For my purposes, the term "internationalism" indicates the primacy of nationality and of the nation-state as foundational principles within a given organization, while "transnationalism" conveys the primacy of an organization's subjects, objects, or goals and methods. Internationalist groups worked among nations; transnationalist groups worked across them. The division between the two categories is not absolute. It may shift depending on an analysis of an organization's agenda versus its accomplishments. For example, in the 1930s the Inter-American Commission of Women took a transnationalist approach in its efforts to secure a hemispheric treaty protecting the legal nationality of women who married foreign-born men, a measure designed to protect women in all American countries. But structurally, the commission was composed of twenty-one women, one from each American nation, and it was created by the Pan American Union, an intergovernmental organization. Furthermore, legislation protecting married women's nationality had to be secured by separate national governments. In these respects the composition of the commission was internationalist in nature. The history of women's organizing across national boundaries suggests that the categories of internationalist and

transnationalist are two points on a continuum rather than either-or definitions, but they are useful distinctions, not least when examining U.S.
women's intentions and accomplishments in Latin America.[10] I refer in this
book to "transnationalism" when appropriate, but I use "internationalism"
to signal U.S. women's inability to dissociate themselves—consciously or
unconsciously—from their national identities and from their assumption
of national superiority over Latin Americans.

For the women I study, internationalism was first and foremost a spirit
and a practice of cooperation among women from different nations to
advance common interests, especially peace. What then made this *women's*
internationalism? First, an assumption by its practitioners that their methods were gendered. Jane Addams, for instance, founder of the Hull-House
settlement in Chicago and later president of WILPF, distinguished between
what she saw as masculine realms of international diplomacy, characterized
by formal, officially sanctioned exchanges among men, and the nongovernmental, less formal, interpersonal modes of exchange among women.[11]
Women, Addams and her supporters argued, were suited by nature and
habit to interact on a personal level. If cultivated properly, those personal
exchanges could grow and flourish to a point at which shared experiences
and shared knowledge of peoples and cultures across national boundaries
could do as much to prevent war as any diplomatic treaty. Addams referred
to this as "human internationalism," to differentiate it from what she saw
as impersonal, formal agreements and interactions among governments.
Other proponents took this gendered argument one step further, claiming
that motherhood endowed women with the authority to promote peace. At
a women's peace conference in 1915 U.S. suffragist Carrie Chapman Catt
encouraged her audience to take up the internationalist banner: "O, my
sisters, this, henceforth, is the especial task of the World's Mothers. . . . It
is for us to foster Internationalism, that promise of the civilization yet to
come."[12] According to Catt, and to other women alarmed by the outbreak
of violence in Europe, women's roles as mothers both authorized and obli-
gated them to explore and endorse alternatives to war.

Second, I use "women's internationalism" to denote cooperation across
borders in the interest of advancing women's status. Doris Stevens, the first
chair of the Inter-American Commission of Women, did not share
Addams's and Catt's belief that women's nature as social beings or their
experiences as mothers drove them to enact internationalism in gendered
ways. During her tenure with the IACW, Stevens used whatever methods

she could to advance her goals of securing hemispheric treaties on married women's nationality and women's equal rights. In some instances she cultivated personal relationships with women in ways that evoked Addams's practices; in others she lobbied male diplomats and drafted legislation just as any nongovernmental agent or organization might do. But her goal, the function of her internationalism, was to recognize and to secure women's rights on a global scale.[13] This was a less idealistic, more sophisticated approach to internationalism, and its adherents were often younger and more politically shrewd in their methods. Clearly, there was significant potential for overlap between these two definitions of women's internationalism, but they remained distinct approaches.

This is a history of internationalism, but it is not an internationalist history. Where other recent works have been concerned with the impact of internationalist ideas in other parts of the world, my primary focus is on U.S. women and their organizations.[14] More specifically, I am interested in national organizations rather than regional ones. There were myriad charitable and service organizations begun along the U.S.-Mexico border in response to the influx of refugees after 1911, like the Pan American Round Table of San Antonio, Texas, but their agendas were local rather than hemispheric. I am also interested in secular groups rather than explicitly religious and missionary ones whose primary purpose was to proselytize. There were hundreds if not thousands of Protestant missionaries in Mexico during the Revolution, significant numbers of whom were women.[15] But they did not see themselves as internationalists like Jane Addams or Doris Stevens, and their goal was to win converts, not to promote peace or advance women's status.

Changing Dynamics

By the 1910s, international organizations and connections among women across national borders were well-established phenomena. As early as the 1830s, educated upper- and middle-class women in the United States and western Europe were exchanging letters and visits in which they discussed their common struggles for women's rights, abolition, temperance, and other causes. These early networks laid the foundations for the organizations that developed by the 1880s.[16] The International Council of Women, established in 1888, was the first organization dedicated to connecting women around the world. Other significant groups included the World Woman's Christian Temperance Union and the International Woman Suffrage Alliance. All these groups grappled with questions about identity, mission, and representation. Whether dedicated to one cause or many, whether claiming to represent nonwhite, nonelite, or non-Western women or not, this "first wave" of women's internationalism sharpened the desire of its participants to advance women's status and to secure a more peaceful world.[17]

The outbreak of World War I lent a new urgency to their efforts. By 1915 the war had sparked a new wave of women's internationalism, one that was more attuned to international relations and diplomacy, and more convinced of the connection between global peace and the status of women.[18] In April 1915 more than one thousand women from every warring nation met at The Hague to discuss bringing an end not only to the current war but to all future wars. In her closing address to the congress, Jane Addams noted with awe and pride that at a time when the "spirit of internationalism had apparently broken down," these women had come together "to protest from our hearts, . . . to study this complicated modern world, [and] to suggest ways by which this large internationalism may find itself and dig new channels through which it may flow."[19] All the participants believed that world peace could not be guaranteed without extending the parliamentary franchise to women, and that women had a responsibility to claim for themselves an active role in international relations. These beliefs were at the core of the organization founded at the congress, the International Committee of Women for Permanent Peace, later reconstituted as the Women's International League for Peace and Freedom.

The nature of women's internationalism was shifting in other ways as well. In the nineteenth century, women reformers often saw themselves as embarking on a grand civilizing mission to spread "Western" culture and ideologies, particularly those centered on domesticity and female moral authority. The World Woman's Christian Temperance Union sought to "liberate" women in China, India, Japan, and other regions by convincing them of their potential power within abstinent, Christian families and societies.[20] Generations of European and U.S. suffragists and feminists relied on and perpetuated assumptions of "Western" superiority and "Eastern" backwardness and savagery as they sought to establish their own moral authority and to argue for their own advancement.[21] Manifestations of this discourse among women have been called "feminist orientalism" or "imperial feminism," signifying the belief that "Western" goals and modes of activism—generally liberal, republican, individualist, and Protestant—were the standards by which to measure all feminisms and all women's status.[22] This literature articulates the ways in which U.S. women assumed their platforms were both superior and universal, and thus were sure to be embraced by Latin American, African, Asian, and Middle Eastern women. I am interested though in their internationalist platforms as well as their feminist ones. U.S. women believed their own methods for securing peace and global cooperation, as well as for securing women's advancement, were superior to any others. Therefore I use the phrase "imperialist internationalism" in addition to "imperialist feminism" to refer to this dynamic.[23]

In many ways, women like Jane Addams and those in WILPF had abandoned the most blatantly imperialistic forms of this rhetoric by 1915. These women internationalists saw themselves as citizens of a world community rather than as agents of Western civilization. They established for themselves an active and influential role in international politics by holding conferences and lobbying governments. WILPF, for instance, devoted much of its time in the late 1910s and early 1920s to urging the Allied powers to redesign the Versailles Treaty to include disarmament, and to pressuring the United States to join the World Court. Although their efforts were only moderately successful, they did earn the respect of government officials in many countries.[24]

Elements of the orientalist ethos persisted, however. Organizations like WILPF that originated in Europe and in the "neo-Europes"—Australia, Canada, and the United States—not only struggled to include women of non-European descent in their ranks but they also persisted in viewing northern and western Europe and the United States as the "core" of their internationalist realms, and Asia, Africa, the Middle East, and Latin America as the "periphery." Membership practices and organizational rhetoric further marginalized vast numbers of women. Annual conferences were held in Europe or occasionally in the United States, and proceedings were conducted only in French, German, or English. Leaders often spoke of their desire to "help" their oppressed "sisters," many of whom were only beginning to "awaken" and realize their desire for "emancipation."[25] As a result of this ongoing orientalism, nonwhite and non-Western women struggled to claim a place for themselves in many international women's organizations and to have their experiences and concerns heard.[26] This was a legacy with which U.S. women wrestled throughout the 1920s and 1930s as they sought to build networks in Latin America. Ellen Starr Brinton's resentment of the charge that all U.S. Americans were guilty of "high-hatting" Mexicans was merely one example among many of U.S. women's struggles to comprehend Latin American accusations of arrogance and superiority.

In addition, disparities among women internationalists were growing. Though many U.S. women shared a desire to establish connections with women around the world and to enjoy peaceful international relations, they were not politically or ideologically homogenous. When it came to the issue of peace, for instance, some were political leftists who were opposed to all forms of war and wanted to see an immediate end to international conflict. Jane Addams and WILPF fit into this category. Others, including Carrie Chapman Catt and the League of Women Voters, were more moderate; they argued for gradual methods of eliminating war through international law. Some women did not oppose war at all on principle, but believed the need for it could be reduced by encouraging friendships between elite women of different countries. A group called the Pan American International Women's Committee wanted to facilitate business among male diplomats and government officials by bringing their wives and daughters into closer contact. Given their close (though informal) relationship with the Pan American Union, the committee was also adamant about remaining "non-political." This set them in marked contrast to groups such as WILPF and the LWV. Other differences among women internationalists centered on their methods. When a WILPF section sprang up in a new country, its members were encouraged to adopt a uniform set of policies and guidelines. The YWCA, by contrast, believed strongly in the need to adapt its program and approach depending on the needs of individual countries into which it was expanding. All of these groups were internationalist, but few of them agreed on the best way to achieve their goals—or on what those goals were in the first place.

The Western Hemisphere

Understanding the broader contexts within which Ellen Starr Brinton was working does not explain, however, why she was in Mexico. Many U.S.

women internationalists took a new interest in Latin America during the early twentieth century. Since the 1820s, when the majority of Latin American countries won their independence from Spain, orators and politicians throughout the hemisphere had claimed that all the new American nations shared an identity distinct from that of the European powers they had rebelled against. Popularized in the 1880s, the term "Pan Americanism" conveyed that sense of unity and common interest. Framing commercial and strategic interests as common to all "Americans" dated back to the Monroe Doctrine of 1823, but it took on new significance after the outbreak of World War I, when it was mobilized as a rhetorical defense against potential German encroachment.[27] Whether explicitly or implicitly, many U.S. women internationalists saw in Pan Americanism an opportunity to reach out to Latin American women by capitalizing on these preexisting ties. Some groups incorporated the word into their names, such as the Pan American International Women's Committee. In 1919 the U.S. section of WILPF established a Pan American Committee. In 1922 the LWV organized the Pan American Conference of Women. The term was a concise rhetorical way to encompass the hemisphere, but it also signaled a unity of purpose and a common identity among "Americans."[28]

But those professions of unity had long been contested. Critics of Pan Americanism, particularly Latin American opponents of U.S. foreign policies, charged that it was little more than rhetorical cover for U.S. dominance and exploitation. The early twentieth century represented the height of U.S. intervention in Central America and the Caribbean Basin. The legacy of the Monroe Doctrine and the Roosevelt Corollary established the Western Hemisphere as the domain of the United States in the minds of many U.S. Americans. While the former aimed to keep European powers out of the Western Hemisphere, the latter effectively sanctioned the policing of Latin American countries by the United States to maintain stability and foster democracy. President William Howard Taft's policy of "Dollar Diplomacy" extended this idea by encouraging U.S. bankers to offer loans to foreign governments in exchange for U.S. control over infrastructure and public finances. Protecting these loans frequently necessitated armed intervention on the part of the U.S. government. By 1922, U.S. troops occupied all or part of Cuba, Puerto Rico, Panama, Nicaragua, Haiti, and the Dominican Republic. These interventions created widespread resentment in Latin America and inspired popular and political resistance.[29] Many women were among the anti-imperialists and pacifists within the United

States who mounted campaigns against such actions. Thus even as they employed and drew on the rhetoric of Pan Americanism, some internationalists also critiqued it.

Inter-American cooperation among women held the potential both to move beyond the problems of Pan Americanism and to re-create them. In her analysis of the founding of the Inter-American Commission of Women, K. Lynn Stoner argued that "inter-American feminists shared motives and a spiritual basis for their alliance. They placed women's issues above national interests, and they sought democratic relations among themselves, with men, and among nations."[30] But it is important to understand the limits of that cooperation as well. U.S. women internationalists were immune neither to the arrogance of imperialist internationalism and feminism nor to the "culture of imperialism" that pervaded the country in the early twentieth century.[31] WILPF, for example, protested Dollar Diplomacy and U.S. economic imperialism in Latin America vigorously during the 1920s, and yet did not question the validity of imposing its own programs and perspectives on Latin American women. Furthermore, like their European colleagues, few U.S. internationalists spoke the language of the women they targeted. Neither Ellen Starr Brinton nor most of her associates spoke Spanish, Portuguese, or any indigenous languages. Inter-American conferences located in the United States were generally conducted in English, and correspondence to and from Latin America frequently had to be translated.

The epitome of the imperial U.S. feminist and woman internationalist was Carrie Chapman Catt. Numerous scholars have pointed out that her tactics for exporting the women's suffrage movement to Latin America closely resembled earlier efforts to "civilize" non-Western women.[32] Latin American feminists from Puerto Rico to the Southern Cone reacted to Catt with frustration and indignation.[33] After analyzing Catt's attitudes toward inter-American cooperation, for example, historian Christine Ehrick concluded that Catt "in no way considered a Pan American women's movement as a union among equals, but as a means to 'civilize' this part of the world and improve the image of the United States at the same time. These attitudes on the part of many North American feminists and the increasingly nationalistic and anti-U.S. rhetoric emanating from many Latin American sectors during these years worked to create a wide gulf between many Latin American feminists and their counterparts in the United States."[34] This was how imperialist feminism manifested itself in the inter-American context—as attempts by U.S. women to "help" Latin American women advance as they had, for instance by securing the vote, and to implement unilaterally their programs for peace and hemispheric cooperation, with little regard for or knowledge of either the cultural differences across the region or the extent of resentment toward the United States.

The potential for a "wide gulf" to emerge was only heightened in Mexico, which among Latin American countries had one of the longest-standing contentious relationships with the United States. Unlike the warring European nations cited by Jane Addams, the United States and Mexico had never shared a "spirit of internationalism." The U.S.-Mexican War of 1846–1848, during which the U.S. army occupied Mexico City, and after which the United States forced Mexico to cede nearly half its land, left many Mexicans very bitter. Some cordial feeling was restored in the 1860s, when the United States helped Mexico evict the French, who had installed an emperor in Mexico City. Between 1876 and 1910, dictator Porfirio Díaz encouraged U.S. investments as part of his plans for economic modernization. U.S. funds helped build thousands of miles of railroads, provided electricity to the major cities, and developed extensive mining industries. A U.S. company first produced oil in Mexico in 1901. Over 10,000 barrels were produced that year; by 1910 the number was over 3.6 million.[35] This level of economic investment led to much more favorable relations between the two governments, but the vast majority of Mexicans suffered under political repression and sank deeper into poverty. By 1910, U.S. owners controlled 27 percent of Mexican land, and U.S. investments in Mexico totaled over $1 billion.[36]

The volatile history of U.S.-Mexican relations intensified with the outbreak of the Mexican Revolution in 1910. Fueled in part by nationalist resistance to the economic domination of the United States, the Revolution represented for many Mexicans an opportunity for political and social change.[37] To U.S. policy makers, on the other hand, it signaled a challenge to decades of uncontested land acquisition and access to valuable natural resources, including copper, silver, iron, and oil. Concerned about the effects of successive short-term governments and the threat of potentially radical land reforms on U.S. property owners and investors—not to mention the danger of European, especially German, influence—Woodrow Wilson and his successors tried to influence the course of the Revolution by supporting or opposing various factions, and by ordering or threatening military intervention four times between 1914 and 1927.[38] The two countries severed diplomatic relations between 1920 and 1923 over the issue of

Article 27 of the revolutionary 1917 Mexican Constitution, which declared all subsoil resources to be vested in the Mexican nation. One of the most dramatic but little known moments of crisis came in early 1927, when both countries seemed prepared to wage war over the implementation of Article 27. Following the peaceful resolution of that crisis, the United States and Mexico resumed some of their old Porfirian patterns in the late 1920s and early 1930s, as the United States again began to expand its financial holdings. But the revitalization of the Revolution under Mexican president Lázaro Cárdenas after 1935, which culminated in the nationalization of the oil industry in 1938, once again threatened the two countries' relationship and the integrity of Franklin Roosevelt's Good Neighbor Policy.

U.S. interference over the course of the 1910s and 1920s in a popular and ostensibly democratic revolution drew criticism from several quarters, but internationalist women in the United States were particularly concerned about its negative effects. Mexico was one of the most significant countries for U.S. women trying to create inter-American networks. Given its proximity and accessibility, it was a logical place to start, and its relationship to the United States demanded the attention particularly of U.S. women peace activists. Mexican women, for their part, began by the mid-1910s to organize and to develop a feminist consciousness. Many of them were eager to reach out to feminists in other parts of the world for solidarity and guidance.[39] Several U.S. and international organizations wanted to take advantage of this moment to establish contacts and extend their work in Mexico, but U.S. interventions hindered their efforts by provoking resentment in both countries. As a result women internationalists also devoted significant time during the interwar period to lobbying the U.S. government to modify its Mexican policy.

Mexico is integral, therefore, to understanding the nature of U.S. women's internationalism during this period. Internationalist ideals, imperialist methods, revolutionary nationalist aspirations, and the contested rhetoric of Pan Americanism coalesced in the interactions between U.S. and Mexican women as they did nowhere else. The interplay between all of these factors was what made it impossible for U.S. women to realize their goals. In the end, their own assumptions of nationalist superiority forestalled their internationalist ambitions. But the ways in which they sought to negotiate these dynamics, and the varied approaches they took in Mexico, illuminate both the possibilities as well as the limitations of inter-American cooperation during this period.

Chapter 1

The Best Kind of Internationalism

Though she was not the first to practice it, the author of the new internationalism in the World War I era was Jane Addams. In her closing remarks to the Women's Auxiliary Conference of the Second Pan American Scientific Congress in January 1916, Addams commended the attendees for fostering "a new type of internationalism." Earlier philosophers and politicians, she argued, had dreamed of "a rather formal undertaking" in which they would "pass resolutions and found a constitution, and so forth and so on." But present circumstances demanded a different approach, one stemming "from the point of view of human experience and mutual interests." Drawing on her experiences at Hull-House, she pointed out that immigrants from Europe and South America and elsewhere came to the cities of the United States every day and eventually learned to live together and understand each other through common interests and activities. If this could be done "by simple peasants from Germany and Italy, Slavs and Latins, Anglo-Saxons and whoever you please—if they can achieve this internationalism—then certainly it can be done by other people living in these various countries." Advances in technology, which made travel and communication easier than ever before, opened up new possibilities for those kinds of exchanges even when the participants did not live in the same neighborhood. "We have an opportunity such as never faced the world before," Addams announced, "to found *human* internationalism."[1]

Addams contrasted her new brand of internationalism with the formal, diplomatic approach that characterized the late nineteenth and early twentieth centuries. Before 1914, the hallmark of this approach was the Hague System, which produced the first international agreements on the laws of war and war crimes, and formed the basis for the beginnings of international law in the early twentieth century. Conservative men increasingly dominated this legalistic internationalism; they pursued contacts with government leaders and eschewed input from ordinary citizens. The minutiae of diplomatic treaties and arbitration agreements were too complex, they felt, to allow for meaningful contributions from most men and women.[2] In 1913, Nicholas Murray Butler, president of Columbia University and head of the Carnegie Endowment, contended, "We must face the fact that our rather scientific and intellectual program is on too high a plane to be understood and sympathized with by large numbers of persons."[3] Addams implicitly painted this approach as "inhuman"—devoid of personal interactions, producing sterile treaties rather than interpersonal understanding and broad commitments to peace.

Her internationalism centered on the activism of ordinary citizens. In the same way that she had mobilized settlement house workers and immigrant residents to transform the neighborhood around Hull House, Addams sought to galvanize peace activists to transform relations among nation-states. Informed by pragmatist philosophy, she blended her commitments to peace and social justice to pursue not just the absence of war but a lasting and just peace.[4] She was the principal architect of the women's peace movement that emerged during World War I and relentlessly pressured the Wilson administration and later the delegates to the Versailles conference to pursue mediation, compromise, and arbitration. Extending to the international realm her belief that "the cure for the ills of Democracy is more Democracy," she wanted arms production, trade agreements, and "foreign politics" brought under democratic control. Addams's human internationalism was a *practice*, not just a theory; it expanded her vision of social democracy to encompass the globe.[5]

And women were its natural practitioners. Addams's gendered belief in women's special mission to preserve peace informed human internationalism. As she explained to her audience at the Women's Auxiliary Conference, "From the beginning of time this understanding of peoples, of natural intercourse, of social life versus political life, has largely been in the hands of women, and therefore it is an obligation which women have in this generation as peculiarly their own."[6] This assertion echoed closely the sentiments both Addams and Carrie Chapman Catt had expressed at the international women's peace conference at The Hague the previous spring. Catt deliberately appealed to the "common bonds" of sisterhood and to women as the "World's Mothers."[7] Such inclusive,

Figure 1. Jane Addams, 1915.
Jane Addams Collection, Swarthmore College Peace Collection.

communal language was prevalent among women in organizations trying to build solidarity across national boundaries during the early twentieth century.[8] Addams's human internationalism represented an opportunity for women to lead the way toward a more cooperative, peaceful world. Women internationalists' qualifications, she felt, stemmed not from legal or diplomatic expertise but from settlement work, from moral reform

campaigns, from agitation for woman suffrage, and most important, from
their inherent nature as women and their desire to connect with women
in other countries to promote global friendship and prevent war.

In characterizing human internationalism as a female enterprise,
Addams also deemphasized its political nature. Her distinction between
"social life" and "political life" suggested that for women the former took
precedence, while men ostensibly retained responsibility for the latter. In
her speech to the International Congress of Women in 1915, she told the
delegates that the solidarity that brought them together in wartime was
compelled by "spiritual forces" and constituted a "spiritual internationalism." Thus, as she distinguished women's internationalism from more
legalistic forms, she also tried to cast it as neutral, steered by women's
natural impulses rather than by great power politics. Even though Addams
often strove to remain nonpartisan, she never intended for her peace work
to be apolitical, as evidenced by her efforts to lobby President Wilson to
mediate the European conflict just a few months after the women's congress at The Hague. Her emphasis on spiritualism portrayed women activists as agents of a higher power, and their activism as a natural duty. At the
same time, it reinforced among women the sense of internationalism as an
imagined community.[9]

Although World War I provided the most immediate and pressing back-
drop for Addams's reformulations of internationalism, it was no coincidence that she delivered an address on the topic at a conference promoting
inter-American cooperation. Many women internationalists in the United
States hoped to extend their work into Latin America, both because of the
long-standing presumed affinity among the nations of the Western Hemisphere and because of the increase in anti-Americanism since the implementation of the Platt Amendment in Cuba in 1903, the declaration of
the Roosevelt Corollary to the Monroe Doctrine in 1904, and the military
occupation of Haiti in 1915. U.S. women wanted both to capitalize on the
unifying rhetoric of Pan Americanism and to counteract the perception
that the United States was an empire in pursuit of hemispheric domination.
Both impulses coalesced around the question of U.S.-Mexican relations in
particular. The outbreak of the Mexican Revolution had led to a succession
of increasingly nationalist regimes bent on curtailing foreign influence in
Mexico, especially U.S. economic influence.

Addams's "human" approach to internationalism dominated U.S.
women's activism concerning Mexico and Latin America for the next

twenty-five years. The women pursuing ventures in the Americas during and immediately following World War I were a disparate group, with diverse goals and expectations, but they were all practitioners—consciously or not—of Addams's brand of internationalism. Four groups in particular were active in Mexico: the U.S. section of the Women's International League for Peace and Freedom, guided during this period by Addams herself and by Emily Greene Balch; the Women's Peace Society (WPS) under the direction of executive secretary Elinor Byrns; the Foreign Division of the YWCA of the U.S.A., headed by Sarah Lyon; and the Pan American International Women's Committee (PAIWC), led by Emma Bain Swiggett. Between 1915 and 1923, members of these organizations worked to establish contacts, to exchange information with Mexican women about their respective programs, to interact with Mexican women in various settings, and to establish branches of their organizations in Mexico City. Their motives and experiences varied, but all these women shared Addams's belief in the power of personal interactions, the sharing of knowledge, and above all the ability of women to further cooperation among nations and reduce conflicts.

As they extended their networks in Mexico, however, U.S. women had to contend with the specter of revolutionary nationalism, not only because by the late 1910s it threatened the diplomatic relationship between the United States and Mexico but because many Mexican women activists drew strength from the ideologies of the Revolution. Some Mexican women were eager to join U.S. women's internationalist ventures, and shared a desire to unite the world's women to work for peace. But they also expected U.S. women to help them achieve their national goals. They were willing to partner with U.S. women, but they expected that partnership to be equal and reciprocal.

Human Internationalists

Who were these new internationalists? Like those who had been active in the transatlantic arena since the mid-nineteenth century, the majority of U.S. women who took an interest in Latin America during the late 1910s and early 1920s were college-educated, middle-class, white, and Protestant. A significant number of them were unmarried, a status not uncommon among women in political and reform movements. Internationalist organizations that required a great deal of travel often had a preponderance of single women members.[10] Few of them were novices when it came to organizing, even on an international scale. They had been and remained active in organizations such as the General Federation of Women's Clubs, the American Association of University Women, and various missionary groups. Many—though not all—were suffragists. All of them felt profoundly the impact of World War I. When the war broke out in the summer and fall of 1914, it came as a shock to many internationalists, who had assumed that the days of war on such a massive scale were long over. As the question of U.S. entry into the war loomed in early 1917, the majority of them supported Woodrow Wilson. Only a small minority maintained a pacifist stance.[11]

Jane Addams herself led one of the most staunchly pacifist of the women's internationalist organizations. The group that became the Women's International League for Peace and Freedom originated in opposition to World War I. For the first few years of the war, women pacifists such as Addams, Rosika Schwimmer of Hungary, Emmeline Pethick-Lawrence of Britain, and others focused on ending it as quickly as possible. In January 1915, representatives from over seventy organizations created the Women's Peace Party in New York City. Their plan called for U.S. mediation among the warring nations; to that end they organized demonstrations and publicity campaigns, flooding the White House with letters and telegrams urging intercession. At The Hague in May, U.S. representatives from the Women's Peace Party helped to form the International Committee of Women for Permanent Peace. After the conference, Addams and several colleagues traveled around Europe, meeting with leaders of both belligerent and neutral nations, trying to rally support for an armistice. But by late 1916 they were growing frustrated, and U.S. intervention seemed more and more probable. Between the U.S. entry in April 1917 and November 1918, women pacifists focused their efforts on hastening a negotiated end to the war and on fending off attacks from pro-war government officials and civilians alike. In the summer of 1919, the International Committee met in Zurich at the same time as the Versailles peace conference to monitor and try to influence the postwar planning. Frustrated with the punitive nature of the Versailles Treaty and the weaknesses of the League of Nations, Addams and her colleagues reconstituted themselves as a permanent organization—the Women's International League for Peace and Freedom. Two

U.S. women, Addams and Emily Greene Balch, were named international president and executive secretary respectively.[12]

Addams and Balch were the most prominent members of a new breed of women internationalists. They belonged to the generation of Progressive women reformers born before 1880 and college educated before 1900 who frequently took an interest in social questions related to industrialization, immigration, public health, social welfare, and other related issues. Addams, for example, founded Hull House on the South Side of Chicago in 1889 as a neighborhood settlement house to coordinate community services and support among immigrant and working-class populations. Balch, an economist and professor at Wellesley College, authored a major study of Slavic immigration to the United States, and also cofounded the Women's Trade Union League. Both women strongly supported women's suffrage, though neither was as active in the movement as some of their contemporaries. World War I brought their pacifist impulses to the fore. They helped organized the International Congress of Women at The Hague and spent several weeks touring areas in Europe affected by the war. Both suffered for their radical pacifist tendencies; Addams was forced to search for new funding for Hull House after opposing U.S. entry into World War I, and Balch's support of socialism got her fired from Wellesley in 1919. Their views heavily influenced WILPF's direction in its early years.[13]

Opposition to World War I was WILPF's raison d'être, but a vocal minority within the organization argued that women pacifists had a duty to protest all wars, not just one specific war. In the fall of 1919, these members resigned from the league to form their own organization. Based in New York City, the Women's Peace Society objected to war on moral grounds, and followed the nonresistance philosophy of William Lloyd Garrison and Mohandas Gandhi. Its official founder and first chair was Fanny Garrison Villard, the abolitionist's daughter, who funded the group for its first several years. But the society's ethos and policies were largely shaped by Elinor Byrns. A practicing lawyer who had once run for local office on the Socialist ticket, Byrns established the society's commitment to total pacifism and universal disarmament. Most of the society's work throughout 1919 and 1920 focused on lobbying the state government in New York and the federal government in Washington, D.C., to end military appropriations and compulsory military training in public schools.[14] Hampered by its small size, small budget, and internal strife between Villard and Byrns, the WPS never approached the scale of WILPF or other women's peace organizations, but its absolute pacifism later proved appealing to Mexican women seeking support within the United States against U.S. military interventions in Mexico.

Opposing World War I was a dangerous stance to take, as Addams, Balch, Villard, and Byrns knew all too well. In the atmosphere of heightened patriotism and xenophobic nationalism that spread across the country in 1917 and 1918, pacifists, feminists, socialists, and radicals of any kind were held in contempt. Opponents of both peace and women's suffrage increasingly linked the two causes with radicalism and socialism in attempts to discredit women like Addams and Balch. Some women activists succumbed to the pressure and pursued less controversial paths. Carrie Chapman Catt, who had been a founding member of the Women's Peace Party in 1915, withdrew from the group and famously threw the support of the National American Woman Suffrage Association behind Wilson and the war effort. She took personal pride in the fact that by 1917, hers was a bourgeois organization, "with nothing radical about it."[15] Within the Left, the split over World War I deepened the divide between socialists, who opposed the war, and progressives, who largely supported it. That split hardened after the Bolshevik Revolution in November 1917; over the next several years, socialists and communists—and those suspected of associating or sympathizing with them—came increasingly under attack.[16]

Not all women internationalists opposed U.S. entry into World War I. While committed to creating a more peaceful world, the Young Women's Christian Association supported Woodrow Wilson's mission to "make the world safe for democracy." This was in keeping with the association's long-standing vision of Christian internationalism and support for missionary work overseas. The YWCA had emerged out of mid-nineteenth-century reform movements in Britain and the United States. Though the movements arose separately in the two countries, they united in 1894 to found the World Young Women's Christian Association, which served as an umbrella organization for all national associations. Although the YWCA of the U.S.A. was not formally incorporated until 1906, members had been active locally since the 1860s—running boarding houses, employment bureaus, and community centers in cities such as New York, Boston, and Dayton, Ohio. During World War I, that kind of experience was in high demand both in Europe and on the home front. Volunteers supplied housing and recreational activities to women's military auxiliaries in France, and opened "hostess houses" across the United States for the families of servicemen. Located near training camps, the houses offered protection to soldiers' wives and children and provided a wholesome, moral environment for servicemen's recreation.[17] The association's ability to provide both relief and moral guidance made it hugely popular among Progressive reformers. By the end of the war, the YWCA's programs, profile, budget, and membership had all expanded dramatically. With over half a million members in 1920, it was the third-largest women's organization in the country, behind only the General Federation of Women's Clubs and the Woman's Christian Temperance Union.

The YWCA's earlier experiences overseas and its shift toward political action in the early 1920s shaped its international ethos as much as did World War I. Association "secretaries," as workers abroad were called, had been posted to India and China since the 1890s. Their encouragement of local initiatives and local leadership, as opposed to imported programs, established a pattern that later associations in Mexico and Latin America would follow.[18] The U.S. association also assumed a more politically active character after 1920. Pressured by working-class members, the YWCA began supporting workers' rights and lobbying for labor laws. More significantly, association leaders created space for workingwomen to articulate their demands and help shape this new direction. No longer was it enough for the YWCA to reform individuals; its emphasis had broadened to include reforming society as a whole through political action for social justice.[19] Not coincidentally, the National Board in the early 1920s loosened the requirement that members had to conform to strict Protestantism, asking instead that they make a "statement of faith" and "take as a model to inform their life individually and socially, the life of Christ." This fueled the association's dedication to pluralism.[20]

On its establishment in 1906 as the YWCA of the U.S.A., the National Board divided its work into two divisions, home and foreign.[21] Before 1914, the main focus of the Foreign Division was on Asia, but after World War I its members turned their attention closer to home. The work of the Foreign Division during the interwar period was steered by Sarah Lyon, who served as its director from 1920 to 1944. Originally from New Jersey, Lyon graduated from Mt. Holyoke College in 1906, and worked for several local YWCAs in various capacities before joining the national staff.[22] She ran the division "with the zeal and efficiency of a general," requiring frequent reports from secretaries abroad and closely monitoring local political situations in those countries. Lyon's influence largely dictated which overseas projects received funding from the U.S. association. She chose her targets selectively. In the early 1920s, for example, Lyon pursued opportunities in the Philippines, because it was a U.S. protectorate, and in Mexico, because of its geographic proximity. She also based her decisions on which projects were likely to become self-sustaining in the shortest time possible.[23] Mexico City, which could boast a significant number of U.S. citizens in residence and where the Young Men's Christian Association had flourished since 1902, seemed a promising target.

Unlike both the Women's International League and the YWCA, the Pan American International Women's Committee was the only internationalist organization born during World War I that did not expressly refer to the war as an impetus for its formulation. It took shape in the wake of a conference organized by the wives of representatives to the Second Pan American Scientific Congress. This Women's Auxiliary Conference, held in Washington, D.C., from December 28, 1915, to January 7, 1916, was attended by wives and daughters of Latin American delegates to the Scientific Congress, as well as a handful of other prominent U.S. women—including Jane Addams, whose closing address on human internationalism inspired many in her audience. Emma Bain Swiggett, whose husband was the executive secretary of the Scientific Congress, took charge of the women's conference and directed the formation of the PAIWC over the course of the following year. Very little is known about Swiggett; she graduated from Indiana University, and married her husband in 1892.[24] She coordinated the committee's work throughout the first decade of its existence, and authored its mission to "stimulate and co-ordinate the work of the women of Pan America for social and civic betterment."[25] Made up of women with little history of political activism (Addams did not join), the Pan American committee was very different ideologically from the Women's International League, the Women's Peace Society, and the YWCA, but its members did believe that greater friendship and cooperation among the women of the Americas would promote friendly relations among their governments. "Pan Americanism embodies beautiful ideals," one member maintained, "and may it not be that after all, the intelligent work of women through favorable avenues of sympathy will be the means of creating in time the real Pan American Spirit."[26] Despite the fact that World War I did not lead explicitly to the committee's formation, the rhetoric of Pan Americanism pervaded calls for hemispheric solidarity in these years, and would have evoked anti-German patriotism among the committee's audiences.[27]

Thus women's internationalism in the late 1910s and early 1920s grew out of both the existing networks of white middle-class women's activism and the immediate crisis of World War I. The Women's International League and the Women's Peace Society arose in opposition to the war, while the Young Women's Christian Association and the Pan American International Women's Committee drew strength from wartime patriotism and mobilization. All these internationalist organizations recognized the power and importance of nationalism and patriotism. Even the peace organizations, which decried the aggressive nationalism that fueled the great power rivalry, understood its significance not only in the United States and Western Europe but also in regions such as the Balkans and the Middle East. But for these U.S. women, the time had come when internationalism had to be equally if not more important than nationalism. At The Hague in 1915, Jane Addams envisioned "a spiritual internationalism which surrounds and completes our national life."[28] Ultimately all these groups sought lasting peace, and believed with Addams that women's cooperative efforts could help secure it. In the meantime, each organization pursued its own methods of putting human internationalism into practice not just in Europe but closer to home as well.

Revolutionary Mexico

As U.S. women internationalists sought to extend their influence in the Western Hemisphere, they looked first to Mexico, not least because its proximity made it more accessible than countries further south. From the East Coast of the United States, travel to Mexico City was usually accomplished via train through Texas, though steamships also made frequent trips between New York and the port of Veracruz. A few intrepid U.S. women even traveled by car. Furthermore, the idea of promoting neighborliness lent itself nicely to broader schemes of interaction and cooperation. Long before the Good Neighbor Policy of the 1930s, U.S. women internationalists invoked the shared border between the United States and Mexico as justification for their work in that country. As Emily Greene Balch wrote to a Mexican colleague in 1921, "I cannot tell how much I feel the need of active cooperation of Mexican women and of earnest and effective efforts . . . between two peoples who are to be such good neighbors."[29] Balch's assertion was all the more compelling given the contentious relationship between the United States and Mexico over the previous ten years, and the fact that in 1921 the two countries did not have a diplomatic relationship.

Two factors prompted U.S. women to strengthen their ties with Mexico, even as those same factors posed significant challenges to their internationalist agendas. First, the outbreak of the Mexican Revolution in 1910 had led to increasingly tense interactions between the United States and successive revolutionary governments. Revolutionary nationalism, especially economic nationalism directed against the United States, proliferated in the early years of the war in slogans such as "Mexico for the Mexicans!" A series of U.S. military interventions and threats of interventions between 1914 and 1919 further inflamed that nationalism. As supporters of peaceful interstate relations, U.S. women wanted to promote goodwill between the two countries in order to counter diplomatic tensions, but the nationalism engendered by the Revolution and stoked by the U.S. government was at odds with their own internationalism. Second, a nascent feminist movement was brewing in Mexico, and many U.S. women used that movement to identify contacts and forge connections with Mexican women. But while not all Mexican feminists cleaved wholeheartedly to a Revolution that tended to marginalize their political roles in society, many of them echoed the political and economic nationalism that was growing in strength and popularity. Their frustrations with the United States created potential points of conflict with U.S. women internationalists over priorities and U.S. policies.

Revolutionary nationalism and U.S. interventions in Mexico escalated in a vicious cycle between 1910 and 1920. Economic nationalism had been building in Mexico during the final years of the Porfiriato, the dictatorship of Porfirio Díaz. Frustrated by decades of partnerships between U.S. businesses and the Díaz regime, which modernized Mexico at the expense of democratic processes and the well-being of poor and working-class Mexicans, reformers pressured Díaz to hold free elections in 1910. After Díaz was ousted in 1911 and his democratically elected successor Francisco Madero proved unable to consolidate power, the United States grew increasingly alarmed about potential threats to U.S. businesses and landowners, not only from the general violence of the war but from campaigns to target foreigners. Repeated attempts on the part of the United States to intervene in and dictate the course of the Revolution only engendered more resentment and hostility. In 1914, citing the illegal arrest of several soldiers in Tampico, U.S. troops occupied the eastern port of Veracruz. Wilson's goal was to land troops on the eastern shore and advance toward Mexico City to force a change in government, but U.S. troops were unable to hold Veracruz, and Wilson was forced to withdraw. In 1915, revolutionary leader Pancho Villa provoked Wilson by attacking the town of Columbus, New Mexico, and killing seventeen U.S. citizens. As a result, Wilson directed General John Pershing's "Punitive Expedition" to invade northern Mexico to break up Villa's army and capture the revolutionary himself. Pershing could not achieve either goal. In 1919 tensions flared again when the U.S. vice-consul in Puebla, William Jenkins, was reportedly kidnapped by Mexican rebels and then accused of having staged the incident to provoke U.S. intervention.[30]

Wilson also feared that anti-Americanism would lead Mexico into alliances with nations at odds with the United States—first Germany, and later the Soviet Union. Between 1914 and 1917, Germany worked hard to establish ties with individuals and groups in Mexico and then to use those relationships to destabilize the Mexican government in order to distract the United States. For instance, in 1915, German agents in Mexico tried to restore deposed military leader Victoriano Huerta to power, in an effort to cause trouble for the United States. In February 1917, German foreign minister Arthur Zimmermann instructed the German ambassador to approach president Venustiano Carranza about a German-Mexican alliance against the United States. The telegram was intercepted and decoded by the British, and subsequently published in the United States, hastening U.S. entry into World War I.[31] After November 1917, many Mexican intellectuals openly expressed admiration for the Bolshevik Revolution in Russia. Two years later, the Mexican Socialist Party changed its name to the Mexican Communist Party; in 1922 the group was accepted as a formal member of the Communist International, also known as the Third International. Throughout the 1920s, U.S. policy makers worried about what they saw as a growing affinity between Mexico and the Soviet Union.[32]

But by far the most contentious issue between the two nations was Article 27 of the 1917 Mexican Constitution. Promulgated by Carranza, the constitution institutionalized the anticlericalism and economic nationalism of his administration. It also elevated the status of the majority of Mexicans by promising sweeping land reforms, and by giving the government unprecedented power to intervene on behalf of workers against employers. Article 27 declared all land and subsoil resources vested in the Mexican nation. To what extent Carranza intended to implement the article is not clear, but on paper it represented a direct and significant threat to U.S. businesses and landowners. In August 1919, the U.S. Senate established a subcommittee of the Committee on Foreign Relations to investigate the Mexican situation. Senator Albert B. Fall, who strongly supported the idea of U.S. military intervention, chaired the subcommittee. The subcommittee released a report in June 1920 recommending that the United States refuse to recognize any Mexican government without an agreement protecting U.S. landowners and financial investments. When Mexican President Álvaro Obregón refused in 1920 to exempt U.S. interests from Article 27, U.S. President Warren Harding severed diplomatic ties and refused to recognize Obregón. The two countries did not restore their formal relationship until 1923.[33]

Revolutionary nationalism and patriotism also grew among ordinary Mexicans, who sought to claim the promises of the Revolution for themselves. This included feminist activists, who began to organize themselves during these years. Many of them were reacting against a late nineteenth-century traditional feminine ideal, according to which women's lives centered on the home and the church, and remained separate from the male spheres of political and intellectual activity. Encouragement for women's political participation first arose among opponents of the Díaz regime. Some Díaz opponents supported expanded education for women and emancipation from the yoke of tradition, particularly as part of a larger effort to attack the power of the Catholic Church. During the Revolution, the Constitutionalists, led by Venustiano Carranza, likewise saw feminists as a potential ally against the Church. None of these revolutionary factions were particularly interested in equality or advancing women's rights. But they did offer feminists a new political language of constitutionalism and representative government to advance their cause. In the mid- to late 1910s, activist women began to co-opt revolutionary ideals of womanhood to argue for greater individual freedoms, greater access to education, and greater dignification of women's influence within the family.[34]

This revolutionary feminism emerged first in the Yucatán, in eastern Mexico. The same month that Jane Addams addressed the Women's Auxiliary Conference in Washington, a very different group of women assembled in Mérida, the Yucatecan capital. In January 1916 the governor of the state, Salvador Alvarado, called two feminist congresses to raise consciousness of women's subordination among Yucatecans and to empower working- and middle-class women to advance their own interests.[35] Yucatán had become a kind of laboratory for testing radical social ideas during the Revolution, thanks in part to Alvarado himself. Venustiano Carranza had appointed him governor in 1915, but his ideas concerning women's issues were more radical than those of most of his party. Alvarado believed all women should receive a solid education, encouraged them to participate in civic life, promoted literacy, and even changed the civil code to allow unmarried women to work outside the home. But the empowerment of women Alvarado sought had its limits; he wanted to elevate women's status in order for Mexico to be seen as a modern nation, but he still believed that a woman's most important role was that of a wife.[36]

The congresses revealed a range of views among Mexican women, but the majority demanded greater access to education and liberation from the "yoke of tradition," even though most did not go so far as to reject marriage and motherhood.[37] Not surprisingly, since the majority of the delegates were teachers, the resolutions of the first congress in January stressed schooling and teaching as the best ways to liberate women and make their contributions to the family and to society more valuable. A few women did express more radical views. Hermila Galindo, a leading Mexican feminist and personal secretary to President Carranza, drew nationwide attention to the congress when she advocated for birth control and access to divorce. Galindo did not actually attend, but in a paper read by a colleague she argued that the new approach to women's education should include instruction on anatomy and hygiene, since women's sex drive was just as strong as men's and they needed to be educated about their own bodies. She also argued forcefully against the sexual double standard, and demanded women's right to divorce.[38] Taken together, these opinions were interpreted by many in the audience, not to mention the press, as promoting free love and sexual equality for women.[39] In fact, most of the delegates were more moderate; they supported Alvarado's plan for expanding women's education, and instead of the right to divorce, they demanded that Alvarado reform the civil code to allow single women to leave home at age twenty-one, as men were allowed to do.[40] Although the focus of feminist activity shifted to Mexico City shortly after Alvarado left office in 1918, these early conferences in the Yucatán marked the first organized feminist activity in Mexico and influenced later feminist conferences in the 1920s.

New feminist leaders emerged from the Yucatán congresses, some of whom would have significant interactions with U.S. women internationalists over the next decade. One of the more radical was Elena Torres Cuéllar.

Torres was a schoolteacher from Guanajuato who traveled to Yucatán to attend the congresses. She was a friend of Hermila Galindo, and read Galindo's paper at the first congress. Enamored with the feminist and revolutionary environment of the region, Torres stayed on in Mérida after the conference. Alvarado, impressed with Torres's motivation and background in education, put her in charge of opening a Montessori school. Torres also became an active participant in the Yucatán Socialist Party.[41] In 1918 she helped organize the Latin American Bureau of the Third International, which aimed to foster solidarity between Russian and Mexican workers.[42] In 1918 or 1919, she moved to Mexico City, where she cofounded the Consejo Feminista Mexicano (Mexican Feminist Council, CFM) in August 1919.

Like Galindo, Torres was frustrated by the limitations of revolutionary rhetoric for women. She saw herself not as a "useful political instrument" for Mexico's modernization, but as an equal citizen.[43] Dedicated to the economic, social, and political emancipation of women, Torres's group became over the next few years the most important feminist organization in Mexico, and the focal point of most interactions between U.S. and Mexican women internationalists. Its goals ranged from equal pay for equal work to civic improvements such as neighborhood inspections and children's parks to political rights and reform of the civil code. The CFM demanded enforcement of the laws protecting women workers that were spelled out in the 1917 Constitution, including overtime pay, safe working conditions, and maternity leave. It claimed equal political rights for women, including the right to vote in local and national elections and the right to run for and hold public office.[44] The CFM platform was not quite as radical as Torres's personal beliefs; there was no mention of birth control or divorce, for instance. But the group's demands did reflect Torres's concern with women as workers, demanding the establishment of wages "considering woman as head of a family," and mechanisms for establishing workplace safety and sanitation.

The Consejo Feminista drew strength and legitimacy from revolutionary rhetoric, even as its members pushed back against its limits and sought international connections to bolster their standing. The group's platform reflected the revolutionary atmosphere in which it was created, incorporating "effective realization of the rights of citizenship granted by the present Constitution and its [enlargement]" and "equal political rights for men and women."[45] Central to Elena Torres's mission was to "aid in the reconstruction of our country."[46] But there was also a clear internationalist cast to the

CFM agenda. The group's call to Mexican women included a demand for cooperation "with women around the world to abolish war, end militarism, and ensure the rights of weaker peoples to live in peace, harmony, and perfect liberty."[47] Torres was eager to establish contacts with international women's organizations, to "promote a feminine entente-cordiale among the women of the whole world in order to bring about permanent peace and international amity."[48] Although it is difficult to pin down the origins of the CFM's internationalist impulses, it is possible they grew from members' understanding that the Yucatán congresses had drawn interest from U.S. and European women, and thus that Mexican women's struggle for emancipation could attract international support. It is also possible that Elena Torres's involvement with the Third International influenced her global thinking as she and her colleagues drew up their platform.

Mexican feminism was thus bound up with the Revolution in important ways, as women like Elena Torres demanded equal access to the new measures of citizenship promised by the 1917 Constitution. Despite their loyalty to the Revolution, however, some Mexican feminists, including Torres, were willing to explore and develop connections with women in other countries, including the United States. Even in the midst of a rising tide of anti-U.S. sentiment, Torres and her colleagues turned in the late 1910s and early 1920s to U.S. women for help in achieving their feminist goals. This suggests that for them, at least, nationalism and internationalism could coexist.

Practicing Human Internationalism

Most U.S. women did not fully understand the nuances of the Mexican Revolution, nor the depth of anti-U.S. sentiment in Mexico. But they did understand the contentious nature of U.S.-Mexican relations, and the potential for those relations to deteriorate as the negotiations over Article 27 dragged on. As the "old" internationalism was breaking down, when diplomacy and formal agreements were no longer sufficient to stem the tide of U.S.-Mexican animosity, U.S. women stepped into the fray to practice human internationalism.

If formal, legal internationalism was measured in treaties and conventions and assessed by examining whether or not they were observed or implemented, the efficacy of human internationalism was harder to gauge.

U.S. women pursued it by establishing contacts with Mexican women, maintaining a correspondence with those contacts, sharing information about themselves and their organizations, sending U.S. representatives to Mexico, recruiting Mexican women to form groups in Mexico City, convening conferences, and implementing a host of other initiatives. That is to say, they pursued the kind of work social activists and nongovernmental organizations have always done, and they did it with limited resources and finite amounts of time and energy. In the early years of this inter-American endeavor, their efforts seemed to pay off.

Any group of U.S. women hoping to expand its work in Mexico needed first to establish contacts in the country. How different organizations sought those contacts, and what kinds of women they hoped to find, varied significantly according to who the U.S. women were and what they wanted to accomplish. Given that the Pan American International Women's Committee had grown out of the Women's Auxiliary Conference and that their main goal was Pan American unity, it is not surprising that Emma Bain Swiggett sought her contacts through the members of Pan American Scientific Congress and the Latin American diplomatic corps. She exchanged numerous letters with Ignacio Bonillas, Mexican ambassador to the United States, and with Henry Fletcher, U.S. ambassador to Mexico, asking for names of Mexican women to whom she could reach out, but neither was particularly helpful. In the end the woman who became her principal Mexican contact was Adelia Palacios, a teacher whose name Swiggett knew because Palacios had attended the first Pan American Scientific Congress in 1908–1909. The YWCA, by contrast, sought out U.S. contacts in Mexico, rather than Mexican women. In other countries, such as China and Japan, part of the association's mission was to serve missionaries and other U.S. women stationed abroad. Although the YWCA's hopes for Mexico were centered more on Mexican women, reaching out to U.S. women and men in Mexico City gave them insight on current political and religious tensions that might hinder their efforts, and on whether a Mexican association would be useful. The YWCA also leaned heavily for guidance and support on the Young Men's Christian Association, which had been operating in Mexico City since 1902.

Both the PAIWC and the YWCA were concerned with recruiting certain types of Mexican women, and avoiding others—especially radical women like Elena Torres and Hermila Galindo. Swiggett remarked to a colleague in early 1919 that though she was frustrated with the slow growth of the

Mexican branch of the PAIWC, she took comfort in the fact that "our one member"—Palacios—"is the right sort and I hope we may soon have others."[49] Swiggett did not expand on what she meant by the "right sort," but given the committee's emphasis on Pan American unity and traditional ideals of womanhood, it is not difficult to imagine that Swiggett wanted members who would not be controversial within the official Pan American community, and whose personal and professional backgrounds were unobjectionable. The YWCA was more explicit. In a confidential letter to the director of the Pan American Union, one official noted that "Some of the Mexican women have become very radical. One of these is Señorita Hermila Galindo. . . . The work of the Y.W.C.A. is very greatly needed to counteract these too radical influences and help Mexican women to develop in a safe and natural way."[50] The association's desire to avoid the feminists who had spoken out about birth control and divorce at the Yucatán congresses indicates that they sought to be of service to Mexican women in more traditional ways, and wanted Mexican contacts who would fit that mold. This approach on the part of these two organizations undercut the implicit universalism of Jane Addams's human internationalism; both groups discounted on principle the knowledge and experiences of "radical" Mexican women. At the same time, both the PAIWC and the YWCA reinforced the emphasis on "spiritual" internationalism in their efforts to avoid ideological conflicts. These groups sought politically safer roads to internationalism.

The two peace organizations, on the other hand, welcomed activist and openly feminist women. When searching for potential recruits in Mexico, WILPF targeted women who had participated in the Yucatán congresses and eventually established contact with Elena Torres. Torres expressed interest in starting a branch in Mexico, and later supported WILPF's efforts while president of the Consejo Feminista Mexicano.[51] As president of the CFM, Torres also reached out to another peace organization in the United States, the Women's Peace Society. How Torres learned of the WPS is unclear, since they were a very small group and were not seeking to expand outside the United States. But in December 1919 Torres contacted Elinor Byrns, the society's executive secretary, because members of the Consejo Feminista were "anxious to come in contact with the various international women's organizations, that they may know more of Mexico and her conditions."[52] Neither the WPS nor the CFM had the resources to do more than exchange letters and information, but they did that with frequency and increasing affection over the next two years. Both WILPF and the WPS sought contacts in Mexico who would help them further their efforts toward peace, and both welcomed the interest of one of the leading Mexican feminists during this period.

Once these myriad contacts had been established, the next step was to implement one of the central tenets of the new women's internationalism—sharing information about the history, experiences, and goals of women in the United States and Mexico. Correspondence was cheap and relatively easy, provided that translators or a common language could be found. Generally, U.S. women wrote in English and Mexican women in Spanish, and all relied on translators within their organizations. A few Mexican women, including Elena Torres and Elena Landázuri, a member of the Consejo Feminista Mexicano who became the principal contact for WILPF, had spent time in the United States and wrote English well. Letters were also occasionally exchanged in French, which until this period was more likely than Spanish or English to be the second language of educated women in the United States or Mexico respectively.

Sharing information about themselves and their organizations was a way for U.S. and Mexican women to discover and establish common interests. Circular letters, pamphlets, periodicals, newspaper articles, press releases, and other media allowed a group's ethos to fit into an envelope. When Rosa Manus contacted Salvador Alvarado, she sent a brief summary of the 1915 peace conference at The Hague. When Emma Bain Swiggett reached out to Adelia Palacios, she included a pamphlet outlining the main achievements of the Women's Auxiliary Conference. U.S. women were not the only ones to follow this pattern. With her letter of introduction to the Women's Peace Society, Elena Torres included a flyer detailing the mission and goals of the Consejo Feminista Mexicano.[53]

Perhaps unsurprisingly, given the distances involved and the fact that Mexico was still experiencing periodic outbursts of revolutionary violence, the process of corresponding and sharing information was not as easy in practice as it was in theory. Letters got lost in the mail. Occasionally, operatives entrusted with messages of introduction or packets of information failed to deliver them for one reason or another. WILPF had a long-standing problem with a member of its California branch, who for several years represented herself as an intermediary for Jane Addams and Emily Greene Balch with the Consejo Feminista, but when Balch finally began corresponding directly with Elena Torres in 1922, they discovered their intermediary had not been fulfilling her duties.[54] Maintaining a regular correspondence was also difficult when various women were ill or absent from their posts for long periods of time. Adelia Palacios endured a long illness during the winter of 1921. Elena Landázuri was away from Mexico City for three months in 1922 during the final illness and death of her mother. Addams and Balch also struggled with ill health. Travel abroad, which was common especially among WILPF and YWCA members, only made regular communication more difficult, since letters often had to be forwarded multiple times before they reached their intended recipients.[55]

Given these difficulties, many women recognized that the ideal way to share information in the pursuit of common ground was in person. Of the four organizations considered here, the YWCA and the Women's International League sent representatives to Mexico; the Pan American International Women's Committee and the Women's Peace Society did not. Their different organizational structures offer some explanation. The YWCA and WILPF were constituted by sections and branches established in countries around the world. The PAIWC, by contrast, was based in Washington and operated primarily through correspondence during the periods between its major gatherings in conjunction with the scientific congresses. The WPS dedicated itself to lobbying in New York and Washington, and never intended to establish national sections in other countries.

The women who traveled to Mexico on behalf of the YWCA and WILPF had varying experiences. WILPF representative Rose Standish Nichols visited Mexico City twice over the course of 1920 to try to start a section there. She spoke with "twenty-five or thirty women" who "seemed interested and eager to form a group."[56] Nichols did not encounter Elena Torres or Elena Landázuri, but another U.S. member, Zonia Baber, met with them both during the same period. Baber, a professor of geography and a close friend of Jane Addams, traveled extensively in Mexico during the early 1920s. She did not know Torres well, but she was well liked both by Landázuri and by Adelia Palacios, with whom she interacted frequently. Two YWCA representatives, Harriet Taylor and Caroline Smith, traveled to Mexico in May 1921 to examine the feasibility of establishing a branch of the association there. They reported that their meetings with various groups of Mexican women and men had been "warm" and "charming," and by the end Smith was convinced that the Mexican people as a whole were "the personification of devotion and love."[57]

The best method for practicing human internationalism was also the most expensive and time-consuming. Organizing conferences, where large groups of women could meet each other in person, exchange information about issues of concern to them, and socialize informally was the most straightforward way to further cooperation. WILPF organized international meetings in 1915, 1919, and 1921, but as they were all held in Europe, it was difficult for Latin American women to attend. The Women's Peace Society was much too small, and had no real reason to be interested in a large-scale conference of its own. But U.S. women who were drawn to Pan Americanism during this period could take advantage of a preexisting network of organizations and conferences. The Pan American Union participated in the International Conferences of American States, which were held roughly every five years except during World War I, though women did not participate significantly in those conferences until 1928. But women had participated in several previous scientific congresses, dating back to 1898. Women comprised 6 percent of the delegates to the First Pan American Scientific Congress in 1909. Most of them were teachers who gave papers and participated in discussions on education in various fields. By the time of the second congress in December 1915, a group of U.S. women—all wives of congress members or diplomats—desired more time devoted to women's education and other issues than the scientific congress could provide. A month before the scientific congress opened, a hastily convened committee sent invitations to the wives and daughters of the men traveling to Washington to attend the Women's Auxiliary Conference of the Second Pan American Scientific Congress. Planning for the conference rested largely in the hands of Emma Bain Swiggett, whose husband was the general secretary of the Scientific Congress.[58]

The idea of human internationalism, conducted through personal exchanges and information sharing rather than treaties and formal agreements, was exactly what the organizers of the auxiliary conference had in mind. Swiggett hoped that in the process of becoming better acquainted and of exchanging views "on subjects of special interest to women as well as on those dealing with Pan Americanism" that a desire would arise "on the part of the women of the Americas for further and harmonious cooperation in the future." The official report of the conference went further in explaining its origins: "It was the belief that such cooperation among women would furnish a powerful factor in developing the means 'to increase the knowledge of things American,' and 'to disseminate and make

the culture of each American country the heritage of all American Republics.' There was a vision of all that a united American womanhood might
do in creating and cherishing feelings of mutual helpfulness and friendship,
and of all it might contribute to a strong spiritual union of the Americas."[59]
Such a mandate echoed Jane Addams's visions of a "spiritual internationalism" to promote cooperation and peace, and of the special role of women
within it.

The program of the conference faithfully executed this mandate, direct-
ing the attendees' attention to "things American" that promoted traditional
conceptions of "American womanhood." Included in the program, for
example, were talks on "Education for Home-Making" and "Advancing
Ideals for the Home." In a speech on "The Changing Emphasis in the
Education of Women in the Southern United States," conference attendee
Elizabeth Colton praised the increasing presence of "domestic science" in
southern colleges. Instead of being taught "ornamental" subjects such as
music, art, and elocution, women were now being taught "practical" skills
such as cooking and sewing. "Home economics," she contended, "are better adapted for the majority of women than curricula such as at Bryn Mawr
and Wellesley Colleges." Blanche Z. de Baralt, a French painter married
to a Cuban diplomat, recognized the "superior intelligence" of "the Latin
American woman," but maintained "it is our conviction that the most
immediate need for the women of Latin America is training in the domestic
sciences; in order to destroy the barrier between man and woman she must
be prepared for usefulness as a skilled home maker as well as an intellectual
worker."[60] This emphasis on women's domestic capacities reflected the elite
makeup of the conference attendees and their distance from the more activist feminism emerging in the United States during the 1910s.

But the traditionalist slant of the conference should not obscure its significance within the context of the new internationalism. Swiggett and her
colleagues believed strongly in the unique power of women to shape inter-
American relations. As wives of prominent diplomatic officials, the organizers were fully aware of the myriad issues facing U.S.-Latin American relations, not least of which were the Wilson administration's interventions in
Mexico. The purpose of the conference was to facilitate diplomacy among
men, first by fostering friendship among women, and second by trying to
create a sense of common purpose. This was not a novel effort on the part
of Swiggett and her colleagues; women had long used their positions as
wives, sisters, mothers, and daughters to further their own and their male

relatives' political agendas. In a context such as this, "Washington women —both well-known and not—appear as political actors in their own right, using social events and the 'private sphere' to establish the national capital and to build . . . extraofficial structures."[61] Swiggett used her position as the wife of a prominent Pan American official to advance not only women's interests but international interests as well.

Indeed, a closer look at the conference agenda reveals the presence of many progressive ideas about women and their potential contributions to international amity. One representative from Texas spoke on "The Solidarity of the World's Womanhood as an International Asset." Fannie Fern Andrews, founder of the American School Peace League and member of the Woman's Peace Party, proposed a "Pan American Bureau of Education" that would stress topics such as "Public Education in a Democracy" and "International Education." Another speech on "Constructive Woman, an Aid to Modern Progress" highlighted the achievements of woman educators, political reformers, and social workers, including Maria Montessori, Susan B. Anthony, and Jane Addams.[62] Addams herself closed the conference with her address on the new internationalism. All these speeches reflected a belief in the power of women to effect change through personal interactions and shared knowledge.

Once a gathering like the Women's Auxiliary Conference, or a visit to Mexico like those by Zonia Baber or Caroline Smith and Harriet Taylor, had done so much to foster new friendships and establish common ground among women, internationalists sought to ensure that their work would continue. The most obvious answer was to form a group—whether a new organization entirely, like the Pan American International Women's Committee, or a new branch of an existing organization, like the YWCA or WILPF—and then to establish an agenda for that group. Emma Bain Swiggett turned the committee that had planned the Women's Auxiliary Conference into the PAIWC. Once she had secured contacts in as many Latin American countries as possible—including Adelia Palacios in Mexico— Swiggett decided that the first issue the committee would address would be child welfare. In May 1918 she sent a letter to all her contacts asking them to compile and share information on infant mortality and maternal health in their countries.[63] The organization's first "Bulletin," which appeared in 1921, centered on child welfare and published much of the information collected by committee members throughout the Americas.[64]

The YWCA and WILPF, meanwhile, continued their efforts to start new sections in Mexico City. The Mexican men and women with whom Harriet Taylor and Caroline Smith spoke were enthusiastic about the prospect of establishing an association in Mexico City. They believed the YWCA "middle-of-the-road policies would attract women from a broad spectrum—Marxists and 'free thinkers,' Roman Catholics, members of the pro-American business community—by offering them a place to serve that was free of partisan politics."[65] Taylor and Smith recommended starting a Mexican YWCA, but slowly, arguing that gathering support and resources from the local community would take time. They noted that the successful organization of a branch of the Young Men's Christian Association a few years earlier was cause for optimism. In fact, the Mexican YMCA had guaranteed Taylor and Smith an "immediate membership" of three hundred women from among the families and friends of their own members. The U.S. association allocated funds, and Smith returned to Mexico City in May 1922 as the new group's first executive secretary. The first members of the board took office in October 1923.

WILPF, for its part, struggled to identify potential members. Both Rose Standish Nichols and Zonia Baber, the representatives who traveled to Mexico City in 1920, made efforts to gather a group of women for a new section, but none of them panned out, likely due in part to Nichols and Baber's personal rivalry. By coincidence, however, they both reported to Jane Addams and Emily Greene Balch that the Mexican woman ideally suited for the task of forming a section was Elena Landázuri. Addams knew Landázuri well; the latter had lived in Chicago for several years, stayed at Hull House on more than one occasion, and traveled to Vienna in 1921 as an official delegate to WILPF's third international convention. She was also a member of the Consejo Feminista Mexicano, and a friend of Elena Torres. Ideally, WILPF leaders in Geneva would have liked to start a Mexican section from scratch, but failing that, Balch was prepared to have Landázuri transform the Consejo Feminista Mexicano into one. She asked her to sit down with Torres and "see what could be done" toward that end.[66] Landázuri promised to do what she could to start a Mexican section, though she gave Balch no reason to believe the council could be transformed. She enclosed a translation of their program, with the certainty that Balch would approve of it, and continued, "I do not think that other groups or individuals will follow the program of the League as near as this group follows it."

However, she noted, "everything that goes beyond what is the general attitude of the public . . . is bound to create a certain antagonistic spirit around
it and I do not want to limit the scope of the W.I.L. to the feminist group."
Landázuri ended though on a positive note. "In view of all this," she concluded, "I have decided to select myself the group that will integrate the
W.I.L. here. I feel very hopeful, because you can sense here in the air a spirit
of renaissance and freedom that has to bear its fruits. I know that the ideal
of the W.I.L. will be understood by many and supported, just give me some
time and I feel that I will offer a strong competent group to support the
League."[67] Landázuri was aware that the Consejo Feminista was not ideal
as a WILPF section because it had an agenda of its own, but she was confi-
dent she could organize a separate group to affiliate with Geneva. Balch
accepted her offer, and sent Landázuri a set of guidelines for starting a
section.

Getting new branches and sections off the ground frequently led to new
trials. With Adelia Palacios as her only contact, Emma Bain Swiggett was
often frustrated with the slow rate of progress in securing Mexican members of the Pan American International Women's Committee. Eventually
Palacios sent several names of other women who might be persuaded to
join the committee, but when Swiggett contacted them, only one responded.[68] The slow progress of the YWCA, meanwhile, was deliberate. In
the wake of Taylor and Smith's reconnaissance trip in 1921, the U.S. Foreign Division decided to proceed carefully for several reasons. First, none
of the U.S. secretaries who might reasonably be asked to live in Mexico City
for a year or two to help get the branch off the ground spoke any Spanish,
and they needed time to study the language. Second, unlike WILPF, which
could hold meetings easily in members' homes, the YWCA needed its own
facility to carry out its mission—part of which was to serve as a boarding
house for young women in the city. Searching out and acquiring a suitable
building took time. Finally, the association did not want to attract undue
attention from the Catholic Church. Taylor and Smith believed that their
main opposition would come from members of the Church hierarchy; ordinary Catholics, they argued, would welcome the group once they understood its mission.[69]

The Women's International League, meanwhile, struggled with whether
to establish a new section in Mexico from scratch, or to join forces with an
existing group, such as the Consejo Feminista. Emily Greene Balch strongly

preferred the former. Her previous experience in other countries had convinced her that when an existing group agreed to become a national section, WILPF's agenda had to compete for attention with the group's previous one. Balch was happy to have Elena Landázuri working on her behalf in Mexico City, and she was happy to hear that the council had voted to become a section, but she was skeptical about how that decision had come about and how well peace would fit with the CFM program. Peace was important to the Mexican group's platform, but it was not central. A letter from Elena Torres in April 1922 confirmed Balch's fears. Torres told her the council was "very interested" in WILPF: "We have gladly accepted the suggestion to form a National Section, but until now we have not proceeded owing to the fact that we have being working in making propaganda in favor of the women questions in social ground, [sic] and because we have not had the appropriate conditions to succeed in this respect, connected with your League."[70] This reiterated to Balch the necessity of Landázuri's forming her own section, since it was clear that WILPF's agenda was not the only one of the Consejo Feminista. Torres's reply indicated that while the council may have been able to adopt the League's agenda on top of their own, their work for peace would never be as central as it would have been to an organization that owed its very existence to those aims. Given WILPF's standard practice of establishing sections from scratch that were entirely focused on peace, affiliating with the Consejo Feminista was probably not the best course of action, but in the early 1920s Balch and Addams had few other options than to continue relying on Elena Landázuri to carry out their work in Mexico.

Despite these difficulties, by the early 1920s U.S. women's efforts seemed to be off to a good start. Steady correspondences had been established. Plans were in the works for both a Mexican section of WILPF and a Mexican branch of the YWCA. The former was officially established in 1922, the latter in 1923. The Women's Auxiliary Conference had been a success, and Swiggett's plans to form the Pan American International Women's Committee were under way. Reflecting the often informal nature of human internationalism, there were very few concrete arrangements in place. U.S. women's internationalism in Mexico was built on personal contacts and information exchange, but it was also dependent for its existence on individual initiative. In other words, women's internationalism had been established but was far from being institutionalized. But these initial steps were important, particularly given that they occurred concurrently with the decline and severing of U.S.-Mexican diplomatic relations in December 1920. Moreover, the fact that U.S. women had met with a notable amount of enthusiasm for cooperation among Mexican women meant that their internationalist efforts had at least a fighting chance to take root and grow. And as they discovered, Mexican women intended to be more than just passive partners in these endeavors.

Mexican Women's Internationalism

Many of the Mexicans with whom U.S. women were in contact advocated for internationalism. The platform of the Consejo Feminista Mexicano demonstrated that its members believed their nationalist and international-ist ambitions could coexist. Elena Torres echoed Jane Addams in her letter to the Women's Peace Society when she declared that the CFM sought an "entente-cordiale" among the world's women.[71] Elena Landázuri, in a speech before WILPF's third international convention in Vienna in 1921, argued for the power of women's organizing to effect change, both within Mexico and internationally.[72] Adelia Palacios continuously reiterated to Emma Bain Swiggett that she was committed to realizing the ideals of the Pan American International Women's Committee.[73] All these women wel-comed and cooperated with U.S. visitors in Mexico, such as Zonia Baber, Caroline Smith, and Harriet Taylor. The fact that the Mexicans with whom U.S. women were in the closest touch shared their basic assumptions about the power of women's internationalism was promising common ground on which to build.

But women such as Torres, Landázuri, and Palacios also made clear that they could and would use the methods of human internationalism to express their own views, and to articulate exactly what they wanted out of these exchanges with U.S. women. These women were prepared to embrace internationalism because they saw it as a means to help them achieve their own goals—some of which overlapped with U.S. women's interests, and some of which did not. The principles of mutuality, cooperation, and equity that underlay human internationalism promised much for Mexican women in this regard. In these efforts, Mexican women focused on two goals. First, they sought solidarity with and guidance from U.S. women on advancing Mexican women's civil, political, and economic status. Second, they wanted U.S. women to take a strong stance against U.S. intervention in Mexico, and to voice their opposition to policy makers in Washington, D.C. Like U.S. women, Mexican women advocated internationalism as a path to peace and a way to secure women's rights, but they saw it as a means to further their nationalist goals, such as an end to U.S. economic exploitation, as well.

Mexican women made clear that while they sought guidance from U.S. women, they did not want to be led, and they would resist any U.S. efforts at imperialist internationalism. Elena Torres distributed copies of the detailed, extensive Consejo Feminista platform as widely as possible among women's organizations outside Mexico. She sent copies to Elinor Byrns of the Women's Peace Society and to the U.S. section of WILPF in late 1919. In addition to wanting to share information about Mexico, the CFM solicited advice and support: "We beg of you to communicate with us directly and to send us all your literature, suggestions, programs of action and any information that may aid us in our new organization, and in return, we shall keep you informed of our progress and development."[74] Torres and her colleagues had put considerable thought and effort into crafting their platform, and they resisted several attempts on the part of U.S. women over the years to alter or narrow their focus. A few representatives from peace organizations wanted the CFM to focus solely on disarmament. Other U.S. women contended that the only way for the CFM to achieve its goal was by focusing on suffrage.

Elena Landázuri attempted to counter these incursions in 1921 in an address to the third international WILPF congress in Vienna, in which she emphasized the unique nature of Mexican problems and the need for Mexican solutions to fix them. Knowing she was the first Mexican woman to address a WILPF congress, Landázuri spent a considerable portion of her time outlining the history of Mexico, especially since the start of the Revolution. She explained that the reign of Porfirio Díaz had been an era of progress and development for some Mexicans, but it had cost the majority of Mexicans their land and freedoms. Some revolutionary leaders had tried to implement socialist policies in order to rectify this situation, with some benefits, but as far as Landázuri could judge, reforms that were "imported" from abroad proved largely inadaptable "to our conditions." On behalf of her compatriots she argued that "We must seek the possibility of social betterment from our own institutions, in forms that arise from the needs of our organizations." She was not speaking only of socialism; Landázuri implicitly rejected the wholesale imposition of any foreign ideology or system of government. The solutions to Mexican problems would originate in Mexico. "We are responsible for the current disarray of our country," she asserted, "but I think we recognize that with shame, which is already the first step toward a better future."

While Landázuri defended Mexican agency, she did not reject the possibility that international groups could offer assistance. She closed with a message to women and men of all nations. If foreigners wanted to "protect" Mexico, they should "take it seriously" among themselves:

> Begin by knowing who we are—read our works, enjoy our art, admire our history, and when you know our soul, you can begin to teach us what we want to know. In a family, you don't leave the children forgotten in a room and only come to realize their existence when they enter the classroom as half-savages and break all the rules. You educate them, you protect them, you guide them. So it is with nations—the young people have the right to question the thinkers, the idealists. Irrigate our virgin and fertile soil with something of the treasure of your love and your wisdom, and with your already skillful hands help us climb to the top.[75]

Landázuri thus walked a careful line between asserting Mexican autonomy and accepting guidance from groups such as WILPF. Outsiders could not hope to "fix" Mexico simply by rigidly imposing their plans and ideals. If they truly wanted to be useful, they had to learn how best to be useful in Mexico, to Mexicans. At the same time, however, Landázuri's family metaphor left intact prevalent assumptions about the inherent superiority of some groups over others—Mexicans were still the "children" in need of education. This tension between asserting autonomy and working alongside organizational leaders was common among women trying to challenge imperialist feminism during the interwar period.[76]

What both Landázuri and Torres demanded from U.S. women, particularly the peace activists, more than anything else was vocal, active opposition to U.S. military interventions in and U.S. economic exploitation of Mexico. In her initial letter to the Women's Peace Society, Elena Torres stated that the Consejo Feminista had originally been founded in August 1919 "as a spontaneous unit of protest against the constant incursions of American troops across the Mexican border," and that they were reaching out to U.S. women's organizations in large part because they hoped U.S. women would speak out against such incursions: "We are especially anxious to come in contact with the various international women's organizations, that they may know more of Mexico and her conditions and perhaps throw the weight of their opinion against the possible recurrence of any international misunderstandings."[77] Torres was careful not to paint all U.S. Americans with an imperialist brush. The CFM was eager to work with U.S. women, as long as they understood Torres's belief that "the ongoing threat for Mexico and for all Latin American countries is the boundless greed of a few U.S. imperialists," who would not hesitate to provoke a war "in order to control Mexican oil."[78] Elena Landázuri made a similar distinction in her address to the WILPF convention: "I must say that if a group of U.S. capitalists is our greatest enemy, we find among the people of the United States our greatest friends."[79]

Torres saved her strongest rhetoric for lashing out against economic exploitation by U.S. businesses. In a statement she sent Elinor Byrns to read on her behalf at a conference in Toronto, Torres contended that discrimination and exploitation were common within U.S. companies based in Mexico. U.S. and Mexican workers in the same jobs were compensated differently, treated differently, and given different benefits. Torres cited the mining and petroleum industries as particularly egregious offenders. Mining companies brought technological advancements to regions such as Guanajuato that should have improved not only production but the quality of life for its workers. Instead they brought only "ruin and misery." Petroleum workers tended to enjoy higher wages, she conceded, but their earnings were offset by extraordinarily high costs of living and a lack of job security. Mexicans were not opposed to progress in methods and machinery, Torres noted, but she questioned the "superiority" of a group of people who brought "the most frightful misery to thousands of families," and who were willing to sacrifice "human interests before all others."[80] Torres demanded that the WPS, and any other groups seeking an ally in the CFM, "castigate severely all those North American citizens who foment revolutions in other countries solely for the purpose of securing arms sales and maintaining the lives of their factories."[81]

Torres's and Landázuri's communications with U.S. women proved that they were more than willing to join internationalist ventures, but they expected to be more than just silent partners. The reactions they received indicated that U.S. women, particularly members of the Women's Peace

Society and the U.S. section of WILPF, took the CFM's concerns seriously, but that they were unlikely to take meaningful action to address them. The WPS lacked the resources and organizational dedication to send Torres much more than their goodwill. Elinor Byrns read Torres's invective against the "U.S. imperialists" to other members of the society, who asked her to assure Torres "that we are not all of us here eager for profits from petroleum and that we are very much ashamed of the people who want to throw us into war with Mexico." But, Byrns noted, "I am afraid that the people who are willing to go to war are now in power."[82] The U.S. section of WILPF passed a resolution in August 1920 favoring "constructive and friendly co-operation with Mexico" and opposing armed intervention, but there is no record that they took any further action.[83] Both groups likely felt hamstrung by their previous commitments to their own peace programs, and by their lack of money and influence with policy makers, but the fact remains that they did not prioritize the Mexican women's demands to the same extent they did their own. U.S. women were drawn to Mexico in part because of contentious U.S.-Mexican relations, but they did not condemn U.S. economic imperialism or exploitative business practices, even when expressly asked to do so by Mexican women.

Both U.S. and Mexican women saw promise and possibility in Jane Addams's new "human internationalism." The Women's International League for Peace and Freedom and the Women's Peace Society saw it as a chance to advance their fight for a permanent peace. The Young Women's Christian Association was eager to extend its mission for social and economic justice to Mexican women and girls. The Pan American International Women's Committee believed that promoting Pan Americanism among women would lead to greater hemispheric cooperation and harmony. By 1922 three of the four organizations (all except the WPS) seemed poised to solidify their new branches and new connections in Mexico. Members of the Consejo Feminista Mexicano, meanwhile, were ready to join internationalist networks as part of their efforts to promote global peace and to recruit allies in their struggles against U.S. imperialism in Mexico. All these organizations employed similar methods that followed on Jane Addams's articulation of human internationalism: personal interactions, exchanges of information, and shared experiences. These internationalist efforts were especially significant in light of the fact that after 1920 the United States and Mexico no longer had a diplomatic relationship. In fact, cooperation among U.S. and Mexican women laid some of the groundwork over the next few years for the restoration of formal diplomatic relations.

Nevertheless, U.S. and Mexican women did not approach the new internationalism in the same ways. Among U.S. women there was considerable divergence in their goals and methods. Women in the YWCA and the PAIWC sought "safe" contacts in Mexico, women who could not be branded as radical or politically inappropriate. By contrast, WILPF and the WPS cultivated contacts, such as Elena Torres and Elena Landázuri, who were more politically active. Mexican women, for their part, were prepared to engage in the methods of human internationalism, but they had a clearly defined agenda that U.S. women did not necessarily share. The Mexican Revolution, the spread of economic nationalism in Mexico, and the resentment against the United States resulting from repeated interventions infused Mexican women's internationalism in ways that posed potential conflicts for U.S. women. Elena Torres and Elena Landázuri wanted to use internationalism to defend their own nation, and to get U.S. women to speak out against theirs. Internationalism may not have been much more than "spiritual" for Jane Addams and her followers, but for Mexican women it was undoubtedly political.

Torres and Landázuri were about to have another chance with a different group of U.S. women. The U.S. League of Women Voters began making plans in 1921 to hold its own hemispheric conference of women. As an organization born out of the victory for women's suffrage, the league seemed to the members of the Consejo Feminista Mexicano like an ideal partner with whom to share their agenda for women's advancement in Mexico. That perception would be put to the test in Baltimore, Maryland, in April 1922.

Chapter 2

The Pan American Conference of Women

In April 1922, more than two thousand women and men from twenty-one American nations descended on Baltimore, Maryland. Convened by the U.S. League of Women Voters, the Pan American Conference of Women (PACW) centered on "subjects of special concern to women," including education, child welfare, and women's political status. But the league also acknowledged another, overriding concern. "Peace among nations is essential to the work that women have most at heart," declared the call to the conference. Seeking to capitalize on the spirit of internationalism flourishing in the early 1920s, the league hoped to further the cause of global peace by fostering "international friendliness": "The League believes that friendliness with our neighbor countries will be stimulated and strengthened when women from all parts of the western hemisphere come together for sympathetic study of their common problems."[1] To that end, league members invited delegates from each of the twenty-one American nations to come to Baltimore—where the league had already planned to hold its third national convention in April 1922—for an inter-American conference.

With this conference, the League of Women Voters became the first U.S. organization to put inter-American women's internationalism into practice on such a large, coordinated scale. Formed in 1920 out of the National American Woman Suffrage Association, the nonpartisan league's early goals included equal status for women under the law and prevention of war through international cooperation. It did not belong to the same pacifist tradition as the Women's International League for Peace and Freedom, but its members shared a belief in women's power to effect political change both nationally and internationally.[2] The Pan American conference seemed the perfect chance to implement the ideals of Jane Addams's human internationalism: women gathered together to

WOMEN OF AMERICAS GATHER AT BALTIMORE

Figure 2. Maud Wood Park, center, opens the Pan American Conference of Women. Maryland governor Albert Ritchie is second from the left.
Chicago Tribune, April 23, 1922.

share information and experiences, engage in personal interactions, build solidarity around common causes, and foster global peace. Unlike the conveners of the Women's Auxiliary Conference in 1916, league members took great pains to learn about the leading women activists in each country, and to extend invitations to them, rather than inviting women simply because they happened to be married to or fathered by a man attending a separate conference. The league guaranteed the participation of women already committed to various causes, women who would be able not only to share information but potentially to implement whatever strategies or suggestions arose in Baltimore. Every Latin American delegate had several opportunities to speak publicly throughout the conference, ensuring that attendees would hear more than just U.S. women's voices. The original list of topics for discussion included not only education and child welfare, but also women's suffrage and the limitation of armaments. These were later modified, though, by the U.S. State Department, which sanctioned but did not sponsor the conference.[3]

The Pan American Conference of Women is thus significant for several reasons. First, it demonstrated how women's internationalism served as a form of gendered diplomacy. By emphasizing "international friendliness" as the goal of the conference, league members made it clear they understood their actions as part of a broader effort to promote peace and understanding among American nations. The diplomatic potential of the conference extended beyond anything the participants themselves hoped would come of it. Both U.S. and Mexican government officials saw the conference as an opportunity to further reconciliation between the two nations, which still did not have a formal diplomatic relationship.

In its sheer size, the conference also illustrated the extent to which women activists across the Americas were committed to the promise of Addams's human internationalism. The reasons for their commitment varied, however. U.S. women, newly enfranchised, wanted to stake a claim, a political voice for themselves in international relations. They wanted to extend and coordinate activism for suffrage and women's rights beyond the United States, and they wanted to further hemispheric peace by bringing together women from across the Americas. Though many Latin American women may well have shared the latter two goals, they were looking for more. For instance, Mexican women, represented in Baltimore by Elena Torres and members of the Consejo Feminista Mexicano, continued to demand that U.S. women use their newfound political power to oppose interventionist U.S. policies and exploitative U.S. business practices in Mexico.

Although U.S. and Mexican women's dedication to internationalism may have been equal, their roles in Baltimore were not. U.S. women had disproportionate power to shape the agenda and the outcome of the conference, more than any Latin American women. The League of Women Voters took it on themselves to direct the proceedings with minimal input from the non-U.S. participants. While professing a mutual desire to learn from each other, conference organizers circumscribed Latin American women's contributions. Even when Mexican women expressly asked to have U.S. policies toward their country included on the agenda, league officials balked. To be fair, the LWV had to operate within a set of constraints—like reliance on the approval of the U.S. State Department—that limited their ability to allow discussion of controversial topics. But the fact remains that the organizers set the agenda and chose topics for discussion based on what they assumed were common concerns of all women in the Americas, while admitting they knew little of women's concerns outside their own country. This imbalance called into question the cooperative nature of human internationalism.

Gendered Diplomacy

The idea for the Pan American Conference of Women came from Lavinia Engle, an active member of the Maryland League of Women Voters. Engle thought that in addition to providing the fledgling league with widespread publicity, such a conference would be an ideal way to promote inter-American cooperation. Secretary of Commerce Herbert Hoover was interested in furthering trade with South America, Engle pointed out to LWV president Maud Wood Park, and would likely help secure support from the Harding administration, while Carrie Chapman Catt could help identify potential delegates using her contacts from the International Woman Suffrage Alliance.[4] No Latin American woman had the right to vote in 1922, and the alliance had branches only in Argentina and Uruguay, but Catt had developed an extensive network of contacts through a survey the group conducted in 1902 on the political status of women around the world.[5] By corresponding with U.S. commercial attachés in Latin America, Secretary Hoover also helped identify politically and socially active delegates, rather than simply extending invitations to the wives of Latin American diplomats.[6] In June 1921, Park established a committee to determine the feasibility of such a conference, decide how many Latin American delegates might realistically be expected to attend, and draw up a tentative agenda outlining the purpose and goals of the conference that could be used to generate publicity.[7]

Reflecting the newfound power of women voters, Park also organized a delegation to the White House. On June 29 she led a group of conference backers, including Maryland and National LWV officials, a representative of the City of Baltimore, and the governor of Maryland, to a meeting with secretary of state Charles Evans Hughes. After securing his approval, the conference committee, chaired by Dorothy Hubert and LWV executive secretary Minnie Fisher Cunningham, began to make definite arrangements.[8] They wrote to members of the Latin American diplomatic corps, asking for the names of prominent women in their countries. In October the U.S. State Department issued invitations on behalf of the league to every Latin American country, asking governments to appoint delegates.[9] The Pan American Union also lent its enthusiastic support. Director Leo Rowe promised Engle and Cunningham he would "keep after" the State Department to issue the invitations promptly and even speak to as many Latin American ambassadors as he could personally, to convey his own belief in the significance of the conference.[10] By October 1921, the conference was beginning to take shape.

Conference planners recognized the significance of their work as women diplomats. The league argued that by convening a group of women to discuss common concerns, they were furthering international cooperation. In other words, this was not just women getting together to discuss "women's issues" separate from international politics. As Engle had originally pointed out, a conference promoting inter-American peace and cooperation was an ideal way for the league to generate publicity and establish a voice for women in international relations. A popular argument for women's suffrage throughout the nineteenth and early twentieth centuries was that women's influence would improve U.S. politics and society by making them more humane and by reducing corruption. After winning the vote in 1920, U.S. women used similar rhetoric to establish their authority over international issues ranging from disarmament to national defense.[11] The Baltimore conference attempted to do the same for diplomacy. Advance press coverage reflected the league's success in this regard. The *San Antonio Express* asserted, "Diplomatic service of this sort heretofore has been entrusted to men; but in view of the new civic position woman has assumed in the United States . . . the time has come when she should enter this larger sphere of action."[12] The *Baltimore Sun* agreed: "Nothing could more strikingly demonstrate how far the world has moved in the last few years from old precedents and customs than this great international gathering of women. For weal or woe, for good or ill, the heretofore politically submerged sex is asserting an equal right with man to guide and govern the earth."[13]

A few months before the conference opened, League of Women Voters vice president Marie Stewart Edwards articulated the organization's own understanding of this gendered diplomacy: "By emphasizing the preservation of the race as a necessary function of government we can perhaps supplement the masculine idea which overemphasizes the preservation of property to the exclusion of other things, and by combining the two we may eventually do away with this queer theory that to protect property and to protect the human race we must create engines for the destruction of both."[14] Edwards saw in the Baltimore conference an opportunity to counteract the prevailing trends in inter-American relations, to put an end to the cycles of violence and aggression like that between the United States

and Mexico. Her characterization of masculine politics as focused on property rights resonated particularly with the Mexican situation, given the
centrality of land and subsoil resources to the U.S.-Mexican dispute. "Preservation of the race," meanwhile, was a common way in which women
peace activists framed their mission, linking their work to their familial and
social roles as mothers.[15] This juxtaposition was at the heart of the role the
LWV envisioned for itself in U.S. foreign policy. The ballot was not only a
chance to improve U.S. politics and society; it was a tool for improving the
world, a way for women to exert authority over international relations.
"The mothering heart and conscience of women have always been at the
service of those close at hand," the league declared. "For the first time in
history these qualities are being consciously directed to meet world-wide
needs."[16] In the weeks leading up to the conference that vision seemed
poised to become reality.

U.S. league members were not the only ones who saw promise in these
new forms of gendered diplomacy. Their government saw an opportunity
in the Pan American Conference to conduct diplomacy through women.
With regard to Mexico in particular, the appeal of "international friendliness" among governments took on special significance, of which the organizers were well aware. The two countries had had no official relationship
since December 1920, and by early 1922 both sides were looking for
potential ways to restore ties. Almost from the beginning of the league's
contact with the State Department and the Pan American Union, the
question of Mexico was a key topic of discussion. Hughes and Rowe recognized the conference as an opportunity to take steps toward reconciliation. Marie Stewart Edwards reported that the secretary of state was
"tremendously pleased with this opportunity for establishing lines with
Mexico which they had not been able to do as yet in a more direct manner."[17] When financial difficulties left the organizing committee wonder-
ing if they should postpone the entire conference, Maud Wood Park
observed that Sumner Welles, assistant secretary of state for Latin American affairs, and Rowe were anxious to have the conference proceed as
scheduled because "it might mean real help in the Mexican situation."[18]
The Department of Commerce was also interested in the trade benefits
that might result from a restored diplomatic relationship. Philip Smith,
chief of the Latin American Division of the Bureau of Foreign and
Domestic Commerce, instructed the U.S. trade commissioner in Mexico

to publicize the conference in Mexican newspapers and gather information on women's activism in Mexico City.[19]

Mexican officials also welcomed the opportunity presented by the Pan American Conference. President Álvaro Obregón knew that for his government to be considered legitimate in the eyes of the world, and to begin to solve the problem of Mexico's massive foreign debt, he would have to reconcile with the United States. On March 22, 1922, less than a month before the conference opened, Obregón told the *New York Times*, "We wish to assume our place in the world of nations. By our efforts to pay our just obligations the Mexican Government is demonstrating that it realizes its obligations and is determined to fulfill them. Naturally recognition is needed. . . . Our desire and our word to resume the payment of interest on our debts should help toward bringing both recognition and closer relations."[20] At the same time, Obregón had to save face in front of widespread opposition to the United States in his own country.[21] The PACW provided him an opportunity to reach out to the U.S. government while deflecting any potential resistance. Sending a delegation of women to meet with other women was a move much more likely to be accepted and forgotten in Mexico than sending a group of oil producers, for example, to meet with U.S. investors. Obregón's support of the conference was so strong that he authorized federal funds from the Secretariat of Public Education to finance the delegation.[22]

Identifying the Mexican women who would represent their country was a long process for Dorothy Hubert and the organizing committee. They relied primarily on the personal contacts of U.S. officials and others in Mexico City. After considering input from the U.S. trade commissioner, the U.S. chargé d'affaires in Mexico City, and the Pan American Round Table (PART), a women's group based in San Antonio, Hubert focused her attention on the Consejo Feminista Mexicano. The trade commissioner called it the "leading national women's organization of Mexico," while the *Woman Citizen*—the organ of the League of Women Voters—extolled Elena Torres as "one of the most brilliant women of the Republic."[23] Torres had dramatically expanded several CFM programs; for instance, by 1922 they were distributing free breakfasts to 6,000 school children a day. The Mexican secretary of education personally appointed Torres head of the Mexican delegation to Baltimore. Hubert wrote to Torres in January, formally asking her to attend the PACW as a Mexican delegate and to raise interest in the conference among her colleagues. Torres agreed, and recruited seven of her colleagues to travel to Baltimore with her.[24] They included a math teacher, a newspaper editor, and two women who had spent several years teaching indigenous Mexicans to read and write Spanish. With the exception of Torres, who came from a working-class family, the Mexican delegates were middle-class, and all but two were unmarried. Several of them had spent time in the United States, including Torres, and spoke English well.[25]

The Mexican delegation's journey to the conference was a veritable public relations campaign, designed to promote Pan Americanism, Mexico, and the League of Women Voters all at the same time. Composed of eight women, the group was one of the largest contingents from a Latin American country. From Mexico City they traveled by train to Laredo, Texas, where the U.S. Treasury Department had instructed customs officials to "extend every courtesy to facilitate the passage of the Mexican women through that port." They were met at the border by Florence Terry Griswold, president of the Pan American Round Table, who, along with several members of her organization, escorted them to San Antonio. After a few days of events and sight-seeing in San Antonio, several Round Table members accompanied the Mexican women by train to St. Louis, where they received "special hospitality" from the local branch of the League of Women Voters. From St. Louis, Torres, Griswold, and the others continued on to Baltimore. The Mexican delegation carried with them a Mexican flag made from silk and hand-embroidered by hundreds of Mexican women. President Obregón had asked them, on behalf of the entire country, to present the flag at the Baltimore conference, and afterward to carry it to Independence Hall in Philadelphia.[26] On April 28, Torres exchanged flags with members of the New Century Club, a prominent Philadelphia women's organization. They in turn presented Torres with a U.S. flag to be delivered as a gift to President Obregón's wife.[27] This was gendered public diplomacy at its finest—the journey and exchange of flags were designed to spread a peaceful and pleasant image of Mexico across the United States, establishing these representatives as friends rather than adversaries. At a time when the two countries did not enjoy a formal diplomatic relationship, these kinds of interactions held great symbolic significance.

In addition to establishing the Pan American Conference of Women as a venue for gendered diplomacy, the pre-conference activities and exchanges also revealed that while all the delegates were dedicated to furthering inter-American women's internationalism, some had more power than others to shape its direction. The process of setting the conference

Figure 3. Members of the Mexican delegation to the Pan American Conference shortly after their arrival in San Antonio. Left to right: Eulalia Guzman, Aurora Herrera de Nobregas, Luz Vera, Julia Nava de Ruisanchez, and Elena Torres. Torres told the *San Antonio Express*, "We are going to work out things which have been overlooked or given up as an impossibility by men."

San Antonio Express, April 16, 1922.

agenda most clearly illustrates this imbalance. Lavinia Engle, who had the original idea for the conference, initially chose the topics for the roundtable discussions. U.S. members of the organizing committee then refined her selections. The task had to be started early; in order to solicit support for the conference from the U.S. State Department, league representatives had to be able to present a tentative agenda. Once they had secured support, they could not stray very far from their initial proposal. With this in mind, Engle chose issues she assumed would be of interest to women throughout the hemisphere. Her first list, submitted to the State Department in July 1921, included six topics: "education, child welfare, women in industry, prevention of traffic in women, suffrage for women, and international friendliness and reduction of armaments."[28] Engle admitted to Maud Wood Park, however, that in setting the agenda she was hampered by her lack of knowledge of Latin America. "I have tried to topic [*sic*] the points for the P.A.C.," she wrote in October 1921. "After all the whole matter boils down to the simple fact that we know practically nothing about any of our American neighbors except Canada and not a great deal about her."[29] Less than a week later Engle, Cunningham, and the other members of the organizing committee supplied Rowe with a copy of the conference agenda—weeks before they had even begun contacting Latin American women about attending. The final list included Engle's first four original topics verbatim. "Suffrage for women" was changed to "women's political status," and "international friendliness and reduction of armaments" was removed entirely, in favor of "women's civil status."[30]

In setting the agenda for the conference, league officials operated under several constraints. One was time—in order for invitations to be sent and acknowledged, and for Latin American delegates to make travel arrangements, they had to secure the cooperation of the U.S. State Department at least six months in advance. Other restraints were not so concrete. Most league members, especially those interested in international relations, were aware of the popular resentment of the United States throughout Latin America. U.S. financial imperialism in Central America and the Caribbean reached its height in the early 1920s, and many league members had already joined a coalition of anti-imperialists opposed to U.S. policies like Dollar Diplomacy.[31] In her original proposal for the conference agenda, Engle argued that one important benefit of the meeting was that it would give Latin American women a chance to get to know U.S. women and to "learn that we are not as bad as we are painted."[32] Her inclusion of "reduction of armaments," along with "international friendliness," would have won approval not only from opponents of U.S. interventions in Latin America within the United States but also from many Latin Americans. Yet neither phrase appeared on the final version of the conference agenda. No record exists of why the change was made, but it is important to keep in mind that the entire project hinged on the endorsement of the U.S. State Department. Despite the groundswell of support for disarmament during the early 1920s, State Department officials were likely reluctant to sanction discussion of the topic at an inter-American conference during a time when the United States was involved in myriad ongoing military interventions in Latin America. Reliance on State Department support also may well have made Engle, Park, and the organizing committee feel they could not encourage any discussions at the conference that might have sounded like criticisms of U.S. foreign policies.

But the fact remains that Engle and the committee chose the topics for
the conference without consulting any Latin American women, or even any
U.S. women with greater knowledge of Latin America, and that they
assumed the topics they chose were of common concern to all American
women. They were not wrong; their issues were important to activist
women throughout the hemisphere, as the delegates' lengthy contributions
to the roundtable discussions proved. But neither Engle nor the committee
took into account the myriad problems unique to Latin America as a whole
and to various countries in particular. Not least among these, despite the
LWV's reluctance to discuss it, was the problem of U.S. imperialism.

The Mexican delegation did not share the league's reluctance. Two
months before the conference opened, the members of the Consejo Feminista Mexicano sent a telegram to the league, begging all U.S. women to
exert pressure on their government to change its Mexican policy. The
concerns they iterated echoed closely the arguments Elena Torres and
Elena Landázuri had been making to the Women's Peace Society and the
Women's International League for Peace and Freedom for over a year.
"The Mexican ground has been bloodied by more than ten years of revolution," they wrote, and "all the implements of destruction have been
furnished by the United States." They charged that American mining
companies continued to exploit Mexican workers, paying them infre-
quently and with devalued currency. The CFM implored U.S. women to
demand action from their government to stop facilitating the devastation
in Mexico.[33]

The lack of response from the league must have been discouraging for
Torres and her colleagues, but they did not abandon their mission. It took
Hubert, chair of the organizing committee, a month just to acknowledge
the telegram. She assured the CFM of the "great interest which we feel in
your statements and of the desire of the LWV to establish and maintain the
most friendly possible relations with the women of Mexico."[34] She gave no
indication, however, that the issue would receive space on the conference
program, and with the removal of "international friendliness and reduction
of armaments" as a roundtable topic, there was no obvious place on the
program to discuss Mexican women's concerns. This did not deter the Consejo Feminista. Elena Landázuri informed Emily Greene Balch that she and
her colleagues were "preparing a memorandum of the situation," in order
to "convey to the American Delegates right information of international
matters." These included oil, land rights, and humanitarian crises along the

border. The CFM was counting on the understanding of league members as women, indicating it was not just U.S. women who saw women's internationalism as explicitly gendered. Landázuri maintained they were approaching the league "because we feel sure that they would understand and act differently than men have." She requested Balch's help in laying the groundwork for the Mexican appeal, "because I feel sure that this little group is going to be of help to the country and the relations of both countries." The CFM communications proved that its members were coming to Baltimore expecting to be heard by U.S. women, and that Mexican women also saw themselves as engaging in gendered diplomacy to improve U.S.-Mexican relations.

An article in the *Woman Citizen*, the journal of the League of Women Voters, just two months before the conference opened bolstered the Consejo Feminista's case that U.S. foreign policies were harmful to Mexico. Part of a series designed to help familiarize U.S. women with Latin America, the article was written by Lily T. Joseph, president of the Texas Federation of Women's Clubs, who had traveled to Mexico the year before. Joseph was highly critical of U.S. foreign policy, identifying "certain of our big interests" as responsible for the Harding administration's failure to recognize Obregón: "Bluntly, the policy which they foster is this: Send our army into Mexico! *Only a few of our American boys will be killed.* If necessary shoot down the Mexicans; but protect our interests, that we may gorge and wax fat upon the wealth that we shall bring out of Mexico."[35] Although Joseph's main focus was on the conflict over Article 27, the CFM would have agreed with her that U.S. business interests were exploiting Mexico. Elena Torres likely would also have appreciated the attention Joseph brought to Mexican poverty. Joseph bemoaned the "sad changes" she witnessed in Mexico City since her last visit before the Revolution. Streets that had once been filled with the "handsome equipages" of the rich and fashionable, soldiers "smart in bright uniforms" defending the National Palace, stately trees, and dazzling buildings had been replaced by shabbiness and "long lines of the impoverished people selling their treasures for a song." She described the poverty she saw in the villages and towns between the Texas border and Mexico City, where crowded markets were filled with people selling "miserable little piles of fruit," "strings of beads," and "tawdry ornaments."[36] Joseph's article helped Torres and the Consejo Feminista by introducing active LWV members to the current situation in Mexico right before they made the trip to Baltimore.

The planning, negotiating, and communicating that went on between the spring of 1921 and the opening of the conference in April 1922 thus revealed several things. First, women and men on all sides saw it as a venue for gendered diplomacy, and particularly as an opportunity for advancing a potential rapprochement between the United States and Mexico. Second, the process of setting the agenda for the conference indicated that some participants had more power to shape the agenda than others, and that some participants' concerns outweighed others. The League of Women Voters hosted the conference; its members took primary responsibility for choosing the roundtable topics and for writing the program. In doing so they had to balance input from Latin American women like Elena Torres and Elena Landázuri against the interests of the U.S. State Department. The article by Lily Joseph strongly suggests that by February 1922, if not before, league members were aware of the situation in postrevolutionary Mexico, but to what extent they would allow Elena Torres and the other Mexican delegates to air their grievances against the United States at the conference itself remained to be seen.

The Official Record

The Pan American Conference of Women officially commenced at ten o'clock in the morning on Thursday, April 20, at the Century Theatre Roof in downtown Baltimore. In welcoming the delegates, LWV President Maud Wood Park drew attention to the cooperative spirit of the gathering, emphasizing the shared nature of women's struggles throughout the hemisphere. "The women," Park declared, "who are turning their thoughts on this conference today realize with us that we women have problems in common that are not defined by national or international boundaries—problems that belong to women all over the wide world, and we believe that in the combined wisdom of the women who are here we shall all receive help in our common problems."[37] This argument that the bonds of gender superseded the bonds of nation and nationality echoed much of the thinking that had gone into conceiving the conference. Park also took pains to convey to the Latin American delegates that the U.S. women she represented wanted that cooperation to be mutual, that they did not intend simply to preach to Latin American women for ten days, but hoped to benefit from their input: "The National League of

Women Voters is eager to learn from the experience of those women who have honored us by their presence today. We realize that we have much to be taught, and we are deeply grateful to you who have taken this long journey to bring us the benefit of what you know about the subjects in which we are also interested."[38] Both sentiments—common interests and reciprocal exchange—followed naturally from the rhetoric of human internationalism.

The male speakers who succeeded Park at the podium affirmed the significance of the gendered diplomacy in which the conference delegates were engaged. Maryland Governor Albert Ritchie asserted that women's "natural" instincts would lend a new cast to this hemispheric gathering: "Previous conventions akin to this have been controlled or influenced by the masculine viewpoint, but here, for the next ten days, we will have the good sense and the level-headedness of women, chastened and heightened by the things which are nearest and dearest to their hearts." Leo Rowe, who as director of the Pan American Union had been instrumental in making the event a reality, emphasized the conference's importance to the cause of Pan Americanism: "One must indeed be devoid of imagination not to appreciate the larger significance of this coming together of the women of the Americas to interchange experience and to assist one another in the solution of these great social problems which are fundamental to our American democracy. This, in every sense of the word, is a continental congress, one giving to the entire world an example of that unity of purpose and that community of ideals upon which the entire Pan American movements rests."[39] Both men thus underscored the League of Women Voters' own rationales for calling the conference: the need for a new kind of inter-American diplomacy and the assumption of a shared set of concerns.

Those shared concerns took center stage for the next three days. Beginning Thursday morning, and continuing through Saturday, the delegates met in a series of roundtables on the predetermined topics: child welfare, women in education, women in industry, prevention of traffic in women, women's civil status, and women's political status. The conduct of the roundtables mirrored the planning of the conference in that U.S. women had a disproportionate influence on the tone and direction of the conversation. Despite Maud Wood Park's insistence that U.S. women were "eager to learn" from Latin American women, a U.S. woman presided over each roundtable; by virtue of her position she had the power to shape the discussions. The league's reasoning behind this move was to have a recognized expert lead each roundtable—all the women except one held official positions in the U.S. government. For instance, Grace Abbott, head of the Children's Bureau at the Department of Labor, led the discussion on child welfare, while Mabel Walker Willebrandt, assistant attorney general at the Department of Justice, led the one on women's civil status. This pattern meant that U.S. women tended to dominate the roundtables (though in some cases this may have been inadvertent). Some roundtable leaders spoke longer in their introductory remarks than others, thereby cutting off time for other women to contribute. Willebrandt spoke for almost fifteen minutes despite the fact that there were thirteen other women participating in the two-hour session. A second U.S. woman participated in each roundtable to share information on the issue, so the United States had two voices on every issue while other countries only had one. The second U.S. woman often spoke last, which meant the United States got both the first and the final words in each discussion.

The roundtable on women's political status exemplified the problem of U.S. dominance. It featured the only woman leader who was not a U.S. government official; at the time of the conference, Carrie Chapman Catt was the president of the International Woman Suffrage Alliance and honorary president of the League of Women Voters. From the outset, Catt made clear that her roundtable would be different, that it would not involve a cooperative sharing of programs in various countries to advance women's political status. To Catt's mind, the Pan American Conference as a whole was "designed to be a conference between those who have already been endowed with the vote and those who do not have it, to see whether there is anything we who are enfranchised may do to assist those who have not yet perhaps begun this movement in their own country." She went on to explain that few Latin American women could speak on the issue, "because the number of those which have begun the suffrage movement there is very limited."[40] In the space of a few moments, Catt shifted the tenor of the conference, from one designed by U.S. women but led by them quietly to one led by them outright.

This imperiousness was not out of character for Catt. She had risen through the ranks of the suffrage movement throughout the 1890s due largely to her political acumen and sheer force of willpower. As president of the National American Woman Suffrage Association from 1900 to 1904 and from 1915 to 1920, she guided the movement to its successful conclusion, though not without provoking frustrations among some of her colleagues. Most notably, after helping to cofound the Women's Peace Party in 1915, she reneged on her commitment to peace just two years later and supported U.S. entry into World War I. Catt had significant experience with international work; in 1902 she founded the International Woman Suffrage Alliance, of which she served as president until 1923.[41] But her international experience was limited almost exclusively to suffrage, which may explain her single-minded focus on the issue at the Pan American Conference. Catt's racial ideologies also influenced her approach in Baltimore. Rosalyn Terborg-Penn has drawn attention to the parallels between the marginalized role of African American women in the U.S. suffrage movement and Catt's and others' "imperializing" views of suffrage movements in Latin America. Catt and many of her colleagues believed that some women "were further back on the evolutionary scale and required more time to develop before they could speak and act in their own right."[42]

Catt's remarks at the roundtable laid bare this attitude. Unlike other roundtable leaders, who made some opening remarks and then turned the podium over to their colleagues, Catt spoke again for almost thirty minutes halfway through the session. This time she directed herself exclusively to the "Spanish-American delegates." Their lack of knowledge about suffrage was excusable, she told them, because they did not have suffrage movements in their own countries, and "probably you who have come here are not particularly interested in this question." But she urged them to reconsider the matter. "It does not matter whether you are interested in this question or not," she argued. "I want you particularly to remember this: There are six continents in the world and there is only one continent where no woman has the vote and that is South America. Will you be content to be the only women in the world without the vote? No!"[43] All their concerns for child welfare, education, social hygiene, and other issues could be addressed if they had the vote, Catt asserted: "You can do a great deal more with the vote than you can without it and you will find that men and women give you a great deal more respect when you have the vote than when you have not got it." She admonished them not to fear the pope's approval, pointing to the millions of Catholic women in Europe and around the world who had secured the vote. Finally, she claimed that the most important thing Latin American women had to do was to ask for help from women who already had the vote, especially U.S. women. Catt and her cohort would do whatever they could, she promised, to help Latin American women win the vote. "And if you are afraid of us," she added, "why just get over it."[44]

Catt's assertion that there were no significant campaigns for the vote in Latin America was belied by the six Latin American women who followed her to speak of suffrage associations operating in Uruguay, Paraguay, Brazil, Cuba, Puerto Rico, and Chile.[45] But each of these speakers admired Catt and deferred to U.S. leadership on the issue. Bertha Lutz, the delegate from Brazil, praised Catt as a "symbol and an inspiration" to all Latin American women, assuring her that "the women of Brazil, and I may perhaps say the women of all South America, hold you in great reverence, esteem, and respect."[46] The Panamanian delegate, Esther Niera de Calvo, called Catt "my best inspirer."[47] Addressing herself to the U.S. delegates, the Puerto Rican representative reported that "as residents of one of the possessions of the United States, [the women of Puerto Rico] say they are your little sisters, and they are asking for your cooperation."[48] Even though the delegates were careful not to antagonize Catt, they defended their own activities for women's suffrage throughout Latin America.

By the end of the day on Saturday, April 22, all the roundtable sessions were completed, and over the next week U.S. LWV members turned their attention during the days to their own internal business. But almost every evening brought a banquet or program designed to include the Latin American delegates. These sessions were important because they extended the gendered diplomatic mission of the conference, and because they gave all the delegates more opportunities to share information about their countries' histories, values, and aspirations. For instance, on Sunday night they gathered for an evening of tribute to "famous women of the Americas." Delegates from each country spoke for a few minutes about notable women from their nation's past. On Tuesday, April 25 they were hosted by the Maryland League of Women Voters, and heard addresses by the governor of Maryland, secretary of commerce Herbert Hoover, and others. The largest of these gatherings took place on Friday in Washington, capping a day-long excursion to the U.S. capital.

Several of the sessions, particularly the trip to Washington, furthered the league's efforts at gendered diplomacy that had begun with the rail journey of the Mexican delegation from Texas to Baltimore. For example, on the opening night of the conference, the 2,000-mile journey of the Mexican flag from President Obregón's wife culminated in its presentation to the League of Women Voters. Ironically, the flag was offered to the league by Florence Terry Griswold, president of the Pan American Round Table of San Antonio, who had accompanied the Mexican delegates from Texas. She presented the flag as a gift from María Obregón made directly to U.S. women, as though the eight women comprising the Mexican delegation had not been involved in the transaction at all. Griswold then used her moment at the podium to highlight the work of her own organization toward establishing better relations with Mexico.[49]

Throughout the conference, the public activities of the delegates attracted much more media attention than the proceedings themselves. Newspapers covered the South American delegates' arrivals in New York and their journeys to Baltimore under escort by LWV members. During the conference the *Baltimore Sun* reported on the attendees' myriad activities, including a driving tour of the city, a visit to the U.S. Naval Academy, a reception hosted by the governor of Maryland, and special church services. These descriptions of Latin American and U.S. women spending time together, enjoying one another's company, conveyed messages of "international friendliness" and enhanced the power of gendered diplomacy more effectively than speeches and pronouncements. The final day of the conference featured a trip to Washington, D.C., where the delegates attended a reception hosted by the Daughters of the American Revolution, dined at the Pan American Union Building, and visited former president Woodrow Wilson. Despite his failing health, Wilson appeared at the door of his home to greet the hundreds of women gathered outside. The delegates also took part in a tree-planting ceremony with vice president Calvin Coolidge.[50] In announcing the events, the *Washington Post* editorialized: "The representative women of the Latin Americas should . . . exert a tremendous effect in bringing the countries of this hemisphere in closer harmony."[51] Thus the *Post* confirmed the significance of these women's activities for furthering "international friendliness" in the Western Hemisphere.

The Pan American conference also continued to receive support from members of the foreign policy establishment, albeit in ways that made clear their views on the subordinate value of gendered diplomacy. During an evening titled "What the Women of the Americas Can Do for International Friendliness" all the conference delegates heard speeches by secretary of state Charles Evans Hughes, British ambassador to the United States Auckland Geddes, and Leo Rowe, director of the Pan American Union. The men who addressed the delegates in Washington commended them for furthering friendly relations among American nations, but made it clear that their work was at best supplemental to that of men. Vice President Coolidge, who had met several of the women at a special ceremony earlier in the day, encouraged future cooperative efforts to address social problems. "There are some problems," he noted, "with which men are peculiarly fitted to deal; there are others which lie within the special province of women."[52] Hughes, the highest-ranking member of the U.S. government to address all the delegates in person, emphasized the important role women could play in politics, though he argued that role was not their most significant: "I have not the slightest doubt that women are to have a highly important influence in our political life, a conserving and wholesome influence. But their most important work, as indeed the most important work of men, is in securing the basis of society itself, and we shall never succeed with any political structure, of whatever name, if women fail in their work upon the foundation of that structure."[53]

Ambassador Geddes tried to strike a less serious tone by assuming a tone of mock parental authority in his speech to the delegates. If they truly wished to make a difference in inter-American relations, he warned, they would have to educate themselves: "What is the matter with you is that you are all too ignorant"—this remark was greeted with laughter and applause—"and unless you get out of that ignorance you are in a positive danger." Friendship was fine, he cautioned, but to effect change the delegates would have to go farther. They had to "understand something about this great mass of economic problems and difficulties which is filling the minds of all the men who are concerned with the international relations at the present time. That means study; it means real hard work on the part of those who would be leaders among women."[54] Geddes's tone was playful and engaging, but he meant what he said. He believed women could make serious contributions to international relations, provided they were knowledgeable enough to compete with their male counterparts.

Rowe, for his part, confessed that he frequently had little faith in men to solve international problems. They were too focused on politics and on competition with other countries. Women, he argued, had to correct those tendencies: "It is almost impossible to expect from this generation that superior viewpoint which means that you help yourselves by helping your brother, and that responsibility, women of America, women of the Americas, the responsibility to carry that principle into the practice of government, into the practice of foreign policy, is a responsibility which rests upon you directly."[55]

All these men seemed to agree in principle with Marie Stewart Edwards and other LWV members that women could be a supplemental force in foreign policy-making. Overlaying their enthusiasm for women's participation, however, was a healthy coating of condescension. Coolidge, for example, distinguished between problems men should handle and those better suited to women, suggesting women were incapable of solving the former. Hughes believed women's duty to the state and to international relations was an important one, but by his definition their role was virtually invisible within the realm of politics. It was in their capacity as women, not as experts, diplomats, or even full citizens, that women were to play their largest role. If women failed in "securing the basis of society" through raising children, politics itself would crumble, but if their influence was lacking in political life, that life would merely be less wholesome. Others trivialized what women had already accomplished. Geddes's tone may have been playful, but he chided his audience for their ignorance, as though those same women had not just spent the better part of a year negotiating the minefield of inter-American relations. As far as these men were concerned, gendered diplomacy was subordinate to "real" diplomacy.

The women in the audience understood this implication fully, but remained undeterred. Lady Nancy Astor—the U.S.-born wife of a British viscount and the first woman to sit as a member in the House of Commons—adopted Geddes's playful tone in retort: "Really the gentlemen, the dear darlings, the gentlemen do trespass upon our good nature. I sat in that box and almost yelled out several times, but I have learned through a hard schooling to keep my mouth shut and it is far more difficult for a woman to learn that than it is to learn economics."[56] Esther Niera de Calvo of Panama countered the marginalization of women's internationalism by arguing that the most important institution for teaching solidarity and cooperation was the home, and that women were naturally suited to educate children in peace and diplomacy: "Woman possesses a flower of good taste, of delicacy, of tact, which she alone knows how to cultivate; it is a spirit of kindliness which foretells the intentions, foresees the desires and perceives the feelings. . . . Therefore, her influence is always beneficial."[57] Brazilian Bertha Lutz reiterated the league's original hope that the conference would promote inter-American peace: "Women of America, let it be our aim . . . to strike hatred out of America and then to wipe war from the face of the earth."[58] Maud Wood Park, in her closing remarks, was more circumspect. She compared herself to a scientific discoverer who had just unearthed "a force for new usefulness that has been long latent." In the "great cooperation of women" begun in Baltimore, she felt, "we are beginning to turn for usefulness in the service of humanity by injecting the love and wisdom that women have stored in the bosom of their own hearts these many years. The families will not lose by this sharing of their love, but the world will gain when this latent force is more and more being realized."[59] Park defended her own and her colleague's diplomatic efforts, while simultaneously promising that women would not abandon their domestic duties in their pursuit of world peace.

Although U.S. women dominated most of the discourse at the roundtables and the evening sessions, there were many opportunities for Latin American women to speak during these events. A member of the Mexican delegation spoke at every roundtable except the one on political status, though her remarks were often brief and adhered closely to the topics chosen by the league. Eulalia Guzman addressed the evening session of the conference on Tuesday, April 25; she spoke for several minutes on the importance of women's education.[60] But what was missing from the official record of the conference was any discussion of what U.S. women could do to pressure their government to change its Mexican policy—the topic that Elena Torres and Elena Landázuri had specifically asked the organizing committee to address. Nor was there any mention of the memo Landázuri had said the Mexican delegation was preparing for the conference. In order to examine further the ways Mexican and other Latin American women tried—and sometimes failed—to shape the agenda and outcome of the conference, it is necessary to look beyond the official transcript provided by the League of Women Voters.

The Unofficial Record

The transcript of the Pan American Conference captured only part of what Latin American women brought to the table in Baltimore, and only part of the process of shaping the agenda and the outcomes. Most significantly, it referred merely in passing to the establishment of the Pan American Association for the Advancement of Women, the group that emerged from a meeting of the Latin American delegates on April 24 and 25, after the roundtables were over and the League of Women Voters had moved on to its own national business meeting. According to a press release issued by the league after the conference, the idea for the association originated with Paulina Luisi, a prominent Uruguayan suffragist. Luisi did not attend the conference herself, but Celia Palidino de Vitale, the Uruguayan delegate, conveyed Luisi's wishes. Vitale "made a strong plea for the acceptance of the plan" to the resolutions committee of the conference, the members of which then agreed she could present the plan to a meeting of the Latin American delegates scheduled for Monday, April 24. With the help of Carrie Chapman Catt, whose attendance the delegates had specially requested, "the plan for the New Pan American Association was made" and adopted by unanimous vote.[61]

But what looked in the official record like a wholly Latin American impulse had more complex origins. The meeting of the Latin American delegates, and the formation of the association, were orchestrated as much by Catt as by Latin American women. In December 1921, as Maud Wood Park and Catt were hammering out details for the financing of the conference, Catt requested an addition to the planned program. She was not actively involved in organizing the conference but constantly exercised her influence behind the scenes to ensure that women's suffrage would be a prominent topic. To that end, she requested the conference planners to schedule a private meeting for the Latin American delegates to which other U.S. women would not be invited, "in order that I may learn what their movement is and what they propose to do."[62] Catt envisioned a meeting of what she called the "really truly Pans" to discuss forming a Pan American organization. "It should be an organizing committee with one member from each country," she elaborated, "and it might have a meeting or two during the convention which would give the Pans the sense that they were still in it while the [U.S.] voters are really preempting attention. . . . Without some such outcome the conference will have lacked object and result."[63] Maud Wood Park and Minnie Fisher Cunningham fully supported the "Pans" meeting separately to form an organization of their own. They did not remark, however, on Catt's opinion that without such a meeting the conference would be pointless. Nor did they refer to Catt's implication that U.S. women were somehow separate from the "really truly Pans," or that the purpose of the meeting was to keep the Latin American delegates occupied while the real business of the conference continued. Moreover, Catt made clear that even though the meeting of Latin American delegates would exclude other U.S. women, she herself would play an active role.

The meeting of the "Pans" took place over several sessions on Monday and Tuesday, April 24 and 25, after the roundtables were over. The minutes that survive are incomplete, but they indicate that both the Brazilian and the Uruguayan delegates were given credit for calling the meeting. Catt's

role was depicted as that of an honored guest.[64] She was "received with
flowers by the rest of the delegates who formed a line for her to pass and
applauded her." The following day she "graciously consented to be present
and to give them the benefit of her valuable advice as to the practical ways
of proceeding to the realization of their idea" of forming a permanent organization."[65] The four questions on the agenda were most likely drawn up
by Catt, since they were the very issues on which she wanted information
from the Latin American delegates: "1. What has been done for women in
your country? 2. What are you doing now? 3. What do you intend to do
next? 4. What help do you need?" At the Monday afternoon session, Catt
addressed the delegates on how to start suffrage work in their own countries, how to get women interested, how to involve the press, and how to
"enlighten the public on the accomplishments in their countries and the
reasons for granting women suffrage."[66] The following day, again under
Catt's supervision, the delegates met to design an organization to coordinate the work in different countries. As Catt had envisioned, the meeting
of the Latin American delegates led to the formation of a permanent organization, the Pan American Association for the Advancement of Women.

The group's stated aims are particularly interesting because they indicate that Catt's influence had limits. Drawn up by Elena Torres and two
other Latin American delegates, the statement demonstrated that while the
conference organizers and the Latin American women shared several concerns regarding women's advancement, their interests were not always
identical:

Aims of the Provisional Pan American Association
for the Advancement of Women:

1) To promote general education among women

2) To secure higher standards of education in all schools for women

3) To secure the right of married women to control their own
property

4) To secure the right of married women to control their own wages

5) To secure equal guardianship of fathers and mothers over their
children

6) To encourage organization, discussion and public speaking among
women and to secure freedom of opportunity for all women to cultivate and use the talents with which God has endowed them

7) To educate public opinion in favor of granting the vote to women or to secure the vote for women

8) To promote friendliness and understanding among all Pan American countries with the aim of the maintenance of perpetual peace in the Western Hemisphere.[67]

Education and suffrage made the list, the latter in weaker terms perhaps than Catt would have liked. Married women in the United States had already won the right to control their own property, which is probably why the LWV never discussed adding the issue to the conference agenda.[68] Securing freedom of opportunity for women was certainly not an issue with which the LWV would have quarreled, but it did not occur to them to include it as a topic for discussion at the conference. The last aim, hemispheric peace and friendliness, was shared by all the delegates, but it would have taken on special significance for the Latin American delegates, many of whom had witnessed U.S. interventions in Latin America firsthand. These goals show that though U.S. women may have controlled the official conference agenda, the Latin American women who attended had a coherent agenda of their own. They were equally dedicated to the project of women's internationalism, and expected to be able to help shape its course.

Mexican women were prominent among them. The experience of the Mexican delegation, also not recorded in the official transcript, illustrates even more clearly that while U.S. women had the power to shape the conference agenda, they could not simply transfer their own concerns to Latin American women. Most important, the topics Mexican women wished the conference to address—aside from those chosen by Lavinia Engle—do not appear in the official transcript at all. This was not for lack of trying, as evidenced by the telegram the Consejo Feminista Mexicano sent to the league two months before the conference, asking for a public opportunity to discuss U.S. policies toward Mexico. To the conference itself the Mexican delegation brought their memo, signed by Elena Torres and Elena Landázuri (corresponding secretary of the CFM but not a delegate to Baltimore), outlining the history of several issues central to the history of U.S.-Mexican relations, including oil, labor, immigration, and the border.[69] Only one of those issues—labor—appeared in any form on the official conference agenda, although the memo revealed that the CFM and the League of Women Voters had different conceptions of the "problem" of labor. Where the latter was concerned specifically with securing protective legislation for women workers, the former was concerned about economic exploitation of all workers. The memo itself appears neither in the official transcript of the conference nor in any of the numerous boxes of material concerning the conference in the LWV papers. This may be because Torres did not read it aloud and therefore it was not entered into the record, or it may be because she presented it at an unofficial gathering or in some other venue during the conference. It is unclear whether Torres had an opportunity to share it, but there is no question that she both wanted and expected that opportunity. Elena Landázuri told Jane Addams that sharing this "statement of the situation" with "as many groups . . . institutions, and people" as possible was the CFM's main goal in Baltimore.[70] Torres herself told one newspaper, "We are not going to the Pan American conference merely to tell the women of the United States that we love them, but that we are willing and anxious to work on friendly terms with them in solving mutual problems. We want to leave the conference satisfied that we have made ourselves understood."[71]

Torres clearly knew her audience; the memo made repeated references to the importance of gendered diplomacy and to the power of women's organizing. The difficulties between the United States and Mexico, she argued, were between their governments, and "not really between the two peoples of the nations; but some problems have arisen that perhaps would have been solved long ago if women had taken a direct interference in their solution." Torres noted that every participant in previous negotiations between the two countries who had been taken at all seriously by the U.S. government had been in some form or another part of either the business community or the "political machinery." Attempts on the part of other nongovernmental groups to involve themselves in diplomacy had been met with apathy or disdain. "Women," she contended, "are much more apt to understand our point of view than either the diplomats or business enterprises, therefore we appeal to them praying to make their influence be felt in organized action." Interactions among diplomats and lawyers often led to "discussions on technicality," but women would not lose sight of what was really at stake: "The human values that the law upholds will find an echo in the mind of the American woman. . . . The miserable life of the poor classes . . . has to be bettered; that is primarily the work of women, and that is why the American women can see through all the clouds of passionate interests and excessive susceptibilities to grasp the greater value the human life."[72] The similarity to Jane

Addams's rhetoric about human internationalism is striking, given the unlikelihood that Torres had ever heard Addams speak on the subject. Torres's appeals to the method were her own, but they demonstrate a remarkable similarity of thinking and a direct appeal to the ethos U.S. women internationalists had been promoting since the peace conference at The Hague in 1915.

The "miserable life of the poor classes" was Torres's main concern. The central argument of the memo was that Mexican workers needed better protections. On the surface, this would seem to have dovetailed nicely with one of the key tenets of the League of Women Voters, which held that women workers had to be protected from the dangers and harsh conditions of industrial labor in order to safeguard their capacity to bear and raise children. But Torres and the Consejo Feminista were concerned with protecting *all* Mexican workers from exploitation by U.S. businesses, and not just so they could produce healthy offspring. Citing reports from the Mexican Department of Industry, Commerce, and Labor, she argued that poor Mexicans were inordinately affected by the foreign policies of the United States. U.S. authorities had no respect for the lives of Mexican refugees and immigrants, Torres contended, while foreign ownership of mines left workers vulnerable to exploitation. As an example she outlined the history of the silver mining industry in the state of Guanajuato. After more than five centuries during which the mines had provided for the people of the region, the largest mine was purchased by a U.S. company in 1900. Intent on increasing the margin of profit, the company ran the mine so strictly that its own workers could no longer afford to live in the local town. "In the course of five years," according to Torres, "the people had been notably impoverished; the cost of life was much higher; . . . men could not afford blankets; nobody was able to work independently, monopoly was felt in all its capitalistic power, which up to date has not been able to reconcile the social interest of the life of the people with the modern methods of work." For a short time the Mexican Revolution promised to alleviate these ills, but those most in need of protection soon learned that successive revolutionary governments were powerless to prevent continued exploitation by U.S. business interests. All the profits reaped from the mines were sent out of the country before the Mexican government could collect its fair share of taxes. At the time of the conference in 1922, Torres maintained, the material situation of the miners remained much as it had been for over twenty years.[73]

Appended to Torres's manifesto on labor and the mining industry was Landázuri's forceful elucidation of the "Oil Question," in which she mounted a thorough legal defense of Article 27 of the 1917 Constitution—the article regarding subsoil resources that was at the heart of U.S. animosity toward Mexico. "We feel sure," she began, echoing Torres, "that the only cause of the difficulties between our two nations is the lack of knowledge of each other's point of view, by the sane elements of both; and that is why we are so earnest about women knowing our situation." If the "sincere" men and women of both countries had access to similar "organs of propaganda" as those who propagated the difficulties, "the work of progress that our laws initiate would be easily carried out." Tracing the present legislation regarding subsoil rights back to the colonial period, Landázuri pointed out that since the time of Spanish rule the land had been vested in the nation itself. Individuals could possess the land only to work it, and a percentage of whatever they produced had to be paid to the crown. Yet in 1920 foreign interests controlled fully 97 percent of Mexico's oil industry. The United States alone controlled 73 percent. By comparison, Landázuri offered, in the same year foreign control of U.S. oil amounted to 4 percent. This dramatic imbalance, she believed, had fostered the general attitude toward Mexico in the United States. "When rights are given which impose no obligations," she declared, "those who receive them are naturally apt to have an attitude of disrespect towards those who grant them."[74] The situation had dramatic effects on poor Mexicans. Like those who worked in the mines, those who lived on land owned by the oil companies had to live with polluted air and water, high rents, and a general disregard for their well-being on the part of the companies. Landázuri argued that only full enforcement of Article 27 could begin to remedy these conditions.

Torres, Landázuri, and the Consejo Feminista Mexicano challenged U.S. women to put their ballots where their mouths were. "You are citizens," Torres reminded them. "You have the vote and know how to use it, it is in your power to make these dreams a reality that would help tremendously to solve the problems between our countries."[75] Nor was she above flattery as she shrewdly co-opted the rhetoric of Pan Americanism. She begged her audience to hear her account with the "high spirit of justice which will be the only one that can avoid future misrepresentations in the international relations of our country." She asserted that U.S. women were possessed of a "spirit of understanding" that would help bring about "a new era of justice and good-will."[76] Torres hoped that by bringing their concerns to the attention of the Baltimore delegates, the CFM would be able to take advantage of U.S. women's newly won political power to begin to address them. Once again, Mexican women pursued their nationalist goals through internationalist channels. Torres counted on her audience to come to the aid of the Mexican representatives by assuming a stronger international role.

Despite Torres's and Landázuri's thorough research and savvy approach, the memo had no discernible impact on the outcome of the Baltimore meeting. If any discussion of their concerns took place, no records of it survive, either in the official transcript or in the LWV archives. This absence is difficult to explain, particularly in light of the fact that before the conference, the organizers clearly understood the significance of the conference in the context of U.S.-Mexican relations. The likeliest explanation is that the organizing committee felt hampered by its dependence on the U.S. State Department. Torres and Landázuri managed in a few pages to strike at the heart of U.S. Mexican policy and expose the reality of the situation surrounding Article 27. Lavinia Engle, Dorothy Hubert, and the others may have worried that publicizing the CFM memo would have embarrassed the U.S. government, which had actively supported the conference.

It is also possible that the league was reluctant to draw attention to the memo because of Elena Torres's status as a communist. In 1922 she was still a leader in the Latin American bureau of the Third International, and a prominent member of the Mexican Communist Party. While the anticommunist Red Scare in the United States had peaked three years earlier, women reformers remained targets for conservatives who believed that organizations like the League of Women Voters represented the encroachment from Bolshevik Russia of "domestic subversion" and antidemocratic feminist militancy. At the LWV convention just a year before the Pan American Conference, the governor of New York had attacked the league as a "menace to our free institutions and to representative government," on the grounds that any nonpartisan, nongovernmental political mobilization signaled a threat to the two-party system.[77] Moreover, since the Revolution and especially in the midst of the conflict over Article 27, Mexico had been frequently denounced as communist by a vocal minority of U.S. legislators. On April 21, as the PACW was already underway in Baltimore, Senator William King of Utah, speaking from the Senate floor, denounced Mexican president *communism*

Obregón and several members of his government as "Bolshevistic."[78] This combination of red-baiting U.S. women reformers *and* the revolutionary Mexican government might well have proved lethal for the CFM memo. The document, with its focus on the exploitation of workers, property rights, and U.S. imperialism, was susceptible to a much more dangerous interpretation by the League of Women Voters than that of a woman sharing the concerns of her countrywomen with a sympathetic audience. Given their own history of being targeted by anticommunists, the league may well have actively suppressed the memo, rather than simply neglecting it.

The Pan American Conference of Women was the first large-scale expression of women's internationalism in the Western Hemisphere. In many ways, it illustrated Jane Addams's hopes for human internationalism: hundreds of women who might otherwise never have met each other were able to gather in Baltimore for ten days to share their stories, their work, and their concerns for the future. They left having formed a group to continue coordinating and promoting inter-American cooperation over the next several years. They also demonstrated the potential for gendered diplomacy inherent in women's internationalism. Government officials in both the United States and Mexico valued the opportunity presented by the conference as a venue for restoring goodwill between the two nations. Diplomacy conducted through women remained subordinate to official interactions in the eyes of most men, but they recognized its usefulness.

But the League of Women Voters' brand of internationalism was prescriptive rather than cooperative. The conference originated in and took place in the United States, and was planned and implemented by U.S. women. As the organizers, league members took the lead in setting the agenda, inviting speakers, and scheduling events. There was room, in theory, for Latin American women to help shape the conference, both during the planning stages and in the meetings themselves. But the league did not solicit input from any Latin American delegates, ignored appeals from the Mexican delegation to discuss U.S. foreign policies toward Mexico, and generally overlooked the nationalist sensibilities of their Mexican colleagues. There was no discussion during the roundtables of how to integrate suggestions or proposals made in Baltimore with existing social programs in the Latin American countries, such as the Consejo Feminista's free breakfasts for school children. Carrie Chapman Catt encouraged the formation of a permanent organization of Latin American women, but she was determined to set their program herself rather than helping them come up with one that reflected their own issues and concerns. At almost every step in shaping the program and message of the conference, U.S. women marginalized the Mexican and Latin American delegates.

In this respect the Pan American conference illustrated the potential for more imperialist modes of interaction that lay embedded in the tenets of human internationalism. True exchange and shared knowledge could only exist when all representatives were given equal time and equal access to the podium. The fact that Lavinia Engle, Dorothy Hubert, Maud Wood Park, and other league officials were operating under a diverse set of constraints should not absolve them of having relegated the Latin Americans to secondary status at the conference.

The League of Women Voters was not alone in its pejorative treatment of women it claimed to embrace and help. Other women's internationalist organizations, such as the International Woman Suffrage Alliance and even the Women's International League for Peace and Freedom, frequently replicated imperialist behaviors even as they denounced the imperialism of their own governments.[79] The LWV exercised its own brand of hegemony over Latin American women by dictating the terms of the conference. They took little trouble to discover or understand the diversity of Latin American women's experiences or the political and social contexts in which they lived. Carrie Chapman Catt, for instance, believed the vote was the only true path to gender equality, but in fact women across Mexico and Latin America had very different ideas about the relative importance of suffrage.[80] The CFM saw it as only one issue among many in their fight for equality. Elena Torres, Elena Landázuri, and the Consejo Feminista Mexico challenged the league to expand the focus of the conference beyond the predetermined topics, to take the nationalist concerns of Mexican women into account at their internationalist conference. The league's failure to do so represented a serious shortcoming of human internationalism. Over the next few years, the Pan American Association and other internationalist projects in Mexico faced similar challenges from Mexican women.

Chapter 3

The Limits of Human Internationalism

In February and March 1923, Carrie Chapman Catt traveled throughout South America in her capacity as president of the Pan American Association for the Advancement of Women. The journey convinced her, she later reported, that despite the challenges of different languages, cultures, and religions, women in the Western Hemisphere had to join forces, not only to promote women's rights but also to secure peace. "I am sure the men will never fetch it about," she wrote to Maud Wood Park, referring to the latter aim, "and they have been at it a hundred years." She foresaw myriad problems, however, including the language barrier—many of the women she met spoke a second language, but it was usually French rather than English—and the influence of Catholicism. Church and state were tied so closely together, she told Park, that protesting a law could be perceived as an attack on the Church: "Large numbers of persons are thus affrighted, and oppose instead of aiding the undertaking which only the boldest dare to lead."[1] In addition, Catt perceived Latin American women as subject to immoral men, outdated laws, and rigid class divisions, and as lacking experience where the women's movement was concerned. "Organization among women is exceedingly backward," Catt reported, "and they have not yet learned how to conduct collective discussion or deliberative meetings." Despite what she saw as enormous obstacles, Catt felt it was "desperately important that we make this Pan American thing go." If both women and men failed to cooperate, she envisioned a hemisphere where the United States stood alone in opposition to the Latin American countries, led by Mexico. "We will be the antagonists and will repeat in the western world what Europe has been doing. . . . This is certain, dead certain to happen unless we set the counter action going. That is why I've become a Pan Am fan."[2]

Figure 4. Carrie Chapman Catt, following the U.S. suffrage victory in 1920.

Schlesinger Library, Radcliffe Institute, Harvard University.

In the wake of the Pan American Conference of Women, U.S. internationalists remained committed to their inter-American endeavors. The three organizations that had been in place before the conference—the Mexican section of the Women's International League for Peace and Freedom, the Pan American International Women's Committee, and the Mexican branch of the YWCA—were slowly gaining traction. The Pan American Association for the Advancement of Women, formed in Baltimore, was now poised to join the other three in reaching out to Mexican and Latin American women to foster hemispheric solidarity. Moreover, the Mexican women with whom U.S. organizations were trying to partner were still enthusiastic about these efforts. Elena Torres and Elena Landázuri, both members of the Consejo Feminista Mexicano, continued to work with WILPF, the YWCA, and the PAAAW. Torres had accepted a vice presidency in the latter group. Adelia Palacios remained the primary contact for the PAIWC, and had begun working for the Mexican YWCA as well.

But the limits of human internationalism began to crystallize during this period. The problems were both practical and ideological. U.S. women struggled to overcome funding shortages, to grapple with a lack of organizational experience among Mexican women, and to reconcile increasingly divergent priorities between themselves and their Latin American colleagues. Mexican women, for instance, remained unwilling to prioritize suffrage to the extent that many U.S. women, especially Catt, wished. In the mid-1920s, they became more suspicious even of causes such as peace and internationalism. Gendered appeals from women like Emma Bain Swiggett, head of the Pan American Committee, to women as the world's mothers or to the solidarity of "Pan American womanhood" no longer resonated among increasingly politicized feminists like Elena Torres. These difficulties also reflected the ideological limitations of human internationalism. It was becoming increasingly obvious that U.S. women's internationalism could not coexist with Mexican women's nationalism in ways satisfactory to either side. Furthermore, the tendency among some U.S. women toward imperialist internationalism and imperialist feminism reached new heights during these years, manifesting itself especially in racialized assumptions about the superiority of "Anglo-Saxon" women and their methods. The presumptions of women like Catt that they knew what was best for Mexican women ultimately drove Mexican women like Torres and Landázuri away from cooperative endeavors altogether.

The nature of human internationalism itself made it particularly susceptible to these shortcomings. Cooperation premised on shared knowledge and personal interactions could not function when one group thought itself superior to another. Between 1922 and 1926, three of four internationalist organizations in Mexico failed. Bookended by the two follow-up gatherings to the Baltimore conference—the first in Mexico City in 1923, and the second in Washington, D.C., two years later—these years witnessed the disintegration of the Pan American Association, the Mexican section of

WILPF, and the Pan American International Women's Committee. None of these groups could overcome the practical and ideological limitations of human internationalism. The experience of the Mexican YWCA, the only one of the four organizations to survive the mid-1920s, suggests that human internationalism could work, but the YWCA succeeded by establishing itself firmly within local contexts, and restricting its scope to addressing local needs. Ironically then, the only internationalist organization to survive did so by deemphasizing its internationalism.

Mexico City, 1923

Elena Torres made the first effort to organize a follow-up to the Baltimore conference. As vice-president for North America of the Pan American Association, she convened the First Congress of the Pan American League of Women in May 1923. Torres wanted to establish an agenda for her section of the organization and to recruit more Mexican members. In this effort she had the clear support of the Mexican government, which subsidized the travel of all Mexican delegates to the conference, and also that of U.S. delegates between the border and Mexico City. Torres invited several U.S. organizations to send representatives, including the Women's International League for Peace and Freedom, the Young Women's Christian Association, and the League of Women Voters. The meeting attracted 179 attendees; about twenty were from the United States and the remainder were Mexican. The U.S. delegation included Zonia Baber, representing the U.S. section of WILPF, Edith Stanton, secretary for the Pacific Coast region of the YWCA, Florence Terry Griswold, president of the Pan American Round Table, who had traveled with the Mexican delegation to Baltimore the year before, and Jessie Daniel Ames, founder and president of the Texas branch of the League of Women Voters. Torres extended special invitations to Maud Wood Park and Carrie Chapman Catt, but both declined in order to attend a convention of the International Woman Suffrage Alliance in Rome, Italy.[3]

The Mexico City conference was Torres's first opportunity to set the agenda for an inter-American women's meeting. Unlike in Baltimore, she did not have to resort to petitioning another group of women to include her issues. She and her colleagues in the Consejo Feminista controlled the platform. Their program for the meeting included, to a greater or lesser degree, all six of the topics that had made up the roundtables in Baltimore: child welfare, education, women in industry, prevention of traffic in women, women's civil rights, and women in politics. But it also listed a host of others. The economic status of women, especially of married women, was a central theme. Paid labor outside the home was only one component of that status; Torres also wanted to discuss "woman as the economic administrator of the home," "the child as an economic problem in the home," and "the social problem of the woman"—single or married—"who wants to obtain her economic independence." Topics on morality were divided into two distinct categories: "the sex problem" and theories of nonresistance. The former centered on the sexual double standard, but also raised questions about sex education for children and adults, and the problems of coeducation. The latter included discussion of peaceful means "for the solution of any problem whatsoever," whether in the home, in politics, or in the international arena.

Significantly, Torres's list of political topics did not include suffrage explicitly, even though Carrie Chapman Catt had expressed a clear wish for the Pan American Association to prioritize the issue. Instead Torres wanted to focus on "woman as a moralizing agent in all public and private service," and to discuss women's civil rights in domestic relations. Her section on international problems did not raise the subject of U.S.-Mexican relations, but did include disarmament and "the abolition of war." She also listed "nationalism and internationalism," though the extant records of the conference include discussion only on the latter.[4] Torres's lack of focus on the vote is not surprising; after a very small push to incorporate woman suffrage into the Mexican Constitution of 1917, there was no organized suffrage drive in Mexico again until the 1930s.[5]

Finally, Torres posed a question that may never have occurred to the planners of the Baltimore conference: "Have the women of all nations in the world, as women, the same identical interests to defend?"[6] This was a distinctively transnational question, one that challenged the assumptions of U.S. activists that their goals were universal. Like women from other colonial, decolonizing, and developing regions, Torres questioned the aspects of imperial feminism that replicated patterns of Western colonialism by assuming universal measures of women's status and progress. Torres's question echoed those from women in other non-Western countries. Women in Egypt and elsewhere in the Middle East, for instance, prioritized Islam as a component of their feminist and nationalist activism, often in the face of derision from European and U.S. women who assumed all Muslim women were oppressed by the veil.[7] There is no record of the conference attendees discussing Torres's question, but the fact that she posed it suggests she recognized the possibility that the answer might be "no," that any transnational bonds of gender might not always take precedence over other identities and priorities.

According to reports from Mexican newspapers and from the U.S. women who attended, the conference was a success—spirited, yet businesslike. Torres was clearly in command. She had sent detailed instructions to the delegates on submitting topics for discussion, preparing their remarks, and confining themselves to strict time limits. She sat on the platform for most of the conference, even while other women were facilitating discussions. At the request of several Mexican delegates, she canceled all sightseeing trips and social events planned for the U.S. delegates. The Mexican women, she argued, "were there to work and not to entertain"—a not-so-subtle reference to the amount of socializing the Pan American delegates had done in Baltimore the year before.[8] She asked delegates to adhere as closely as possible to the five general areas of discussion she had outlined—economic, social, moral, political, and international topics—but within those she wanted the delegates to be able to address the issues of most concern to them.

Given this flexibility, the resolutions passed by the delegates reflected the discussions that took place at the conference more closely than they reflected Torres's original agenda. Four main themes emerged in the conference resolutions: improving women's economic status, reenvisioning women's contributions to public welfare, eliminating the sexual double standard, and promoting internationalism. The biggest overlap between Torres's intentions and the final outcome was the issue of women's economic status. To improve the status of women already in the paid labor force, the attendees resolved to petition the federal government of Mexico to establish industrial and commercial schools for women, to ease the overcrowding in clerical fields. They resolved to make a study of the conditions of domestic servants, and to secure better legal and financial protections for them. They also asked Congress "to simplify the Mexican Constitution to stipulate that the work of women receive the same remuneration as the work of men, and that wages paid be in relation to the cost of living." To protect women as the primary "administrators" in the home, they resolved to form consumers' cooperatives. They demanded adequate support for women whose husbands had abandoned or divorced them.[9] The delegates also emphasized the significance of women's organizing, and the need for improvements in women's civil status. "The social conditions in all parts of the country require the coordinate help of all the forces of women," they declared, and therefore resolved to stimulate and promote "the creation of groups of women who have social tendencies, leaving them the absolute liberty to select that type of organization which is most adequate and best suited to their aims and circumstances." In order to empower these organizations further, the delegates asked their state and federal governments "that all work of public welfare be placed exclusively in the hands of women, just as all military work is placed exclusively in the hands of men."[10] This comparison of the national welfare and the national defense was especially striking. By equating the two, the delegates were asserting that women's contributions to the general welfare of the nation were on a par with service in the Mexican army.

These concerns for women's economic status and women's roles in public welfare reflected some of the central debates among Mexican feminists in the wake of the violent phase of the Revolution. Following the establishment of the 1917 Constitution, the main challenge facing Mexican feminists was how to argue for their own citizenship status. Revolutionary citizenship was based on an implicitly masculine subject, and required the public exercise of three components: military service, civic engagement, and paid labor. Throughout the late 1910s and early 1920s, feminists debated whether they should try to challenge the citizenship ideal to include elements such as women's unpaid labor and reproductive roles, or try to position themselves as gender-neutral subjects who could meet the citizenship requirements as well as any man.[11] The conference resolutions reflected something of a compromise between those two positions, as the delegates sought to elevate and equalize labor women already did, both inside and outside the home, and to argue for an expanded definition of civic engagement that would include women's organizing and welfare work. The last point suggested that the delegates were also seeking to articulate a gendered alternative to military service, to find another way in which women could serve the revolutionary state.

Debates among the delegates concerning these first two categories of resolutions were not especially contentious. The same could not be said for the resolutions that fell under the broad description of "moral." The majority of the delegates agreed on the inclusion of resolutions demanding greater

sex education in schools and an end to the sexual double standard. But potential answers to other moral questions were not so unanimous. For example,
citing the fact that "the cost of marriage by the Church is in many cases
prohibitive," the delegates recommended "an enlarged viewpoint to be able
to judge justly, unions that have not received legal sanction but are the result
of high ideals held by the united parties." Florence Terry Griswold, president
of the Pan American Round Table of San Antonio and a U.S. delegate, protested that the conference was sanctioning illegitimacy. The resolution was
defeated by a vote of 58–27, and Griswold later congratulated herself on
having "saved the Congress from the depths of immorality."[12]

But by far the most contentious issue at the conference was birth control. The final conference resolutions contained several statements about
this "real social problem," including the need for more scientific information to be available to more women and the concomitant needs for better
prenatal and postnatal care, higher literacy rates, and instruction on the
"social responsibility of parenthood." The delegates were careful to tie these
statements directly to other resolutions on morality. In the same section
they resolved "that all possible forces be stimulated to raise the moral level
of the Mexican people," and reiterated again the need for a single sexual
standard for men and women.[13] Perhaps unsurprisingly, this portion of the
conference drew more negative attention from the conservative press in
Mexico City than any other. The country's leading Catholic newspaper
described Torres, Landázuri, and Guzman as "unsatisfied old maids who
were preaching 'free love' for their own satisfaction," and claimed that as
school teachers they would "put these atrocious ideas into the minds of the
children."[14] Its editors branded all women attending the Congress as mili-
tants and therefore distinct from "real" Mexican women.[15] Another Mexico
City newspaper castigated the delegates as "unpatriotic" for even allowing
discussion of birth control.[16] It is important to point out though that the
few women at the congress who did support issues like birth control
received a disproportionate amount of the press coverage. Knowing how
volatile the issue was, Torres managed to keep discussion of it to a mini-
mum. Most of the delegates, in fact, did not support birth control, but
that did not stop newspapers in Mexico City from labeling the congress as
radical.

The important point is that Mexican women directed the conference.
Most of the U.S. delegates did not take an active role in the debates over
women's economic status, public engagement, or morality. "Except for the

one section on internationalism," remarked LWV delegate Jessie Daniel
Ames, the entire conference was "purely Mexican." Notably, the only resolution not authored by a Mexican was the one on internationalism. Originally drawn up by Zonia Baber, the WILPF representative, it centered on
the evils of war. "War is the greatest enemy of civilization," she argued. Its
most insidious effects were the promulgation of books, stories, songs, toys,
games, works of art, and other cultural forms that commemorated and
celebrated war. These created a "war psychology," Baber argued, that
formed "in the minds of little children an emotional background for war"
that demanded expression later in life. She therefore proposed resolutions
urging parents, teachers, and others to "disarm the nurseries," and urging
governments to "take steps to abolish all financial and political causes of
war, to outlaw war . . . [and] to maintain an abiding peace by friendly
association and cooperation with all nations of the world." The only portion of the section on internationalism that originated within Mexico was
a resolution to reform the Mexican prison system and to abolish capital
punishment.[17]

Although on the surface Baber's resolutions may have seemed innocu-
ous, they provoked much debate. Baber reported back to WILPF that the
first objection came not from a Mexican woman but from Griswold. She
asked, "Would you take away all the great War heroes from our children?
All of the greatest things in science have been the result of War. What
would our history be without our wars?" In response, she received no
applause and no support. Baber described Griswold as "out of harmony
with the meeting" and was personally ashamed that the Round Table
women were "still militarists."[18] But a handful of objections from Mexican
delegates carried more weight with Baber. One woman, in opposing a separate resolution on greater friendship with women in the United States,
declared "daily events demonstrate to us that across the Rio Bravo they are
very far from loving us." As evidence, she pointed to "active campaigns
against Mexico, the deprecatory names that, generally, are used in the
neighboring country to insult us, the wide dissemination of denigratory
films and the little attention that the North American government has paid
to the many remonstrances of our government, protesting this conduct."
Sustained applause greeted these remarks.[19] Baber heard similar frustrations
in many of her conversations with Mexican women, but she struggled to
understand the connections they were drawing between her resolutions

against war in general and U.S. aggression toward Mexico in particular. Like many internationalist impulses originating within the United States, Baber's resolution did not take into account the widespread and often virulent anti-Americanism in Mexico. Mexican women in 1923 were as exhausted by violence as anyone, but supporting a pacifist resolution from a U.S. woman seemed too much like abdicating their right to self-defense against the United States. Baber's resolution eventually passed, but she made clear in her report to WILPF that the women with whom she spoke "all fear the United States, and were not at all reserved in telling me so."[20]

Aside from the discussions on internationalism, many of the twenty U.S. women in attendance reported feeling removed from the proceedings. Only two spoke any Spanish, which meant the rest relied on translators. Elena Landázuri handled most of the translations, but she was overburdened and had other work to do during the conference. Because the conference centered primarily on issues of national concern to Mexican women, U.S. women often did not feel right voting on the resolutions, even though as official delegates many of them were entitled to vote. As Jessie Daniel Ames reported, "The position of the delegates from the United States was an anomalous one. They belonged officially and had a voice and a vote, but the proceedings were so entirely Mexican in their nature that the voice and vote, when exercised seemed an impertinence."[21] Every U.S. woman did note, however, that the Mexican women went out of their way to make them feel welcome.

But as Ames—who was unusually clear sighted about Mexican attitudes toward the United States in general, and toward the U.S. delegates to the congress in particular—summed up the proceedings: "If the conference was intended to bring together in understanding sympathy the women of the United States and Mexico, it probably failed." Ames recognized more clearly than any other U.S. woman present the problems prohibiting cooperation between U.S. and Mexican women. First, she understood how difficult it was for many U.S. women to appreciate the challenges Mexican women faced, and to recognize the ways in which those challenges differed from the ones facing U.S. women. In her report to the LWV, for example, she tried to contextualize the debate over common law marriages and illegitimacy. Fearing that Griswold's attitude would be taken as characteristic of all U.S. women at the meeting, she maintained that "the Mexican women were attempting in a courageous way to deal with one of their most difficult problems, handicapped in the outset in a manner completely incomprehensible by the women from this country."[22] Ames also reported on press hostility toward the congress. The Mexican government, she noted, was outwardly more sympathetic, though Ames remained skeptical. Rumors circulated among the Mexican delegates that President Obregón had pledged fifteen million pesos (seven and a half million dollars) toward carrying out the congress proposals. Ames did not understand how the Mexican women could believe it was true. "The faith of the Mexican women in their Government is unbounded," she wrote. "Of all the situations facing the delegates from the United States, this faith in the party in power in the Government was the most difficult to comprehend. Not only do the women of this group believe in the good intentions of the Government, but apparently they believe in its omnipotence."[23]

Ames argued that U.S. women internationalists could not continue their current approach to fostering inter-American cooperation. Feminist leaders in Mexico looked to the League of Women Voters for guidance, she maintained, but the league had not lived up to the leadership role it established for itself at the Pan American Conference of Women. She seemed almost embarrassed for her organization that they had sent her as their representative. She knew very little about what had happened in Baltimore, knew very little about Mexico, and spoke no Spanish. "It is our duty to learn more about the people whom we would help before we offer criticism or advice," she pointed out. "Otherwise our presence in their meetings amounts to an impertinence." She offered several suggestions for changing league policy in the future with regard to such meetings. Delegates should be chosen who spoke Spanish and had some knowledge of Mexico, in order to "greatly lessen suspicion and hostility." The Mexican women needed practical guidance more than anything, Ames felt. She described Torres, Landázuri, and Guzman as "open-minded fair thinking women who wanted to know how to get results but were untrained and unprepared." They needed training in convention organization and parliamentary rules of procedure. Without changes to league practice concerning future delegates, it was "not possible for the women of the United States to help the Mexican women."[24] Ames's opinion of Mexican women as "courageous" but "untrained" was likely shaped by her personal experience of living in Texas, where she was realizing firsthand the effects of racism in limiting women's political reforms. According to her biographer, Ames began in the early 1920s to cross the "psychological bridge" that would lead her from the women's suffrage movement toward a life-long anti-lynching campaign.[25]

Jessie Daniel Ames was one of the few U.S. women active in inter-American affairs to recognize and articulate not only what it felt like for U.S. women to be among the marginalized rather than the marginalizing but also the ways imperial feminist patterns actively hindered true cooperation among U.S. and Mexican women. Her observation that voting on resolutions seemed "impertinent" may well have echoed the way Elena Torres and other Mexican women had felt in Baltimore, where the proceedings had been U.S. American rather than Mexican in nature. Certainly her inability to speak Spanish drove home her position as an outsider, regardless of her status as an official delegate.

Most importantly, Ames understood that she did not understand Mexico. Unlike Carrie Chapman Catt and other imperial feminists who assumed the universality of their agendas, Ames was not prepared to advocate "helping" Mexican women until U.S. women learned something about the women they were trying to help. These reservations are striking amid a sea of assertive opinions from her U.S. colleagues. Where other U.S. women were prepared to charge ahead with plans for cooperation without questioning their appropriateness, Ames suggested caution. Without the kind of understanding she advocated, the project of human internationalism itself was presumptuous. Most U.S. women did not speak Spanish and knew little about Mexico. As Ames pointed out, this was hardly promising ground on which to build a cooperative and equitable internationalist project.

This congress of the Pan American Association for the Advancement of Women marked the first anniversary of the Baltimore conference, and could have signaled the institutionalization of inter-American women's cooperation. Elena Torres and other Mexican women set their own agenda, ensuring that the issues most important to them would at least receive a proper airing. Mexican women were able to participate fully in the proceedings, and U.S. women were not allowed to dominate the discussions or control the outcome. But on the whole the conference did not bode well for the future of inter-American cooperation among women. It replicated some of the shortcomings of the Baltimore conference, including the language barrier. Most important, U.S. and Mexican women were not really collaborating to solve problems or to address issues in either country. Mexican women were prioritizing their own issues, just as the League of Women

Voters had done in Baltimore. They were certainly entitled to do so, and those issues were significant. But the lack of mechanisms for true cooperation to address them made it seem more as though U.S. women were attending a national conference of Mexican women, rather than an international one. As a Mexican endeavor, the First Congress of the Pan American League of Women was a success. As an inter-American one, it was less so.

Practical Limits

The 1923 conference in Mexico City highlighted the practical and ideological challenges facing women's internationalism. All four U.S. organizations in operation in Mexico by this point—the Pan American Association for the Advancement of Women, the Women's International League for Peace and Freedom, the Pan American International Women's Committee, and the Young Women's Christian Association—had to navigate concrete difficulties, including language barriers, communication problems, a lack of organizational experience among Mexican women, struggles to find adequate funding and capable leaders, and the increasingly divergent priorities of U.S. internationalists and Mexican feminists. Of the four organizations, the first three failed to maintain their presence in Mexico past 1924, and by 1925 the Pan American Association and Pan American Committee had both disintegrated entirely. The only group to persist was, significantly, the least internationalist in its daily practice—the Mexican branch of the YWCA, which mitigated its practical challenges by restricting its scope.

The 1923 conference in Mexico City was not the only evidence that all was not well with the Pan American Association for the Advancement of Women. While Elena Torres and her colleagues were preparing for the conference, Carrie Chapman Catt embarked on a concurrent inter-American venture in her capacity as acting president of the Pan American Association for the Advancement of Women. Though her approach was different from Torres's—instead of organizing or attending another conference, Catt undertook a month-long individual tour of South America—she encountered dilemmas similar to those exposed in Mexico City. When the association first convened in Baltimore, the plan was to arrange another full-scale meeting somewhere outside the United States in two or three years. Conferences like Torres's in Mexico City were meant to be regional affairs only.

PAAAW

But the association as a whole was soon suffering from a lack of direction and leadership.

Catt was the first to draw attention to this problem. Originally appointed honorary president of the association in Baltimore, she agreed in 1923 to serve as acting president for one year. She subsequently embarked on the tour, visiting the only remaining populated continent on which no woman had the right to vote. She traveled to Brazil, Uruguay, Argentina, Chile, Peru, and Panama, where she met with government officials, spoke to women's organizations, and conferred with women leaders. Catt's publicized accounts of the trip, particularly a series of articles she wrote for the *Woman Citizen*, conveyed her satisfaction with the people she met and her optimism about the future. She declared that Brazilian women were well organized and "actuated by noble aspirations."[26] In Chile Catt found a small but dedicated group of "very earnest-minded women" who she predicted would "'carry on' with increasing effectiveness."[27] Like the women gathered in Mexico City, she deplored the moral double standard evident in every country, and noted with concern that it tended not only to disadvantage women in marriage but also to condemn to ridicule those women who spoke out in support of women's equality and need for opportunity. She recognized—perhaps for the first time—the lack of widespread democratic traditions and the extent of Latin American resentment of the United States. "Under these conditions," she acknowledged, "the vote is far less important to these women than individual liberation from code and custom."[28] She advised U.S. women to respect the differences between North American and Latin American "civilizations," and to offer what assistance they could as Latin America awaited "the emancipation of women from the seventeenth-century customs into the light and freedom of the twentieth century."[29]

The practical difficulties facing the Pan American Association, however, were readily apparent. The biggest problem was that no women's organization could afford to host the next planned conference. Unlike the League of Women Voters, which relied on dues and the generosity of members for funding, Latin American organizations got their money from their governments. Officials in both Argentina and Brazil, the most likely candidates to host another Pan American conference, had refused such requests. Most of the women targeted for recruitment, meanwhile, were single working women who could barely afford membership dues, much less any further contributions.[30]

Catt's frustrations in the wake of the South American trip led her to resign her position with the association less than a year later. In her letter to the League of Women Voters—the group under whose auspices the Pan American Association had been formed in Baltimore—Catt suggested forgoing the plan to hold one hemispheric conference in favor of two regional ones, one in Cuba for the Central American and Caribbean countries, including Mexico, and one in South America. "I can see no other solution," Catt admitted, "to a forward movement among these women." But she refused to give up all hope for a larger gathering. "I feel keenly that by hanging on and continually petting the women of these various countries," she reported to the league, "we might be able to pull off a Pan-American Congress somewhere within the next four or five years. I think such a Congress would be useful even though it did not become permanent." Further reports on the status of women in the Americas were under way, she noted, and "a comparison of these reports, with a determination to work for improvement, would be useful even if the movement went no further." Her replacement, she urged the league, should be young, energetic, and patient: "There is an opportunity for a woman to do great work, but anyone who places a time limit on anything to be done with Spanish America will get the disappointment of her life."[31]

Although suffrage had been her central focus at the founding of the Pan American Association in Baltimore just two years earlier, Catt did not mention it in her letter to the league. The barriers to women's organizing she saw during her tour dimmed her hopes for a hemispheric suffrage movement. In addition, her concern with Pan Americanism reflected the redirection of her own agenda from suffrage to peace work. In 1923 she had resigned as president of the International Woman Suffrage Alliance; two years later she established the Committee on the Cause and Cure of War.[32] Without the weighty leadership from a figure like Catt, the Pan American Association stalled. No clear candidate emerged to replace her, and the challenges of planning and funding the next hemispheric conference appeared insurmountable.

The Mexican section of the Women's International League did not have to contend with the difficulties of planning a conference, but U.S. representatives faced similar problems with getting Mexican women to commit to their organization. Since 1921, Jane Addams and Emily Greene Balch had been relying on Elena Landázuri to launch the Mexican section. Landázuri had not attended the Baltimore conference with the other delegates from the Consejo Feminista, choosing to remain in Mexico City to continue her work for both WILPF and the YWCA. By spring 1922 she felt "really ashamed" at not having been able to start a section yet, but she told Balch that she was meeting with interested women on a regular basis. "I feel that we must make patient work and go slowly rather than hastily," she wrote in May 1922. She did not want a group that would be "merely nominal," but one committed to its cause.[33] In the meantime, Landázuri was working to incorporate peace work into the agenda of the Consejo Feminista, of which she was now the corresponding secretary. The Consejo had secured support from the national Secretariat of Public Education for a series of lectures on peace in local schools, and several members had published articles promoting peace in newspapers and magazines across the country. By July Landázuri was more optimistic about the chances for a WILPF section. "Group women" in general were "pretty indifferent," she reported to Addams, but "there is a group of women now who are going to do something." Elena Torres had just departed on a South American tour to establish contacts with women's groups. Eulalia Guzman, another Baltimore delegate, was traveling to Europe to attend the International Congress on Moral Education in Geneva, and planned to stay at WILPF's Maison Internationale. Landázuri was optimistic that she would be able to start a section within six months. She hoped one result of these travels would be that Mexican women could "hook" their "little body of women with the groups in Europe, the groups in Latin America and in Saxon America."[34] Addams and Balch were not disturbed by the delay; Balch thought Landázuri "quite splendid."[35]

Both Addams and Balch knew that the personal connections established between U.S. and Mexican women were integral to the success of Landázuri's efforts. To that end they hoped to secure a more permanent liaison between the two sections. In September 1922 Zonia Baber, Addams's friend from Chicago and an active member, became chair of the U.S. section's Pan American Committee, and secured Landázuri's participation on it.[36] Over the next several months Baber continued to try to recruit members in Mexico, but her main contribution as chair of the committee was to attend the conference in Mexico City in May 1923, and report on it to the U.S. section. As other U.S. representatives had done before her, Baber commuted back and forth between the two countries, rather than establishing a permanent residence in Mexico City. Without a long-term presence in the city, there was no way for the U.S. section to maintain consistent pressure on Elena Landázuri or the Consejo Feminista to take the final steps toward becoming officially registered as the Mexican section.

In the summer of 1923, Addams and Balch sent another representative to Mexico City, who had a more radical proposal for starting branches in Mexico and other countries like it. Anna Melissa Graves was a teacher and writer from Maryland who spent several months in Mexico City agitating for peace. She pointed out to Balch that some of WILPF's own policies might be hindering its progress in Latin America. For example, league guidelines prohibited foreign citizens from being members of national sections. Graves argued, and Elena Landázuri agreed, that such rules should be reconsidered in Latin America, where the most active pacifists were usually foreigners.[37] Overcoming entrenched divisions based on nationality would be a challenge, but Graves pleaded with Balch to help change WILPF's policies as an example for others to follow: "Shouldn't we do everything that we can . . . to kill this dangerous sense of separatism?" Establishing new policies regarding sections, she argued, would finally allow for a strong, permanent Mexican branch. Without such action, she told Balch, WILPF would become a cause of the very problem it was trying to solve.[38] Balch responded that the rules limiting membership to national citizens sprang more from custom than from anything else, but gave no indication she would make an effort to change it.[39]

Landázuri never did succeed in establishing a permanent section of the Women's International League in Mexico City. Whether this was due to a lack of time and resources or to a lack of constant support from the United States is unclear, but after 1923 the organization had no active presence in Mexico for six years. The logistical problems posed by WILPF regulations about membership likely contributed to this; Mexican women needed more flexibility regarding membership rules, guidelines, and finances before they could begin to overcome the ideological barriers between themselves and international work. Human internationalism, with its emphasis on personal connections and shared experience, could not work without adequate resources and flexibility.

Among U.S. internationalist groups, the Pan American International Women's Committee faced the most significant restraints, including a lack of funding, a weak institutional structure, and a stubborn reliance on its self-defined "semi-official" status relative to the Pan American Union. Unlike WILPF or the YWCA, which could rely on membership dues, or *finances*

Catt, who enjoyed support from donors and foundations, the Pan American Committee had few sources of steady income. The group's primary source of support was one donor, an elderly Massachusetts woman named Cornelia Crane. As a result, Emma Bain Swiggett, executive secretary of the committee who had organized the Women's Auxiliary Conference in 1916, and the other members of the committee relied on the intergovernmental organization to which they were attached—the Pan American Scientific Congress—for opportunities to plan and carry out large-scale gatherings like the auxiliary conference. Swiggett hoped to be able to organize another auxiliary conference for the next scientific congress, but the date of the latter was uncertain throughout the early 1920s.

The committee's potential impact was especially diluted because Swiggett was the only active member. She had almost no help in coordinating and executing the committee's activities, and she chose to define its work narrowly. She claimed that since her group enjoyed "semi-official" status relative to the Pan American Union, it could not involve itself in any controversial political questions. As an auxiliary to the Pan American Scientific Congress, which was itself an auxiliary of the Pan American Union, Swiggett believed the committee was attached to the Union as well. When a women's group in Texas solicited the committee's support for a proposal to establish an International Court of Arbitration for the Western Hemisphere, for example, she declined on the grounds that the committee was not authorized to endorse such a measure.[40]

Although Swiggett may have felt personally and professionally constrained by these circumstances—her husband, Glen Liven Swiggett, was president of the Scientific Congress—the "semi-official" rationale inhibited any real input from Mexican and Latin American women on what direction the committee's work should take. As the Mexican representative to the PAIWC, Adelia Palacios followed Swiggett's lead, working solely on her issues and events. Throughout their entire correspondence, the only time Palacios made any small demand on the committee to address an issue important to her was in 1924, when she asked Swiggett if it would be "possible for the committee to work on the loan to Mexico?"[41] Swiggett's response was sympathetic but firm: "As to your personal question in regard to the loan to Mexico, it is not possible for our Committee, on account of its semi-official connection, to take any step that would not be misunderstood and do more harm than good. I regret this."[42] She did not elaborate on what misunderstanding or harm might result from any effort in support of the loan, but her reluctance to involve the committee in questions of foreign policy in any small way was clear. Palacios dropped the issue.

Lacking adequate funds for a follow-up to the Women's Auxiliary Conference, the committee settled in 1923 for coordinating a hemisphere-wide celebration of Columbus Day. In lieu of one large gathering, women assembled in twelve American cities to discuss common themes and share in common activities. The event was thus more inter-American in form than in function. Each assembly featured speakers on "Our Debt to Women of the Past," "The Demands upon Women of the Present," and "The Obligation of Our Women to the Future."[43] Each opened with a written greeting from Antoinette Hughes, wife of Secretary of State Hughes and the nominal head of the Pan American Committee. Calling on "the common bond of womanhood," she encouraged participants "to confer regarding those things which are of peculiar interest and value to women" and to devote themselves to "forging new bonds of amity."[44] In Washington, Swiggett, Hughes, Eleanor Lansing, and other diplomatic wives discussed women's past and present contributions to education, religious and humanitarian work, industry, and public life. In Mexico City, Adelia Palacios gathered speakers on education, child welfare, and women's contributions to journalism.[45] Unlike the original Women's Auxiliary Conference, however, there was no mention in either the United States or Mexico of the contributions women could make to diplomacy, or even of future plans for cooperation. The program was more a celebration of women's "common bond" and "common interests" than a prescription for putting them to use. In contrast to the 1916 conference, the Columbus Day celebrations privileged style over substance when it came to women's internationalism.

Although Swiggett did not officially dissolve the committee for another two years, the Columbus Day celebrations constituted its last significant activities. The only other notable gathering took place at the Second Women's Auxiliary Conference, held in conjunction with the Third Pan American Scientific Congress in December 1924 in Lima, Peru. There Swiggett demonstrated again her determination to restrict the committee's scope, informing the U.S. ambassador to Peru that participants would "demonstrate the capacity of the American woman to study and settle the problems which most directly concern her," including "the education of the family, social welfare, organization of women's work, the most important questions of government and hygiene of the home, etc." She reiterated that those subjects would be the only ones discussed.[46] Her determination to keep the committee apart from "political questions" led her to reject offers of collaboration from both the League of Women Voters and from the Women's International League, even though joining forces with one or the other might have kept Swiggett's committee alive in some form. By refusing to discuss any diplomatic or political questions, and by clinging to empty platitudes about Pan Americanism, Swiggett and the committee retained their dedication to the spiritual nature of human internationalism, but they lost any force or effect they might have otherwise had. This mindset made most U.S. women apathetic toward or outright disdainful of the organization; one representative in Lima called the meeting an "awful bore."[47] Swiggett formally dissolved the group in 1925.[48]

In marked contrast to the Pan American Association, the Women's International League, and the Pan American Committee, the YWCA encountered few of these practical difficulties. First, the YWCA took a different approach to personnel. Rather than placing heavy responsibilities on Mexican liaisons to organize and motivate a branch of their organization, as the Pan American Association did with Elena Torres and the Pan American Committee did with Adelia Palacios, or sending U.S. representatives to Mexico for a few months at a time, as WILPF did with Zonia Baber and Anna Graves, the Foreign Division of the U.S. association sent Caroline Smith to live in Mexico City for three years. From 1922 to 1925, Smith established the association's presence in the city, and was able to oversee the early years of the Mexican branch's development in person. As a result, she was able to establish a much closer working relationship with Elena Landázuri, who served both WILPF and the YWCA during 1922 and 1923, than Jane Addams or Emily Greene Balch had been able to do. The fruits of this relationship were evident in the early success of the Mexican association. After the board of directors was formally invested in October 1923, the membership rolls grew quickly. Within a year the association had 78 active members and 121 associate members, and counted no fewer than 386 women among those who regularly visited the association or took part in its activities.[49]

The second thing the YWCA did was limit its scope. In her report to the Foreign Division in October 1924, Smith commended the board for not overreaching and for restricting its efforts to three main functions: education, protection, and recreation. The first category included classes for women and adolescent girls in English, training in "mother craft" for new mothers, and a small circulating library. Under the second heading fell both the boarding house for travelers and local women, and an ad hoc employment bureau functioning out of it. The final category encompassed the work that would become the main YWCA focus over the next several years, but began only as a small "experimental recreation club" that gathered young women together for physical activities and educational excursions.[50] Unlike, for instance, the broad agenda of Elena Torres's 1923 conference, the association focused on a set of clear, tangible goals.

Third and most importantly, Caroline Smith and her colleagues were determined to "Mexicanize" the YWCA as soon as possible. In practical terms, this meant putting Mexican women in positions of leadership and allowing them to shape the association's programs, while Smith and other non-Mexican women provided logistical and financial support. Three-quarters of the board of directors was made up of Mexican women. As early as March 1923, Landázuri reported to the Foreign Division that among her colleagues, many of whom the YWCA was then targeting to be active in the association, most saw "mother craft," health education, and activities for girls as the most pressing needs for women in Mexico City.[51] By the time the board members officially took up their posts seven months later, Landázuri already had a mothers' club, a student club, and a service club for girls set up and ready to go with new members.[52] The mothers' club was one of the association's most successful early endeavors. Over forty women joined; together they coordinated classes and training programs for new and expectant mothers, and they soon opened a free clinic at the YWCA headquarters for mothers and infants.[53] All these services had been proposed and largely developed by Mexican members. But almost all the funding for them came from the Foreign Division of the YWCA—a circumstance Smith recognized might well become the strongest barrier to full independence for the Mexican association.

The YWCA thus offers an important contrast, particularly to WILPF. Both branches had been established directly from the United States, rather than from their international headquarters in Europe. Both relied on their U.S. branches for funding and staff or volunteer support. And both looked to Elena Landázuri as their primary Mexican contact. But while WILPF struggled to get its Mexican section off the ground, the Mexican YWCA showed great promise during the mid-1920s, precisely because it allowed local members to shape the organization to fit their own needs and desires, rather than imposing on them an agenda and a formal structure.

The practical difficulties encountered by the Pan American Association, the Women's International League, and the Pan American Committee all illustrate potential weaknesses of human internationalism. As a method, it was dependent on personal interactions and the exchange of knowledge and experiences. When those broke down, or when there were insufficient opportunities to foster them, internationalism could not be sustained. Without strong leadership, either from institutions or from individuals, there was often no way to ensure that interactions continued on a semi-regular basis, and that the fruits of those interactions were given space and resources to blossom. A single conference was not enough, if there was little effort to capitalize on it. But while human internationalism depended on some sort of institutional structure, it also could not work if that structure were too intrusive. Organizations had to remain flexible enough to adapt to local contexts. When WILPF and the PAIWC had to choose between maintaining existing standards and practices or experimenting with new ones in the hopes of sustaining their work in Mexico, each chose the former course. There may not have been one "right" way to practice human internationalism, but some were more successful than others.

Ideological Limits

U.S. women internationalists' own prejudices and assumptions also circumscribed their effectiveness among Mexican and Latin American women. Some of these ideological limits had been apparent since the 1910s. In Elena Torres's and Elena Landázuri's early exchanges with the Women's Peace Party, the Women's International League, and other groups, it was clear that U.S. and Mexican women were talking past each other. Torres and Landázuri repeatedly asked U.S. women to speak out against their country's exploitation of Mexico, and U.S. women consistently failed to do so in any meaningful way. U.S. women's tendency toward imperialist internationalism continued in the wake of the Baltimore conference. At the 1923 conference in Mexico City, Jessie Daniel Ames observed that this kind of internationalism was hardly international at all. During the mid-1920s, U.S. women's internationalism and Mexican women's nationalism continued to diverge. But it is also important to consider to what extent U.S. women's assumptions about Mexican women in particular, and about Latin American women in general, hindered the furtherance of inter-American cooperation.

The widening ideological divide between U.S. women's international-ism and Mexican women's nationalism was best illustrated by the experi-ence of Anna Melissa Graves, the WILPF representative who spent several months in Mexico City in 1923. Graves advocated not only global peace and women's rights but the abolition of the nation-state altogether. This made her one of WILPF's most *trans*nationalist activists. Graves not only wanted to work across nations rather than among them, she desired the end of nations. Nationalism was the true enemy of peace, she believed, and only when men and women opened their eyes to its dangers could world peace become a reality. In 1923 she spent eight months in Mexico, teaching English and representing WILPF. She hoped to succeed where previous attempts to establish a section had failed, but her "absolutist" stance, as Emily Greene Balch referred to it, frequently affected not only her interac-tions with Mexican men and women but with WILPF itself. Referring to WILPF's policy of not allowing foreigners to become part of national sec-tions, for instance, she charged that WILPF "perpetuates the causes of war by perpetuating the causes of separatism."[54]

Graves believed, however, that the biggest obstacle to organizing in Mexico was not WILPF policy but the prevalence of Mexican nationalism directed at the United States. Among many Mexicans, that nationalism intensified in 1923 as the two countries drew closer to a settlement of the dispute over Article 27 and the restoration of diplomatic relations. Since 1920, both U.S. and Mexican envoys had met repeatedly to try to negotiate an agreement that would satisfy both the Mexican government and the U.S. businesses and landholders whose property was vulnerable to nationaliza-tion under the article. By the end of August, the two countries had reached an unofficial accord that favored the United States. But while the arrange-ment restored friendly relations between the governments, it did not do so for their people.[55] Graves repeated to Balch a conversation she had had with a Mexican lawyer, Rafael Mellon, whose radical transnationalism she greatly admired. Graves had observed a "marked increase" in nationalist sentiment in Mexico in the five months she had been there, and lamented the impact she felt it had had on several Mexican women associated with WILPF. Mel-lon agreed. "I am so distressed that I do not know to whom to turn," he told Graves. "I have had absolute faith in Elena Landázuri for five years, but she has changed, and so has Srta. [Eulalia] Guzman. They are both convinced nationalists today." When Graves asked him why, he responded, "because the U.S. has forced us to give up our Revolution and we know it." Graves concurred with this assessment, explaining to Balch, "Every strike, every counter-revolution, and every more extremely radical revolution was fomented and capitalized in the U.S. until in order to save itself from fomented uprisings, this Government yielded and renounced its constitutional right to take land from the landholders who had stolen it from the people in order that the government might give it to the people." Graves deplored this "defection," but admitted she understood it. "Of course," she continued, referring to Landázuri, "she doesn't realize the defection. She still says she is a Pacifist and honestly believes herself to be one. . . . [But] she makes inflaming speeches on nationalism and Mexico's right to a national soul—and doesn't realize that inflamed 'sore' nationalism—nursing a grievance—is as disintegrating as inflamed aggressive-chauvinistic nationalism."[56] For Graves, the only true path to peace was to renounce entirely nationalism and national identity, regardless of the history or geopolitical status of one's nation. Her commitment to transnationalism was so strong that she was prepared to lay blame for any failure of global cooperation on both imperial aggressors and their targets.

Graves was not blind to the plight of countries like Mexico, which she believed suffered greatly under the domination of the United States. "Given the throttling of Mexico," she continued, "the increase of nationalism here is not surprising. That is what a pacifist and internationalist is up against in Mexico."[57] Like Carrie Chapman Catt, Graves drew a parallel with Europe. If WILPF members in particular, and the United States in general, wanted to avoid the same nationalist path throughout Latin America that had led to the disintegration of Europe before World War I, they had to act at once. "Latin America may escape this curse of Europe," she wrote to Balch, "but not unless its mind is turned immediately. It has never been national until now—and though nationalism is rampant now it is not deeply rooted yet." Latin America had the potential, Graves believed, to advance the "civilization of the West" and become the next center of global culture. But if countries like Mexico dedicated themselves to "cultivating this poison of nationalism" they would self-destruct, she predicted: "No one is immune to the evil hysteria which nationalism produces."

Graves's transnational views on global cooperation and peace activism were extreme compared to most of her colleagues, but her observations on Mexico pointed to one problem facing WILPF and unintentionally confirmed another. The former was the need for flexibility. The way WILPF organized national sections had been established in Geneva among women

from developed countries with experience of popular political participation. That strategy did not work as well in countries like Mexico, which had
no comparable democratic traditions and different models of mass political
participation. The women Graves and Landázuri recruited were unused to
the formal organizational procedures and rules of order that WILPF followed.[58] Graves's attack on Mexican nationalism, meanwhile, though more
intense than either Balch or Addams might have liked, stemmed from most
members' fundamental lack of understanding concerning the Mexican situation. Supporting a leftist, antiwar, internationalist group like WILPF ran
contrary to many Mexicans' idea of what their country needed most at that
time—active, vigorous nationalism to defend their sovereignty against U.S.
intervention.[59]

   While Anna Graves attributed Mexican women's reluctance to join
forces with U.S. women to their increasing nationalism, other U.S.
women advanced different interpretations. On her tour through South
America on behalf of the Pan American Association, Catt sought to
explain to her colleagues why she found little real support for continuing
the organization. Her desire to "make this Pan American thing go" coex-
isted uneasily with her prejudices toward Latin Americans. In her report
to the Leslie Commission, the U.S. endowment that financed the trip,
Catt bemoaned the state of affairs in the countries she had visited: "This
continent has the least modern women's organization of any of the six. I
did not find in South America one woman with the comprehension, the
energy and the firm resolve to lead the woman movement. . . . Many are
convinced of the need of a changed status for women, but every woman
willing to assume direction of a movement to effect that change, is certain
not to be of pure Spanish descent and is usually classed as unorthodox
and both of these attributes damn her and her cause in the eyes of the
masses."[60] With her friends she was less guarded. Latin American women
all cared more about their appearance than they did about their rights,
she told Maud Wood Park. "The women have gone daft on dress and
fashion I have never seen so much 'style' as here and women's thoughts
and ambition are centered on dress."[61] To a group of "American friends,"
she complained, "There wasn't much time for organizing and the South
American mind is slow." She had done the best she could to help conceive
a movement, she told them, "but I am not sure but the infant has already
expired."[62] Finally, to her close friend Mary Garrett Hay she wrote, "The
climate and the inherited racial tendencies make the people languorous

and willing to put things off until tomorrow. They eat too much. . . .
Sweets are plentiful and desserts are very sweet. The women are therefore
fat and probably less easy to move."[63]

Although Catt publicly acknowledged that Latin American women
would have to follow their own path to emancipation, in private she was
frustrated, condescending, and racist. She recognized the difficulties they
faced, including myriad social and cultural barriers based on gender. In her
public statements she seemed patient and willing to make allowances for
the political and cultural differences between the United States and Latin
America. But her private remarks belied any public appearance of patience
and understanding. South American women were unwilling to do what
needed to be done to further women's emancipation, she thought, not
because they were inexperienced, but because their "racial tendencies"
made them backward and sluggish. In private Catt made no mention of the
lack of democratic traditions in most of Latin America, and nowhere did
she refer to the fact that this lack was perpetuated by U.S. political and
economic hegemony. → not unusual thoughts

Catt's racialized interpretations of the difficulties she encountered in
South America were not all that unusual for her time. There are other
examples scattered throughout U.S. women's observances and reports of
their encounters with Mexican and Latin American women. One U.S.
YWCA member attributed her struggles to organize Mexican women to
what she saw as a negative racial characteristic. "Perhaps you know that
state has a touch of the oriental in it," Brudena Mofoid wrote to Harriet
Taylor in 1923. "The women become very slow and heavy, very dignified
and stupid, [and] concern themselves with affairs of home. It is not in good
taste to be active and progressive."[64] Mary Wilhelmine Williams, arguing
in the 1930s that WILPF should focus its efforts on establishing a strong
branch in every state of the United States instead of bolstering its Mexican
section, noted that in the event of another world war a strong pacifist network in the United States would forestall American involvement better than
a strong inter-American network. "Our Latin sisters would be a very weak
reed to lean on in a crisis," she contended.[65]

Other U.S. women internationalists resorted to popular, stereotypical
assumptions about the differences between "Anglo-Saxons" and "Latins"
to explain situations they encountered in Mexico. Emily Greene Balch
relied on such assumptions in a letter to Elena Landázuri about organizing
a branch of WILPF in Mexico. "I do not believe," she wrote, "that Latin

women will be able to work along just the same lines as Anglo-Saxon
women or organize in just the same way. Let them follow their own natural
lines and be strong in their own way, though of course all that they can
achieve in the matter of businesslike habits, which I do not think are very
natural to . . . women of the Latin race, makes life just so much easier for
everybody."[66] Balch's assumptions about what was "natural" to one race or
another were clear. U.S. women were inherently "businesslike" and efficient; Latin American women were not.

The notion that there were fundamental differences among human
beings, and that those differences could be ascribed to a biological notion
of "race," was prevalent throughout the United States and Western
Europe—as well as Latin America—in the first decades of the twentieth
century. Race was seen as a fixed, "natural" category, marked by innate
traits and characteristics that could be passed on through generations. In
the United States, these beliefs were not only used to justify segregation and
discrimination toward African Americans, Native Americans, and immigrants, they also gave rise over time to the identification of a superior
"Anglo-Saxon" race.[67] Many of the white U.S. women who made efforts to
cooperate with Latin American women were very much products of their
time in their adherence to this scientific racism. It had already been the
source of division and discord between white and black activists in the
United States.[68] In their inter-American work, these racial ideologies
appeared most often in U.S. women's reliance on a distinction between
themselves as "Anglo-Saxons" and all Latin American women as "Latins"
to explain the myriad organizational and ideological differences they
encountered in their work. These were more than convenient labels; they
signified a long-standing belief among U.S. Americans that Latin Americans
were "naturally" inferior and less "civilized."[69] The "Latin" label, of course,
also erased all differences of nationality, ethnicity, and race among Latin
Americans themselves.

A handful of U.S. women attributed these "Latin" characteristics to the
influence of Latin America's European heritage. The "Black Legend" of
Spanish influence—the demonization of Catholic Spain and its colonizers
as cruel and intolerant, and the reliance on their legacy to "explain" the
lack of development and modernization in Latin America—was popular
during the interwar period. "Spain has left her seal on everything," Florence
Terry Griswold informed a U.S. audience. "Her religion, her customs, her
social beliefs are found in all lands south of the Rio Grande. Women have

lived in this atmosphere and conservative spirit, bound to the old traditions, which have not permitted some of the South American countries to
introduce any new ideas."[70] Griswold's interpretation of Spanish religion
and tradition as the barriers to progress, to "new ideas," was supported
by other U.S. women as well. Catt stated her perceived shortcomings of
Catholicism more bluntly. In most Latin American countries, she argued,
"the church is often too political to be altogether spiritual and the state is
too religious to be altogether political. Weak religionists get to be heads of
governments and strong politicians to be heads of the church at times and
both play havoc with that delicate mobile thing we call civilization. The
total effect is to set up demoralizing standards which have prevented the
growth of a high grade of morals."[71] Thus religion became for Catt a marker
of civilization, and Catholicism became a potential barrier to moral—and
by extension racial—"progress."

By contrast, others focused more on what they saw as the problem of
indigenous influences in Latin America. Mary Wilhelmine Williams complained about the predominance of "aboriginal blood" in Latin America
that stymied the development of intelligence and social organization.[72] Caroline Smith, who helped start the YWCA section in Mexico City, noted
that among indigenous and mixed-race populations in Mexico, "the experience of continuous motherhood, sexual over-indulgence, general under-
nourishment and wretched housing and sanitary conditions" contributed
to the suffering and mortality of Mexican children. Amid these conditions,
she further observed, "only the native vitality of the Indians and their
extreme fecundity has kept the race from extinction."[73] The assumption
that any indigenous influence was a negative one was common in the early
twentieth-century scheme for the evolution of civilizations, and whether
Smith knew it or not, the argument that civilizations would advance as
indigenous (and African) populations stopped reproducing and died out
was widespread even in Latin America during the 1920s.[74] But that decade
also witnessed the growth of new ideas about race among Latin Americans,
including pride in their mixed heritage, from writers such as Gilberto
Freyre in Brazil and José Vasconcelos in Mexico. U.S. women's confusion
at this development was evident in Catt's remark in 1923 that among other
factors worthy of study in the region was "the enigma of the mixed races."[75]
For white U.S. women internationalists, accustomed to a binary distinction
of race, the complex racial categories in Latin America remained an
"enigma."

racial complexities

U.S. women's racial perceptions of Latin American women were also influenced by their class perceptions. The higher the class from which a Latin American woman came, the more European, or "whiter," U.S. women presumed her to be, and vice versa. This is illustrated in the contrast between Elena Landázuri and Elena Torres, who both had extensive contacts with a wide range of U.S.-based organizations. Landázuri was from a privileged background; Torres was not. That distinction, along with significant differences in their personalities and activities, was reflected in the ways many U.S. women perceived each of them. Landázuri was often described in U.S. women's correspondence with words such as "delightful," "obliging," and "exquisite." Several U.S. YWCA members in particular were impressed with her background; they boasted that she represented the "aristocratic element" in their Mexican office. One YWCA representative recalled that on seeing Landázuri singing and playing Mexican folk songs on the piano, "my whole idea of Mexico and Mexican life shifted like a kaleidoscope and the women of Mexico because suddenly real to me."[76] One wonders what her "whole idea" of Mexico and its women had been previously, but the implication here is that she did not expect Mexican women to be as cultivated as Landázuri. Torres, on the other hand, was described by many correspondents from WILPF and the YWCA as "forceful," "fiery," and "radical." Jane Addams noted that under her leadership the Mexican WILPF section "got into trouble almost as soon as it was born, largely because [Torres] was a birth-control and communist advocate, shocking the correct Spanish ladies within an inch of their lives."[77] Even though Addams's remark seems slightly bemused rather than disparaging of Torres, she did distinguish Torres from the "Spanish" women in the group. Other U.S. women were quite as supportive. YWCA official Edith Stanton noted of Torres, "She has some of the crudities of a person who has had to fight her way up from childhood. . . . She is young in years as yet and probably the coming years will bring a certain softness which in many ways will add to her strength."[78]

There were, of course, exceptions to this pattern of assumed racial and class hierarchies. Some U.S. women interpreted Mexican women's less-than-enthusiastic responses to organizing overtures not as inherent laziness or indifference to women's issues, but as manifestations of a deep underlying resentment toward the United States and its citizens. In a speech given shortly after her return from a month-long trip to Mexico, Addams argued that "the strain between Mexico and the United States rests on the fear of aggression from a stronger nation which may be so easily betrayed into the evils of modern economic imperialism." WILPF also tried to address the issue on an organizational level. At its international conference in 1924, WILPF issued a statement of its goals, which included "social, political, and economic equality for all without distinction of sex, race, class, and creed."[79]

A more common approach, however, was to avoid the issue of race entirely by falling back on the idea of Pan Americanism as a unifying ideal within which race was not assumed to play a role. U.S. women who wanted to deemphasize differences between themselves and Latin Americans frequently employed such rhetoric. Florence Terry Griswold of the Pan American Round Table was particularly savvy in this regard. In an effort to promote cross-cultural understanding, the PART focused on public school curricula. "We consider," Griswold announced in 1923, "that now is the time to begin educational propaganda of the sort that will mould the minds of coming generations into the sound principles of international amity, so that in the future, we may be one for all and all for one." In order "to bring about the understanding of Americanization in its broadest sense," PART members wrote to the presidents of every American nation to ask that "a general plan for Americanization be adopted throughout the Western Hemisphere."[80] In an address in Mexico City in 1938 Griswold evoked the "melting pot" metaphor for the entire region: "We appreciate that this Hemisphere is but a melting-pot where a distinct nationality is being formed. . . . As we view it, Pan Americanism means all America."[81]

Members of the Pan American International Women's Committee also invoked Pan Americanism on a regular basis. One explained the significance of a 1916 inter-American women's conference as "an opportunity to become acquainted and to exchange views, not only on subjects of special interest to women, but on all matters pertaining to Pan Americanism. . . . It was the belief that such cooperation among women would serve as a powerful factor in developing the means 'to increase the knowledge of things American.'"[82] In her opening remarks for the 1923 Columbus Day celebrations PAIWC chairwoman Antoinette Hughes, wife of U.S. Secretary of State Charles Evans Hughes, emphasized the similarities among women by calling on the "common bonds of womanhood," which existed "irrespective of differences of race and language." The languages of womanhood and of Pan Americanism, Hughes suggested, transcended any spoken language.[83]

This articulation of Pan Americanism elided and obscured differences among women, including nationality, culture, and race, and assumed a universal history and experience based on that of white U.S. women. In practice, Pan Americanism served to deny a specific racial or ethnic identity to Latin American women, because U.S. women tended to assume that the "common" ideal most closely resembled themselves. The PART plan for "Americanization," even in its "broadest sense," could easily have been read by women in Latin America as a program for extending the culture and values of the United States throughout the hemisphere. Certainly the PART showed no awareness of the antipathy toward the United States already prevalent in Latin America by the 1920s. The PAIWC choice of Columbus Day as a moment for hemispheric celebration was equally problematic. In most Latin American countries the day's proceedings were poorly attended, and most of the audience members were elites.[84] Even an organization like WILPF, which in many ways was attentive to the threat of U.S. hemispheric hegemony, over-relied on the label "Pan American" to characterize all American women. Pan Americanism was popular among U.S. Americans during the 1920s and especially into the 1930s as an ideological bulwark against potential threats from Europe and Asia, but as David Sheinin has argued, "Pan Americanism has always been U.S. led, the friendly face of U.S. dominance in the hemisphere."[85] In these instances it was also like another side of the "civilizing" coin—it benevolently brought Latin American women under the umbrella of "American" civilization.

Once again, the contrast provided by the Mexican YWCA is illuminating, since the organization managed to sidestep most of the discord the others encountered and remain intact throughout the 1920s. The YWCA plan for "Mexicanization" was a departure from the approaches of either WILPF or the Pan American International Women's Committee in that it was founded on the idea that Mexican women must shape the association for themselves, rather than come together in order to serve the needs of an external organization. The YWCA was also the only one of the three U.S. groups that was consciously striving to reform and reconceptualize the very notion of "internationalism" during this period. These discussions were association-wide; they included but were not limited to the Foreign Division. In 1925 a group of representatives from several different YWCA staff groups met to devise "a more practical and concrete method of presenting internationalism to our membership. . . . This is recommended in light of the statements made in this meeting by both the finance and city secretaries that in its present form it is losing attractiveness and force."[86] Several members of the group reported that their constituents were bored with lectures on peace, and with pageants designed to promote cross-cultural understanding and goodwill. "Often our world fellowship program is shallow," they noted, "full of pleasant phrases and sentiment. The approach to world fellowship has frequently been paternalistic, giving of our largess to world needs. This paternalism is antagonistic to the social approach to international responsibility."[87] The YWCA pursued this "social approach" in Mexico, as the organization strove to create an association based on the needs and desires of local women, putting them in charge of its operation as much as possible. Though the Mexican association did not come up in this discussion about the future of the YWCA's international work, that the Foreign Division designated it as a priority for funding and staffing over the next several years suggests they recognized its potential not just as an association but as a model for others. In both its Mexican program and its overall ethos, the YWCA showed more flexibility and adaptability than WILPF. Their approach represented the antithesis of imperialist internationalism.

Not all U.S. women were as exasperated by their experiences in Latin America as Carrie Chapman Catt on her tour in 1923, nor did they write off Latin American women as "fat" and "less easy to move." But Catt's sentiments signaled an assumption of the superiority of her own ideas and methods that underlay many interactions between U.S. and Latin American women during the 1920s and 1930s. In particular, the language of Pan Americanism represented the ideological underpinning of imperialist internationalism and feminism in the Western Hemisphere. U.S. women like Catt and the members of the PAIWC who sought to emphasize the unity of the Americas used it in ways that effectively erased any real or potential differences among women. By contrast, the YWCA rarely invoked the phrase, instead focusing much more explicitly on developing programs within local contexts rather than hemispheric ones. It is not surprising that the women internationalists who adhered to the Pan American ethos were largely unsuccessful at creating lasting relationships and organizations throughout the Americas.

Washington, D.C., 1925

Despite her resignation from the Pan American Association for the Advancement of Women in 1924, Carrie Chapman Catt coordinated one last event on its behalf the following year. The All-America Women's Conference represented the last chance not only for the association but also for institutionalizing inter-American women's internationalism, and for any chance at cooperation involving Catt and Elena Torres. By this time, both the Mexican section of WILPF and the Pan American International Women's Committee were effectively dead, and the YWCA had localized its efforts to Mexico City. If any broader organization were to survive, it would have to grow from this gathering.

The size of the conference indicated that fewer women prioritized inter-American cooperation than had done so three years earlier. Held in Washington, D.C., from April 29 to May 2, the conference was much smaller than the one in Baltimore. Only twenty-five women representing thirteen countries assembled in the Columbus Room of the Pan American Union Building. Morning and afternoon sessions were complemented by evening dinners hosted by the American Association of University Women, the League of Women Voters, and the Young Women's Christian Association. The conference was likely timed to coincide with the quinquennial meeting of the International Council of Women, which began in Washington on May 4, and was attended by all the delegates to the All-America Women's Conference. The League of Women Voters played a much smaller role than it had in Baltimore three years earlier. Belle Sherwin, the new president of the league, addressed the delegates and attended many of the sessions, as did Maud Wood Park, but it was Catt who was in control.

As she had in 1923, Catt still wanted to "make this Pan American thing go." Despite her earlier lamentations over the future of inter-American cooperation, Catt made one more attempt to establish a common program for action among all American women. As she wrote to a friend before the meeting, "Latin Americans do not at all like to be told or shown how to do things, so I am planning to show them some things that I think will be useful without appearing to do so."[88] The agenda for the four-day conference included many of the issues that had been discussed in Baltimore, such as education, women in industry, and the legal status of women. Most of the officer positions were still held by their original occupants, including Elena Torres as vice-president for North America. She attended as the official Mexican delegate, and was one of only two Mexican women at the conference.

Catt ensured that the focus of the conference was on the future. As the main organizer, she was not beholden to anyone else for input on the agenda, and could steer the conference largely as she wished. She opened the proceedings by declaring the Pan American Association untenable as it was then constituted. Her travels through South America had convinced her that the difficulties and expenses involved in attending annual meetings were too great. She reiterated the importance of a Pan American women's organization, but suggested drastic changes were in order if such a group were to succeed. The chief object of the meeting, she argued, was to decide how to proceed. Catt proposed several possibilities, including meeting only every five years, affiliating with either the International Woman Suffrage Alliance or another group, or disbanding entirely and allowing the women's movement to develop independently in each country. After Catt's speech, the delegates voted to set aside the program for the rest of the day to focus on this question, but failed to arrive at a decision and planned to continue the discussion the next day.[89]

The range of issues Catt identified as important to American women's activism was more diverse than it had been previously, suggesting she had grown more flexible in her approach to inter-American organizing. That evening Catt gave a dinner in the delegates' honor at the Hotel Washington. After the meal, she introduced twelve women she had invited to speak on "A Dozen Wishes for Every Intelligent Woman":

The First Wish (Education)—Denied for ages.
The Second Wish (Prosperity)—Denied for 3000 years.
The Third Wish (Wages)—The world laughed at it.
The Fourth Wish (Freedom of Opinion)—Scandalous, they said.
The Fifth Wish (A Happy Home)—For both.
The Sixth Wish (Motherhood)
The Seventh Wish (Guardianship)—Justice long denied.
The Eighth Wish (Healthy conditions in Community)—Very modern.
The Ninth Wish (Schools for All)
The Tenth Wish (Goodwill, friendship, and understanding through-out the Western Continents)—For which we all pray.
The Eleventh Wish (Perpetual Peace for the World)—It must come.
The Twelfth Wish (The Vote and what we did with it)—It did come.[90]

Catt chose topics that reflected a broader spectrum of interests than she had at the 1922 Baltimore conference, where she limited herself to suffrage.

Three years later it was still significant; she selected it as the culmination of the evening's discussion. But it followed issues ranging from domesticity and maternalism, to education and health care, to wages and guardianship of children, to peace and international goodwill. This suggests that despite Catt's desire to direct the course of inter-American cooperation, she now recognized that American women had more diverse goals than simply the right to vote. In fact, this range of topics reflected Elena Torres's agenda in Mexico City more closely than it did the LWV agenda in Baltimore.

The following afternoon, April 30, Catt proposed establishing a new organization to replace the PAAAW. The delegates agreed to call it the Inter-American Union of Women. They proposed several revisions to the "Aims of the PAAAW," which were eventually adopted, along with a revised leadership structure. The new aims were broader than the original ones. In place of three resolutions on the rights of married women and equal guardianship of children, for instance, was a single resolution on "the social welfare of women and children." The vote was no longer singled out as a goal, rather the delegates resolved "to obtain and enforce civil and political rights for women." The resolution on international friendliness and understanding remained virtually untouched. Bertha Lutz of Brazil was elected president, and Esther de Calvo of Panama was elected vice-president at large; the delegates resolved to hold another conference in either Brazil or Panama in three years' time. Belle Sherwin replaced Elena Torres as vice-president for North America; Torres was elected to the newly formed board of directors. Finally, the executive board passed a resolution thanking Catt for her "self-sacrificing, generous, and inspired leadership."[91]

Despite her seeming shift away from a domineering approach relative to the goals of the new organization, Catt's closing speech to the conference betrayed some remaining vestiges of imperialist internationalism. She had one crucial piece of advice to share with the Latin American women: "do everything possible to keep the women together and . . . as little as possible to drive them asunder." Urging them to avoid questions such as divorce and prostitution, which had divided the women's movement in other countries, she encouraged them to learn from the mistakes of their predecessors: "When our movement [in the United States] was under way the women could not see the end, and they got bewildered by the many problems that surrounded them. . . . The membership split over a minor question and remained apart in this country for twenty years. The movement was very much weakened because of it." In particular, Catt worried about "one new and vexing condition in the world that was not here when we were going through our [suffrage] movement, and that is this great conflict of industry vs. capitalism." Class consciousness, she argued, created nothing but hate, and hate created war. In order to achieve emancipation Latin American women had to keep clear of the "industrial movement" and try to secure support from both workers and capitalists. The women's movement would only succeed if they carefully excluded all divisive issues.[92]

Catt's concern for the divisiveness of class consciousness likely stemmed not only from her knowledge of what had split the U.S. suffrage movement in the late nineteenth century but from her experience with anticommunism in the United States. Anticommunist fervor again swept the country in the mid-1920s, and women internationalists and peace activists were among its primary targets. In April 1923 a pamphlet entitled "Peace at Any Old Price," by Richard M. Whitney, president of the American Defense Society, claimed that WILPF was controlled directly by the Soviet government.[93] In March 1924 the *Dearborn Independent* printed a two-part article titled "Are the Women's Clubs Used by Bolshevists?" The second installment featured a detailed diagram outlining how a few "key women" with links to "world communism" controlled an extensive network of women activists. The "Spider Web Chart," as it came to be known, claimed to prove that the international socialist movement had infiltrated a wide range of organizations in the United States, including WILPF and Catt's own League of Women Voters.[94] Any appeal to peace or internationalism was vulnerable to interpretation as weak, unpatriotic, and even treasonable. Activist U.S. women defended themselves vigorously, but the accusations forced them all to tread carefully in their public remarks. Catt would almost certainly have been considering the political climate as she addressed the Latin American women in Washington.

But Elena Torres must have been seething as she listened to Catt. Three years earlier she had explained to the delegates in Baltimore that capitalist aggression was at the heart of the problems facing Mexican women. Torres was still a member of the Mexican Communist Party in 1925, and had always dedicated herself to supporting workers' rights. Yet in Washington she found herself listening to Catt tell her that she and her comrades would never be able to achieve emancipation unless they gave up the "industrial movement." For Torres, and for other feminists with strong ties to socialism and communism, there was no distinction between the two.[95] Furthermore, to Torres agitating against capitalism meant agitating against the

United States. Hearing Catt tell her audience to avoid the conflict of "industry versus capitalism" could have sounded to Torres like an endorsement for continued U.S. hegemony in Mexico. Emancipation for Mexican women would have meant little to Torres if her nation as a whole were still oppressed. Whatever her reaction, the Washington conference marked the end of Torres's documented association with Catt and the League of Women Voters. Although she was named to the Inter-American Union of Women board of directors she never participated in the organization. After her return to Mexico she dedicated herself to working for the Communist Party and Secretariat of Public Education.[96]

The Inter-American Union, however, barely lasted one year. Members of the executive board returned to their respective countries hoping to convene their next conference in either Brazil or Panama within two or three years.[97] Bertha Lutz reported she had been "received with enthusiasm" and many women were "eager to work."[98] Esther de Calvo though was disappointed to find "our women seemed to be less interested than ever."[99] She hoped that convening another conference sooner than planned, in conjunction with Panama's centenary celebration of the first Pan American Congress in 1926, would jump-start the Inter-American Union, but she could garner very little material support from Catt, from the League of Women Voters, or from any other U.S. organizations. De Calvo's frustrations, expressed in a letter to Catt, likely summed up those of other Latin American internationalists like Elena Torres: "You know, Mrs. Catt, I have had such a strong desire to have women from your country here, that the United States is the only American Republic where I have sent more than three invitations. . . . According to the program adopted last April in our Conference in favor of our ideals of fraternity and friendship between the women of the Americas, I have worked very hard, but I have to feel quite disappointed with the results of my work in the United States."[100]

De Calvo's letter captured the bind in which Latin American women internationalists found themselves with regard to U.S. women. They could not sustain an organization like the Inter-American Union, which traced its origins to the United States, without significant structural and financial support from U.S. women. But nor did they want simply to be led by the United States, to suffer the arrogance and presumptions of leadership from women like Catt. If U.S. women were not prepared to cooperate on a more equal footing, such an organization was doomed. Speeches like the one Catt delivered in Washington proved how empty Pan American rhetoric could be if it served only to mask instructions and directives from U.S. to Latin American women.

By 1926, little remained of the myriad endeavors U.S. women internationalists had begun in Mexico ten years earlier. The Pan American Association for the Advancement of Women, the Mexican section of the Women's International League for Peace and Freedom, and the Pan American International Women's Committee were all defunct. The Mexican branch of the Young Women's Christian Association was flourishing, but promoting internationalism played little part in its daily activities. U.S. women's efforts had been stymied by a range of problems, including a lack of resources, divergent priorities, and their own imperialist tendencies.

Human internationalism was especially susceptible to these kinds of practical and ideological limitations. A method centered on personal interactions and shared experiences was more vulnerable to inequitable partnerships if one group thought itself superior to the other. The promotion of goodwill through personal exchanges and shared knowledge could only work if the participants involved spoke the same language—literally as well as figuratively. Very few U.S. women internationalists spoke Spanish, and while Elena Torres, Elena Landázuri, and Adelia Palacios spoke English, not all of their colleagues and few of their constituents did. But the languages of a spiritual internationalism and a political nationalism were also in conflict. U.S. women were trying to bring Mexican women into their internationalist fold, to incorporate them into agendas that had already been established. WILPF in particular worked hard to make its Mexican section conform to preexisting standards. Mexican women were seeking help to articulate their nascent feminist and nationalist demands. They had no interest in an internationalism that professed itself above politics. This set up an intrinsic inequality in their interactions with U.S. women.

It was no coincidence that the two most successful ventures of the mid-1920s were also the least international. Both the 1923 conference of the Pan American Association in Mexico City and the Mexican YWCA were primarily Mexican efforts; they reflected the agendas and desires of Mexican women to a much greater extent than did such U.S. efforts as the Pan American Conference of Women. Mexican women focused on their own needs, requesting guidance and cooperation but not directive leadership from U.S. women. There was little work done either at the 1923 conference or within the YWCA, for instance, to build sustained programs for cooperation that brought U.S. and Mexican women together as equals on a regular basis. Some women deployed rhetoric about Pan Americanism to that end, but they could not bring about egalitarian internationalism in practice.

Although the YWCA continued to flourish over the next few years, other U.S. women internationalists needed time to regroup. Neither Emma Bain Swiggett's Pan American Committee nor the Pan American Association ever reformed themselves, but by the end of the decade WILPF had begun to renew its efforts in Mexico City. In the meantime, a diplomatic crisis between the United States and Mexico commandeered all women internationalists' attention.

Chapter 4

The Peace with Mexico Campaign

Throughout the winter of 1926–1927, war loomed between the United States and Mexico. The conflict centered on Article 27 of the 1917 Mexican Constitution, which declared all subsoil resources to be vested in the Mexican nation. This represented a serious threat to extensive U.S. ownership of land and control of petroleum reserves. Though accurate numbers on U.S. investments are difficult to come by, the *New York Times* estimated in February 1927 that U.S. holdings in Mexico totaled more than $1.265 billion, including more than $270 million in oil lands and refineries, and more than $140 million in rural properties.[1] After ten years of failed negotiations over how U.S. businesses and individuals might be compensated or even exempted, the article was due to take effect on January 1, 1927.

Simultaneously, several other factors fed the growing clamor for U.S. military intervention. Local and regional outbreaks of violence threatened the safety of U.S. landowners and their families. U.S. policy makers suspected that Mexico wanted to dominate Central America, and they took Mexican support for anti-U.S. forces in Nicaragua as a provocation. Moreover, prominent Catholic groups in the United States denounced Mexican president Plutarco Elías Calles's war against the Cristeros, rebels in the western state of Michoacán who resisted anticlerical measures by the Mexican government in 1925 and 1926. All these factors stoked fears of strengthening ties between Mexico and the Soviet Union, and of Bolshevist influence in the Western Hemisphere.

Exerting influence over U.S. foreign policies was a secondary rather than a primary concern of the women who followed the tenets of human internationalism in the 1910s and early 1920s, and one they did not always pursue actively. The U.S. section of the Women's International League for Peace and Freedom criticized the U.S. handling of the Jenkins incident in

1919, and expressed frustration when the United States severed diplomatic relations with Mexico in 1920. In 1922, the LWV hoped the Pan American Conference of Women in Baltimore would help further negotiations between the two countries. But neither group ever rose to the challenges set by Mexican women such as Elena Torres and Elena Landázuri to protest U.S. economic exploitation in Mexico. U.S. women's refusal to discuss Article 27 and U.S. ownership of Mexican natural resources in venues like the Baltimore conference had long frustrated Mexican women activists.

The crisis of 1926–1927 was too severe for internationalists to ignore, however. As relations between the two countries deteriorated over the course of 1926, U.S. women peace activists were integral to nationwide efforts to mobilize opposition to a war with Mexico, and to convince President Coolidge and Congress that there was little popular support for a war. Carrie Chapman Catt's newly-formed organization, the National Committee on the Cause and Cure of War, drew attention to the crisis at its national conferences, while members of the U.S. section of WILPF and the National Council for the Prevention of War (NCPW) started letter-writing campaigns, coordinated press releases, and lobbied members of Congress. In the late spring of 1927, after the most serious threat had passed, these women congratulated themselves on having persuaded Congress to avert war by marshaling public opinion against it, effectively steering U.S.-Mexican relations onto a more peaceful course. Of course, women's efforts alone did not prevent war, but they helped harness and intensify public pressure on policy makers in Washington.

More significantly, the crisis of 1926–1927 prompted many—though not all—U.S. women internationalists to incorporate politics into their activities and to foreground diplomacy in their work. It fostered their ability to mobilize public opinion in a political crisis through women's and other peace organizations. In the process, these women began to move beyond the explicitly gendered, "spiritual" internationalism Jane Addams had counseled in 1916, and toward more modern, sophisticated strategies for promoting hemispheric cooperation and advancing women's agendas. The skills U.S. women developed during the crisis of 1926–1927 enabled them to launch a new phase of women's internationalism in the late 1920s.

"Mexico Is on Trial Before the World"

The course of U.S.-Mexican diplomatic relations between 1922 and 1926 mirrored in many ways the deteriorating relationship between U.S. and

Mexican women over the same period. During his tenure from 1920 to 1924, former president Álvaro Obregón made significant progress toward securing formal U.S. recognition—which had been withdrawn on his election in 1920—by slowly reversing many of the steps earlier governments had taken toward nationalizing the oil industry. In 1921 the Mexican Supreme Court ruled that Article 27 was not retroactive, effectively wiping out the threat of land seizures. Obregón also courted the U.S. banking industry, looking for help solving Mexico's debt crisis and for future investors in its economy. Those bankers in turn pressured the U.S. government to recognize Obregón.[2] But there were still significant obstacles to be overcome, including popular resentment in each country against the other.

Of the four women's internationalist organizations active in Mexico during the 1910s and 1920s, the only one that regularly spoke out against diplomatic and military hostilities between the two countries was the Women's International League for Peace and Freedom. Prominent U.S. WILPF members were among those who protested President Coolidge's continued failure to recognize Obregón. In May 1923 WILPF national secretary Amy Woods called all members' attention to a set of resolutions that the international office had already passed promoting liberty of commerce and opposing U.S. investors' claims to government protection abroad. She also encouraged her colleagues to reconsider the reasons for the U.S. failure to recognize Obregón. The "average citizen or newspaper man" would claim it was due to Article 27, and its threat to U.S. financial interests. Woods contended that a close reading of the article revealed a more "reasonable nature" than the average citizen assumed. The constitution did not give the government the right to confiscate or expropriate any foreign-owned property without "full indemnity." It allowed the government to concede ownership rights to foreigners, provided they promised not "to invoke the special protection of their own governments." Finally, Woods pointed out that the Mexican Supreme Court had declared that the article was not retroactive. Despite this, the U.S. State Department persisted in applying pressure, "in many and devious ways, to have this article abrogated or amended in such a way as to give American citizens extra privileges expressly denied even to Mexican citizens."[3]

Woods and her colleagues were somewhat appeased on August 31, 1923, when the United States announced the restoration of diplomatic relations with Mexico. The two countries signed an unofficial pact, the Bucareli Agreement, which stipulated that land claims would be submitted to special

Bucareli
Agreement

commissions to determine their validity, set forth guidelines for compensating U.S. property owners, and reaffirmed that Article 27 was not retroactive. But the agreement was never presented to the Congress of either country, and was dependent on the goodwill of both sides for its execution. It served its purpose though in paving the way for the reestablishment of the official relationship between the two governments.

The diplomatic détente collapsed less than two years later, when U.S. president Calvin Coolidge learned that the Mexican Congress was drafting two new laws that did not conform to the Bucareli Agreement. The first piece of legislation, known as the Alien Law, restricted the geographic locations in which foreigners could own land. The second, which worried U.S. officials more, required the owners of oilfields to relinquish any titles to property acquired before 1917 in exchange for government concessions limited to fifty years. The law also stipulated that such concessions had to include a "Calvo clause," asserting that owners and investors were not entitled to special privileges merely because they were foreigners. The U.S. government's interpretation of these new laws was that the new Mexican president, Plutarco Elías Calles, was attempting to steal land and capital from foreigners in an industry that their work and ingenuity had created. With the support of the White House, U.S. oil companies decided not to comply with the new legislation, asserting they would not relinquish land under any circumstances.[4] In June 1925 a press release from U.S. secretary of state Frank Kellogg set the tone for the next two years of diplomatic exchanges, threats, arguments, and negotiations. The Coolidge administration would continue to support the Calles government, Kellogg announced, "only so long as it protects American lives and American rights and complies with its international engagements and obligations. The Government of Mexico is now on trial before the world."[5]

The conflict between the United States and Mexico in Nicaragua complicated the situation. Between 1912 and 1925 U.S. Marines occupied Nicaragua under the policy of Dollar Diplomacy. These years were marked by relative political and economic stability because the United States orchestrated a series of rigged elections that kept the compliant Conservative Party in power. But U.S. hegemony also kept the vast majority of Nicaraguans poor and disenfranchised. When President Coolidge withdrew U.S. troops in 1925, years of popular frustration and resentment of an illegitimate government boiled over. A rebellion led by the opposition Liberal Party, combined with struggles for power among Conservatives, alarmed Coolidge to

Nicaragua

the point that he ordered the return of U.S. marines less than a year after their withdrawal. Many observers in the U.S. State Department claimed that Mexico was trying to supplant the United States as the dominant power in Central America. Beginning in 1924, the Mexican government provided military and financial assistance to anti-U.S. interests in Nicaragua. "The action of Mexico in the Nicaraguan crisis is a direct challenge to the United States," Secretary of State Kellogg reported to the Senate Foreign Relations Committee.[6]

Concerns in the United States about Calles's anticlericalism and potential communist sympathies continued to escalate. In 1926 Calles faced a widespread rebellion in the western state of Michoacán. Catholic workers and peasants, calling themselves Cristeros, rebelled against what they saw as attacks by the Mexican government on their property and on the Catholic Church. On August 1, in response to widespread protests and disturbances, Calles put into effect regulations dramatically curtailing the power of the Church. In response, Mexican bishops suspended church services throughout the country.[7] This marked the beginning of three years of violence in Michoacán and the surrounding region. In the United States, much of the press portrayed the conflict as the result of the brutality of the Mexican government against its own peasants. Mexican leaders were depicted as opposing both the Church and the entire notion of private property. Catholic leaders in the United States lost no time in pressuring their own government to decry the suppression of the Cristero Rebellion. Coolidge consistently maintained that the struggle between the government and the Church did not warrant U.S. intervention. The controversy, however, fueled rapidly growing anxiety and anti-Mexican sentiment in the United States, particularly regarding the issue of private property.

Rumors of Bolshevism in Mexico had not abated since the early 1920s, and the actions of the Calles government concerning the Church and private property were interpreted by many in the United States as further evidence of Soviet influence. In August 1926, the American Federation of Labor, citing Calles's treatment of the Church, argued that 90 percent of the antireligious sentiment stemmed from "ultra-radical forces." "There is no difference at the present time," they continued, "between the Governments of Russia and Mexico."[8] The Knights of Columbus leveled further charges. A pamphlet on "Red Mexico," published in 1926, declared "The Mexican attack on the Catholic Church . . . is an attack on the established principles of civilization and humanity. . . . The Mexican problem is not alone a Catholic problem. It is the problem of liberty-loving, fair-minded, free men everywhere."[9]

Such reports inflamed anticommunist crusaders, even though the potential threats to the United States were overblown in the popular press. Many Mexicans did feel an affinity for the theoretical principles of the Soviet Union, which led to the establishment of a diplomatic relationship between the two countries in 1924. But the two countries were never as close as State Department reports suggested.[10] Most reports in the United States of Mexican communism were either exaggerated or fabricated entirely. The most notorious example was when newspaper magnate William Randolph Hearst published documents claiming to prove the existence of a Mexican Red Army, documents that later turned out to have been forged. But in the wake of the first Red Scare in the United States, rumors could do plenty of damage.

Finally, racialized assumptions about Mexicans and Latin Americans pervaded diplomatic discourse in the mid-1920s to an even greater extent than they did the perceptions of some U.S. women internationalists. The State Department in these years was a den of disdain and contempt for Mexicans and for Latin America as a whole.[11] Francis White, the department's chief Latin Americanist, warned a group of incoming students at the Foreign Service School to expect corruption and instability if they were posted to a nonwhite country: "Political stability in these countries [is] more or less in direct proportion to percentage of pure white inhabitants. The greater the percentage of white inhabitants and the more temperate the climate the more stable the government."[12] Another official informed Secretary of State Charles Evans Hughes in 1923 that "Mexico is and will continue to be governed by an Indian race of low civilization, and it would be a fundamental error to deal with such a government as with that of a highly civilized white race, or to expect to obtain justice by the mere force of logic when justice conflicts with national aspiration."[13] These attitudes were perhaps best represented by U.S. ambassador to Mexico James Sheffield, who once observed that the motivations of Mexico's leaders "are greed, a wholly Mexican view of nationalism, and an Indian, not Latin, hatred of all peoples not on the reservation."[14] Taken together, the conflicts over oil and in Nicaragua, which were fueled by religious, anticommunist, and racist ideologies, alarmed many people in the United States, particularly peace activists and women internationalists, who watched the escalation of tensions between the United States and Mexico with trepidation.

Women Peace Internationalists

Many U.S. women internationalists considered themselves part of the international peace movement that flourished in the wake of World War I. Determined never to see such a war repeated, peace activists in the United States focused in the 1920s on using the new U.S. status as a world power to create a permanent peace. Liberal intellectuals, Protestant ministers, lawyers, socialists, labor leaders, and others formed broad coalitions to pressure the United States to lead the way toward global disarmament and arbitration of international disputes. Most shared a belief that peace was the "necessary reform" if the modern world were to survive its own industrial and technological advancements.[15] They also shared a distrust of the partnership between government and the banking industry that had flourished in Latin American under Dollar Diplomacy.[16] Despite these commonalities, the peace movement was not uniform or cohesive. Some groups advocated the outlawry of war altogether, while others stopped short of an entirely pacifist stance. Some focused on U.S. participation in international organizations such as the League of Nations and the World Court, while others concentrated on education. Among the many groups either composed entirely of women or in which women occupied leadership positions that took an active interest in U.S.-Mexican relations, three national organizations led the way. Carrie Chapman Catt made the issue part of the agenda of her new organization, the National Committee on the Cause and Cure for War (CCCW), which focused on educating the public as well as on direct action protests. The group at the forefront of the popular Peace with Mexico campaign was the National Council for the Prevention of War. The NCPW was a mixed-sex group in which women occupied several prominent positions. The U.S. section of WILPF also took a strong interest in Mexico, driven primarily by executive secretary Dorothy Detzer.[17]

Catt established the National Committee on the Cause and Cure of War in April 1924 as a clearinghouse for the "peace interests" of the nine largest women's organizations in the country. Though she is more often remembered for her work on behalf of woman suffrage, Catt was not a newcomer to the peace movement. She had been an original member of the Women's Peace Party, the precursor to the U.S. section of WILPF, but had fallen out with Jane Addams and other party members when she supported Woodrow Wilson's decision to enter World War I. She had never been as radically pacifist as Addams and WILPF, and still felt in the mid-1920s that

Addams's group was too leftist for most U.S. women. According to Charles DeBenedetti, the CCCW neatly filled Catt's prescription for a women's peace agency that was active but modest. Neither radical nor conservative, it was "constructive," Catt boasted.[18] Its early agenda included lobbying for the United States to join the World Court and organizing a national peace conference. Catt's primary focus throughout the organization's existence was on education.[19]

When she announced that the first Conference on the Cause and Cure of War would convene in January 1925, Catt signaled her intention to keep her distance from other peace organizations like WILPF. She kept the list of invitees to those organizations interested in peace but for which it was not their primary goal, such as the League of Women Voters, American Association of University Women, Women's Trade Union League, and Woman's Christian Temperance Union. No "peace society" received an invitation. Noting that there were over seventy-five such groups in existence by late 1924, Catt protested she could not invite one without inviting them all. "These societies," she told the *New York Times*, "to which 'we the people' should normally look for instruction and guidance, have not yet seen the wisdom, apparently, of a common procedure. . . . The women's organizations calling this conference, on the other hand, have wished to avoid old controversies which have existed between other organizations and to start their investigations into the possible causes and proposed cures of war quite free from such handicaps."[20] Essentially calling the peace movement disorganized and ineffective, Catt positioned her new group as a new alternative. Over the next two years her committee devoted its time and energy to peace education, working through programs already established by its member organizations.

Following this pattern, Catt limited the topics discussed at the Second Conference on the Cause and Cure of War, in December 1926, to the principles, not the machinery, of peace. These included security, arbitration, and disarmament, with reference to Asia and Europe as well as Mexico and Central America. In choosing speakers Catt looked for "impartial" experts on policy, not politicians or activists with agendas of their own. It was therefore somewhat surprising that the man she chose to address conference attendees on Mexico and Central America was Carleton Beals, a journalist who had written frequently on the injustice of U.S. interventions in the region. Predictably, he lashed out in his speech at the political and economic crimes perpetrated against Mexico by the U.S. government and U.S. businesses. The recent land and oil laws, he argued, represented the

Mexican government's attempt "to rectify by legal means the wrongs for which we are in no small part responsible." The Monroe Doctrine, he argued, had been maliciously misapplied to satisfy the "territorial, political, and economic schemes of the United States. . . . With it as an excuse, we have frequently clutched for Mexican territory, Mexican wealth and favorable privileges and concessions." Beals laid the blame for these attitudes at the feet of Woodrow Wilson and his ambassador to Mexico, Henry Lane Wilson (no relation). The latter Beals declared an "inefficient meddler" who had "spilled a river of blood across Mexican history."[21]

Beals's last comment provoked an angry response from Ambassador Wilson, even as it revealed the contradictions inherent in Catt's mission. Wilson denied all the charges and demanded that Catt omit the offending remarks from the published transcript of the conference.[22] Catt was torn; privately she agreed with Beals, but she worried that if she published the conference proceedings without the edits, Wilson would sue the Carnegie Endowment for Peace, which financed the publication. "The whole question of the relations of the United States of Mexico," she wrote to Nicholas Murray Butler, president of the endowment, "and vice versa, is so obscured by politics and political faces to be saved, that it will always be difficult to get at the truth. Mr. Beals was fearlessly frank and probably truthful, but he might have been a bit less harsh without impairing his story."[23] To her colleague and friend Josephine Schain, Catt wrote, "Whoever would have thought that that nice young Mr. Beals, who looks as shy as a high school graduate, could have got us into so much trouble. I am inclined to think that all he said is more or less true, but he did say it in rather a tantalizing way."[24] In the end Catt edited the offending remarks out of the published transcript. Her decision, even though she agreed with Beals's perspective, showed her unwillingness to take a controversial stand on the Mexican question.

Catt still harbored the belief, prominent among human internationalists in the 1910s and early 1920s, that she could keep her committee above politics. But as the Mexican crisis escalated, this approach made her committee increasingly ineffective as those women and organizations willing to engage politics and politicians directly, rather that attempt to remain impartial observers, took center stage. Catt and the CCCW maintained their moderate, non-pacifist position throughout the 1920s. Joan Jensen portrayed her as the "prototype of the right-wing leadership of the peace movement," mostly because of her conservative position regarding the outlawry of war before 1928, and her reluctance to engage in overtly political activism.[25] Catt deliberately distanced herself from the more radical pacifist branches of the movement. In large part this was because she knew it made her less susceptible to Red Scare attacks.[26] Nonetheless, she was forced to defend herself from charges of disloyalty and Bolshevism throughout the mid-1920s. In countering such attacks before the Second Conference on the Cause and Cure of War in 1926, Catt positioned herself and her organization as no further left than the president himself: "There is no one in the coming conference who is any redder or any pinker than Mr. Coolidge. . . . So nearly as I can judge, the general attitude of the conference on the cause and cure of war is about the same attitude which the President of the United States repeatedly has expressed in his public addresses."[27] In aligning so clearly with the Coolidge administration, Catt demonstrated her determination to chart a centrist path to peace. That path kept her removed from much of the more overtly anti-imperialist activism concerning Mexico and Nicaragua over the next year.

The central voice of the peace movement by the mid-1920s was the National Council for the Prevention of War. The NCPW grew out of the National Council on the Limitation of Armaments, which had been organized in support of the Washington Naval Conference in 1921. Like Catt's National Committee, it was a clearinghouse for other peace organizations, though its membership was mixed-sex and generally had a more radical approach to ending war. In fall 1922, the group was made permanent, and changed its name to the National Council for the Prevention of War. Frederick J. Libby led the council from 1921 until his retirement in 1954. A Quaker and convinced pacifist from Maine, Libby expanded the council between 1922 and 1927 to include a program on peace education, a legislative department, and a student forum.[28] Though never as radical as groups such as the War Resisters League and the Women's Peace Union, which advocated the outlawry of war altogether, the council was more willing to challenge the Coolidge administration and the State Department than Catt and her committee.[29] Catt, who had agreed to be listed as vice-chair of the council at its inception, asked to have her name removed from the organization letterhead in April 1926.

Like other peace organizations in the United States, the NCPW became concerned about the situation in Mexico as they watched tensions escalate throughout 1926. Libby saw more at stake than oil, Nicaragua, and the Church. In his 1969 autobiography, he remembered his reaction to an editorial from a popular magazine proposing that the United States simply wipe out the U.S.-Mexican border, invade, and take over the country, and another that suggested Mexico should abandon its revolutionary constitution in favor of semicolonial rule by the United States. This "perennial 'manifest destiny' argument," he noted, came from a "small but persistent section of American public opinion."[30] Under Libby's direction, the council's work on Mexico was carried out over the next year by associate director Laura Puffer Morgan. Morgan's interest in international relations began while helping her journalist husband gather information for his newspaper articles throughout the 1910s. After his death in 1921, she devoted herself full-time to several voluntary organizations, including the National Council of Women and the American Association of University Women, as well as the NCPW.[31] The bulk of her work centered on liaising with representatives of other organizations affiliated with the council.

One of the most important of those organizations was the U.S. section of WILPF. As early as May 1926, U.S. members were publishing information on the Mexican land and oil questions, and warning that unless the Coolidge administration took steps to resolve the situation it would only grow more contentious. At its annual meeting that month, members of the U.S. section passed resolutions urging the U.S. government to establish treaties with every American nation promising the peaceful settlement of disputes. They also argued that present circumstances demanded attention on the part of U.S. citizens as well as the government: "The members of the [WILPF] recognize that in the relations between the United States and the peoples of Latin America we have a continuing problem of great seriousness, that we are at least in some degrees aware of the mistrust with which we are regarded and that we urge our membership to inform themselves as to the historical grounds of this feeling." Further resolutions pledged that WILPF would do "whatever possible" to strengthen friendly relations with Mexico in particular.[32]

Nearly all WILPF activity throughout 1926 concerning the Mexican crisis was coordinated by Dorothy Detzer, who served as the executive secretary for the U.S. section from 1924 until 1946 (see Figure 5). Originally from Fort Wayne, Indiana, she lived at Hull House while attending the Chicago School of Civics and Philanthropy during the 1910s, where Jane Addams introduced her to WILPF. She went to work for the organization in 1924. Detzer's personal antiwar sentiments stemmed in large part from watching her twin brother Don suffer and die from the effects of having been gassed during World War I. After working overseas with various

Quaker missions for three years (though Detzer was not a Quaker herself), she moved to Washington, anxious to find work with a peace organization. At the suggestion of Frederick Libby, she applied to WILPF, where her intelligence and dedication soon made her invaluable. Throughout her tenure she was recognized as one of the most effective "cause" lobbyists in Washington.[33] Her primary issue was economic anti-imperialism. Since February 1925 she had been working closely with Senator Edwin Ladd to craft a resolution compelling the U.S. government to refrain from "directly or indirectly engaging the responsibility of the Government . . . to supervise the fulfillment of financial arrangements between citizens of the United States and sovereign foreign Governments."[34]

Despite their common concerns about the escalating tensions between the United States and Mexico, U.S. women internationalists were little more unified in their approaches to the crisis than they had been to organizing Mexican women. Catt and the National Committee took a centrist approach, while the National Council for the Prevention of War and the U.S. section of WILPF were more radically pacifist. More important, Catt's desire to keep her committee above politics and her reluctance to take a strong stance against U.S. policies kept her removed from the most active arenas of the peace movement over the next several months. The NCPW and WILPF, who were not only willing but eager to engage the politics of U.S. foreign policy, took center stage as the Peace with Mexico campaign took shape toward the end of 1926. Women such as Laura Puffer Morgan and Dorothy Detzer proved themselves keen to abandon apolitical internationalism and adopt new tactics and strategies in their efforts to articulate clear opposition to war.

Mobilizing for Peace

As the U.S.-Mexican crisis escalated during the last half of 1926, women internationalists began to employ new tactics and strategies to mobilize opposition to any potential armed conflict. They organized letter-writing campaigns, they solicited and issued press releases, they called mass meetings, and they lobbied members of Congress and the Coolidge administration. All of these activities were designed to pressure policy makers to submit the dispute over Article 27 to international arbitration. Unlike Carrie Chapman Catt or earlier human internationalists, these women no

Figure 5. Dorothy Detzer.
Women's International League for Peace and Freedom Records,
Swarthmore College Peace Collection.

longer relied on formal conferences or on small-group interactions among women to promote peace and cooperation. They employed modern and sophisticated methods to achieve a recognizable political goal, much the same way that other nongovernmental organizations continued to do later in the twentieth century.

Throughout the rest of 1926, Morgan, Detzer, and thousands of other observers watched nervously as U.S.-Mexican relations deteriorated. Envoys from both countries continued to meet but failed to resolve the oil issue. Representatives of both governments and the U.S. petroleum industry tried to negotiate U.S. compliance with the new oil laws. Both sides exchanged diplomatic "notes" in which they held firmly to their positions. In an address to the Mexican Congress on September 1, however, Calles expressed a slightly more conciliatory attitude, which oil executives interpreted as a sign that he would eventually agree to soften the oil law. Ambassador Sheffield urged Coolidge to push harder for resolution on the oil issue while Calles, who was facing widespread violence over his position on the Church as well as an armed rebellion from Yaqui Indians in the north, was weak and distracted. But both presidents held their ground as December 31, the deadline established by Mexico for U.S. oil companies to relinquish their property titles in favor of fifty-year concessions, approached. U.S. officials and oil executives waited to see if the Mexican government would confiscate all Mexican oil fields, as by law it was allowed to do.[35]

Both countries also continued to manipulate events in Nicaragua. In mid-November the United States oversaw the "election" of president Adolfo Diaz, a former occupant of the position who had proven highly accommodating to U.S. interests. He obediently castigated Calles's efforts "to force on Nicaragua Mexican influence" in his inaugural address, but the U.S. State Department continued to receive reports of Mexican assistance to Juan Sacasa, the leader of the Liberal rebellion. Diaz begged the U.S. government for more aid, claiming Mexico was on the brink of invading his country. In a "manifesto" issued December 11, he announced, "It is understood from reliable sources that it is the plan of the Mexican government that the vessel *Superior*, now being outfitted by officials of the Mexican Government with an armed expedition, should proceed soon to Nicaragua under the escort of Mexican gunboats for the purpose of making war against the constitutional government of Nicaragua." Sacasa vociferously denounced Diaz's claim. Carleton Beals supported Sacasa, charging that the U.S. State Department had orchestrated the manifesto. Kellogg though held fast to his assertion that Calles was trying to extend a Bolshevist empire throughout Central America.[36]

Accusations of Bolshevism in Mexico reached a new peak during these months, fueled by Catholic organizations in the United States and by the State Department. Catholic groups had already made known their conviction that Calles's anticlericalism was a sure sign of his affinity for the Soviet Union. In September, the announcement that the USSR had appointed a high-profile and controversial woman as its new ambassador to Mexico—

the first woman to be appointed to such a position in the Western Hemi-sphere—stirred up new fears of communist agitation and propagandizing in the United States. Alexandra Kollontai was a Bolshevist writer and intel-lectual who had spent several years in the United States campaigning for communism and women's rights. She planned to travel to Mexico via New York, but the State Department denied her a visa, claiming "she has been actively associated with the International Communist subversive move-ment." When she finally arrived in Mexico in December, she was greeted enthusiastically, and voiced her desire to improve relations between the Soviet Union and Mexico, particularly through trade. She denied she was an agitator or a propagandist, but suffered continued accusations from U.S. observers who claimed she was only using Mexico as a base from which to direct communist operations in the United States.[37]

U.S. women internationalists watched all of these developments closely, but they also made clear they would do more than just observe. Detzer used the December 1926 issue of *Pax International*, the WILPF newsletter, to keep members informed about the situation and lay out WILPF's plan of action. "It is now an established fact," she wrote, "that the difficulty involves not alone the land laws of Mexico and the control of her subsoil resources, but the inevitable 'entente' developing between Central Ameri-can countries for the protection of their right against infringement by the United States." Detzer blamed Dollar Diplomacy for the underlying prob-lem: "This growing resistance and wretched fear which have developed among Latin American countries have come not through the processes of imagination, but as the direct result of the American investors and the inevitable marines."[38] On December 14, she wrote to Secretary Kellogg, asking him to clarify his argument that Mexico's actions constituted a threat to U.S. national security, and to explain the legal grounds on which the U.S. government could risk the lives of U.S. soldiers when one Latin American country interfered with another.[39] Just two days later, Kellogg declared he would not renew diplomatic discussions with Mexico before the December 31 deadline. "Our present relations with Mexico are really very serious," Detzer wrote to the international WILPF office in Geneva. "The State Department is as rigid as ever on its stand against Mexico, which involves something deeper and thicker than oil and that is the whole policy of private property." According to a strict interpretation of Marxism, she pointed out, Mexico was "no more Bolshevist than the United States," but if one gauged Bolshevism in terms of a country's attitude toward private property, then "the Central American countries are developing a very different conception from that of the United States. It is this new development which is apparently at the bottom of the difficulty now." Detzer was frustrated at the number of organizations in the United States, groups that could normally be counted on to work for peace, who were now "panic stricken at the very suggestion of 'red.'" If there were no crisis soon, she predicted, it would come later, but a crisis of some sort was inevitable.[40]

WILPF and the NCPW began campaigns to mobilize opposition to a military resolution of that crisis. Detzer kept in close touch with Libby and Morgan, who were gathering information on local and national peace organizations. They learned what those organizations had been doing in their cities and states, and encouraged them to publicize their position in support of arbitration and pressure their senators to do the same. Libby agreed with Catt and the delegates to the Second Conference on the Cause and Cure of War that the matter should be settled through arbitration, without severing diplomatic relations and without lifting the arms embargo. But unlike Catt and her committee, the NCPW asked its member organizations to voice their opposition to armed intervention. Libby urged them to pass resolutions decrying U.S. policy, and then send those resolutions to President Coolidge, Secretary of State Kellogg, and Senator William Borah, chairman of the Senate Foreign Relations Committee.[41] The NCPW also worked hard to publicize the impending crisis in the hope of stirring up popular opinion against a war. Morgan urged her contacts to submit editorials decrying the use of military force to their local newspapers, and pressured newspaper editors to print them. In these efforts they focused particularly on specific sectors of the population, including workers, farmers, and women.[42]

Morgan was responsible for most of this correspondence, coordinating with other women's and mixed-sex organizations, as well as church groups and the press. She wrote to Sidney Gulick, head of the Federal Council of Churches, to express her concern that a resolution passed by the council urging peace with Mexico made no mention of the possibility that the U.S. government might lift its arms embargo against Mexico. This would be dangerous, she argued, because an increasing number of newspaper reports and editorials cited violence against the Church in Mexico as evidence of a growing Bolshevik presence. Several people, including the counselor of the American Embassy in Mexico, had told Morgan that lifting the embargo would be "the most serious step that our government could take" in Mexico. She pressured Gulick to include this issue in all future Council statements about the situation. Morgan also wrote to Katherine Gerwick, executive secretary of the Young Women's Christian Association, asking her to arrange for the copresidents and a few members of the executive board to send telegrams to President Coolidge urging him not to use force in dealing with Mexico, and not to lift the arms embargo. She informed both Gulick and Gerwick of the NCPW's plan to send a deputation in person to Coolidge to discuss the Mexican question. Even if he refused to see them, she pointed out, "The mere fact that it is asked for is sufficient to carry the idea to him, which is the most important thing at the present time."[43]

All of Morgan's efforts were part of the larger NCPW strategy to harness public opinion concerning Mexico. At a meeting on December 20, the executive committee passed a series of resolutions concerning how to proceed. Their plan included contacting every member organization, asking them to release an official statement opposing a war with Mexico, to send telegrams and phone messages to President Coolidge urging him to submit the matter to arbitration, and to encourage as many of their state and local branches to do the same. The council launched a massive publicity campaign in the press, sending information and releases to publications large and small. They reached out to clergymen, asking them to include a plea for peace with Mexico in their New Year's Day sermons. This was directed in particular at challenging the widespread propaganda of the Knights of Columbus, the organization behind many of the reports of atrocities committed against the Catholic Church in Mexico. By the end of 1926 the Knights had raised over a million dollars for their "educational campaign" to inform the U.S. public about the extent of Communist influence in Mexico. "With the combination of religious passion and the cry of communism," Morgan observed sadly, "we have a problem on our hands to maintain the peace."[44] Frederick Libby argued that Mexico's "extreme nationalism" rendered absurd the accusations that it was being controlled by the Third International. The NCPW's main focus, he felt, had to be on getting the U.S. and Mexican governments to submit their disputes to arbitration. He urged all members to send telegrams to President Coolidge pressuring him to opt for arbitration over any other solution. "The time to prevent serious trouble with Mexico," he argued, "is now."[45]

When December 31, 1926 came and went, and not one of the oil companies had complied with Article 27, peace activists feared their work had been in vain. On January 4, Calles ordered his attorney general to "take action" against the companies that had not yet filed property claims.[46] Four days later, he announced that if the United States withdrew its diplomatic recognition over the issue, it would lead to revolution in Mexico, and indicated that he would be willing to submit the matter to arbitration at The Hague "if it were necessary to make such a sacrifice to avert more serious difficulties."[47] Coolidge, apparently unwilling to take Calles up on his lukewarm offer, declared in an address to the U.S. Congress on January 10 that a full-scale intervention of Nicaragua was justified in part because Mexico was arming rebels there.[48] Adding fuel to the fire, on January 12, Secretary of State Kellogg presented a report to the Senate Foreign Relations Committee entitled "Bolshevik Aims and Policies in Mexico and Latin America." Once again citing Calles's shipment of arms and munitions to Sacasa in Nicaragua, Kellogg asserted that Mexico was moving to install a Bolshevik regime in Nicaragua that would be hostile to the United States.[49] If Kellogg could not resolve his frustrations with Calles directly, it seemed he was prepared to start a proxy war against Mexico in Nicaragua.

In response to this escalation of hostile rhetoric from the Coolidge administration, peace organizations ramped up their mobilization efforts. On January 12, thirty-five people representing a dozen groups met in Washington as the Committee on Peace with Latin America (CPLA). Libby, who chaired the meeting, proposed calling a mass meeting to discuss what should be done with regard to the situation in Mexico. Support for the idea was unanimous, although attendees disagreed about its purpose. Some thought the meeting should address the question of Nicaragua as well as Mexico; others wanted to restrict discussion to the arbitration campaign. Libby pointed out that since the two issues were so closely intertwined it would be nearly impossible to prevent discussion of both. Morgan and Detzer agreed. Morgan reported a conversation she had had with a Democratic senator, who told her he expected the U.S. ambassador to Mexico would be withdrawn in the next two weeks, thereby severing diplomatic relations between the two countries. "Only a general uprising of the people will prevent it," she argued, adding that the mass meeting should not be limited to passing resolutions but should also provide information on the whole situation. Detzer, who had argued from the outset that the problems with Mexico and Nicaragua were closely related, urged authorizing a deputation to President Coolidge to discuss whatever resolutions were passed at the meeting.[50]

Statements of support were already pouring in to the NCPW from across the country, many of them from women's organizations. The YWCA pled for arbitration. The Council of Women for Home Missions reaffirmed the importance of "good will" in international relations, and urged the president and secretary of state to apply the principle in their dealings with Mexico. The League of Women Voters pressed Coolidge to accept arbitration "in the interest of international harmony." The Women's Trade Union League demanded that Coolidge submit the matter to arbitration immediately. They argued "that rights of American citizens to make money out of oil concessions land lumber fruit or any other resources of other countries are a subject which is never a justifiable cause of war yet our country, [yet] our sister republics in Latin America are apparently in peril of that very terrible outcome of the present controversy with Mexico and Nicaragua." Statements also came in from the Fellowship of Reconciliation, the American Friends Service Committee, the United Christian Missionary Society, the Federal Council of the Churches of Christ, and dozens of other religious, peace, and labor groups. Taken together, these statements of support represented the opposition of more than ten million people to a war with Mexico.[51]

As time was crucial, the NCPW mass meeting convened only four days after the CPLA meeting, on January 16. Over sixty representatives of national organizations concerned with peace met at the Friends Meetinghouse in Washington, D.C. Led by Samuel Guy Inman, Ernest Gruening, Libby, and Detzer, the attendees discussed the oil law, the alien land laws, the Church, and Nicaragua. Inman and Gruening were recognized authorities on Mexico, whose primary role was to provide information and background on the events leading up to the present crisis. Both men argued that all four issues could be settled through arbitration, a sentiment with which the rest of the attendees agreed. Mexico had already offered to do so, they noted. The State Department was clearly angling for war, argued Gruening, but with little understanding of what they were asking. "If we go to Mexico," he declared, "it would be a greater disaster for us than for Mexico." Gruening also pointed out triumphantly that public opinion was already against war. He called not for "crystallization but expression" of that sentiment. To that end, Morgan agreed to continue the CPLA's nationwide telegram and letter-writing campaign. Detzer asked every organization represented at the meeting to send letters to all its members, asking them to write to President Coolidge, as well as to their local newspapers, supporting a Senate resolution declaring that the United States would not use military force to collect private debts.[52]

After several hours of debate, the Committee on Peace with Latin America produced a strong statement opposing the use of force in resolving conflicts both with Mexico and with Nicaragua. They encouraged President Coolidge and Congress to withdraw U.S. troops from Nicaragua as soon as possible, and protested "any attitude toward the Mexican government savoring of coercion, or which might jeopardize the existing friendly relations between the two countries." "No excuse will exist for coercive measures," the resolution proclaimed, under which they included moving troops and warships toward Mexico, lifting the arms embargo, and severing diplomatic relations, "until these peaceful methods have been fully tried and entirely exhausted." Attendees also adopted a plan of action. In the coming days and weeks, their organizations, under the banner of the Committee for Peace with Latin America, would devote themselves to securing nationwide support for their resolution. Such activities included circulating news releases and petitions, asking citizens to send telegrams to the White House urging arbitration, writing newspaper editorials, and organizing deputations to meet with President Coolidge.[53]

Opposition to possible war came not only from peace organizations but also from within Congress. Many of the sentiments expressed at the meeting could also be heard on Capitol Hill, particularly from a congressional bloc known as the "peace progressives." Led by Senator William Borah of Idaho, this influential group of legislators argued that Coolidge and Kellogg's policies of aggression and accusation were not the solution. Mexico and Central America did fall within the U.S. sphere of influence, they felt, but U.S. leadership was best exercised through friendship and diplomacy rather than, as Borah put it, the "suicidal . . . old doctrine of force."[54] Senator Clarence C. Dill of Washington declared on January 14 that with regard to Mexico and Nicaragua, "as a matter of principle we should be fair and we should be just. As a matter of policy we should play the part I believe it was intended for this Republic to play, that of a great, powerful neighbor, that will insist upon justice as well as insist upon the protection of the rights of its citizens." Although most of these men would not have agreed with the charges of U.S. imperialism levied by the NCPW and other peace activists, a few did. Robert La Follette of Wisconsin called U.S. action in Nicaragua "unconscionable," and denounced Kellogg's claims of Bolshevist influence.[55] In late January, several senators supported a resolution from Lynn Frazier of North Dakota, stating "the President should not employ the armed forces in resolving the Mexican dispute during the congressional recess." When the resolution did not muster enough votes, the peace progressives presented a watered-down version authored by Joe Robinson of Arkansas. The Robinson Resolution, which declared merely that the U.S.-Mexican dispute was a proper subject for arbitration, was unanimously approved by the Senate on January 25.[56]

Despite the weakened language, Detzer saw in the resolution the undeniable influence of the peace organizations and women's initiatives. "There is no doubt but that the Senate vote . . . was the result of pressure brought by the people through the Peace organizations and through the press, which has been very good," she reported to the WILPF office in Geneva. "Never has organization counted so much and there has been a really remarkable response."[57] While Detzer and her colleagues struggled in early 1927 to extend their message to the White House, they had clearly found a receptive audience among members of the Senate. This is significant, though not entirely surprising, given the close working relationship between the "peace progressives" in the Senate and representatives of the major U.S. peace organizations, including Detzer, that persisted throughout the 1920s.[58]

The Committee on Peace with Latin America worked hard over the next several weeks to keep up the pressure on Congress and the president, even though the tension showed few signs of subsiding. Just two days after the Robinson Resolution passed the Senate, Coolidge rejected the idea that the oil question was suitable for arbitration.[59] Clara Mortenson Beyer, a young labor activist from California who had been appointed executive secretary of the CPLA, worried that a break in diplomatic relations would soon follow. She reported over a dozen conversations with members of Congress, all of whom told her they thought Coolidge would act as soon as Congress adjourned on March 1. Throughout February, Beyer worked constantly to keep the letters and telegrams flowing to the White House, and to distribute as much literature as she could as widely as possible. She also urged editors across the country to keep news of the situation in the public eye, noting "the influences disrupting friendly relations with Mexico work better in the dark."[60] She considered trying to keep Congress in session by asking the NCPW's Senate allies to block an appropriations bill, but at the same time she worried that waiting even until March would be costly. "Delay itself," she wrote to a friend at the League of Women Voters, "is a menace to peace."[61]

As March approached, peace activists' fears were nearly as high as they had been the previous December. On March 1, the NCPW news bulletin announced "Crisis with Mexico Enters Second Phase." Congress had adjourned, Coolidge was holding firmly to his belief that the land and oil questions could not be arbitrated, and the director of the Associated Petroleum Producers in Mexico had announced that he would rather the United States go to war than yield to the Mexican government. On March 7, the U.S. War Department announced plans to hold a military demonstration in May along the U.S.-Mexican border, a move Libby saw as the first step toward amassing troops for an armed intervention in Mexico. The U.S. State Department, for its part, threatened to lift the U.S. embargo on arms to Mexico, a sign interpreted by the peace organizations as a U.S. plan to arm a rebellion against Calles. Calles, for his part, was so concerned about the possibility of a U.S. invasion that he ordered his military commander along the Gulf Coast to be prepared to set fire to the oil fields there.[62]

In response, the Committee on Peace with Latin America once again stepped up its efforts. Libby urged all NCPW affiliates to send another round of telegrams and letters to President Coolidge, advising him that U.S. Americans and Mexicans alike were interpreting the United States' planned military maneuvers in Texas as preparation for war. On March 16 a CPLA delegation including Detzer, Morgan, and Beyer presented a petition to Kellogg, signed by 11,385 people, renewing the demand for arbitration.[63] Immediately following the meeting with the secretary, the CPLA held a conference at the Council headquarters in Washington. Representatives of the member organizations agreed to continue publicizing the latest developments, and also discussed plans to organize a nationwide protest against lifting the arms embargo.[64] Afterward Beyer reported to the CPLA membership at large on the conference proceedings. The January telegram campaign had produced the greatest volume of wires and letters to Washington since the Naval Conference in 1921. "Nevertheless," she noted, "pressure from the other side has been gradually changing the attitude of the press throughout the country and the Administration will need further evidence that public opinion has not changed similarly if the issue is to be settled finally by arbitration."[65] In a letter to a friend, Beyer lamented, "This Mexican tangle . . . seems to get worse from day to day. The actions of the State Department are incredible. . . . There is no dealing with such people."[66]

Women internationalists and their allies mobilized on an unprecedented scale during these months to oppose war with Mexico. Employing new tactics such as publicity campaigns, mass meetings, letter writing, and lobbying, they embraced the political nature of organizing. This was not internationalism that sought to spread goodwill and deter militarism through personal interactions across borders. This was a sophisticated, strategic campaign to marshal public opinion in opposition to a specific conflict. As it became clear there would in fact be no war between the United States and Mexico, these internationalists agreed with Dorothy Detzer that their efforts had had a significant impact.

The Crisis Abates

Despite Clara Beyer's forebodings, over the next several weeks and months the likelihood of war lessened. This was due to several developments. U.S. bankers worried that a military conflict would threaten Mexico's ability to repay its substantial foreign debt. Tensions in Nicaragua eased when former secretary of war Henry Stimson managed to negotiate a settlement with the Liberals (though this would later prove temporary). Some of the more flagrant rumors of Bolshevism in Mexico, like the Hearst story of a Red Army, were discredited. On the Mexican side, Calles, facing not only the Cristero rebellion but a nationwide economic crisis, was more eager to settle Mexico's dispute with the United States than he had been a year earlier.[67] And the diplomatic relationship between Mexico and the Soviet Union noticeably cooled. By March 1927, Calles was beginning to repress the activities of the Mexican Communist Party and to distance himself from the Soviets. Soviet ambassador Alexandra Kollontai denied daily rumors that she was about to be recalled by her government, but reports in the United States claimed Calles himself had ordered her to stop spreading Soviet propaganda. Over the next few months she lost favor with many Mexicans who preferred improving Mexico's relationship with the United States to strengthening its ties to the Soviet Union. She left Mexico in June.[68]

But also important was Coolidge and Kellogg's realization that a war with Mexico had little popular support. This awareness was evident in Coolidge's April 25 speech to the United Press. "We do not want any controversy with Mexico," he asserted. "We feel every sympathy with her people in their distress and have every desire to assist them."[69] Facing a lack of support for a war, the Coolidge administration withdrew its defense of the oil companies' hardline stance, leaving them no choice but to try to find another solution.

An important change in the U.S. diplomatic roster helped the oil companies identify that solution. After denying for over a year that he had any plans to quit his post, Ambassador Sheffield resigned on July 8, 1927, citing poor health and personal matters.[70] In September, Coolidge announced Dwight Morrow as his replacement. A banker who had been employed by J. P. Morgan for over thirteen years, Morrow had already been involved in quiet but direct negotiations with the Mexican treasury minister to work out a peaceful settlement to the oil crisis.[71] Reaching Mexico City on October 23, Morrow wasted no time in evincing a much softer, more cordial approach than Sheffield had ever displayed. His instructions from Coolidge were to keep the United States out of a war, but not to yield on the claims of the oil companies. After a series of meetings with Morrow in November 1927, Calles agreed to amend the 1925 oil law, removing the fifty-year limit on concessions as well as the "Calvo clause."[72]

U.S. women peace activists believed that their efforts to harness public opinion and use it to exert influence over the U.S. government deserved a great deal of credit for the peaceful resolution of the Mexican crisis. In a speech to the Indiana Council on International Relations on April 30, Laura Puffer Morgan pointed to the Robinson Resolution. "I have it direct from one of the Democratic leaders," she reported, "that action was taken then only in response to the popular demand." Referring to a poll of newspaper correspondents covering the State Department, Morgan pointed out that the majority believed the lack of aggressive action was "due to the popular interest."[73] Detzer also believed both the CPLA and WILPF had had a tangible effect on events. "Having been on the inside of the situation from the beginning," she reported to the U.S. membership in May, "I think I can say dogmatically that without this first small committee and the intensive efforts put forth by it, the vote of 79–0 in favor of Arbitration in the Senate would never have been secured. One of the oldest correspondents in Washington told me that it was the greatest outpouring of public opinion he had ever seen in more than fifteen years' experience."[74]

U.S. women's efforts were not the only factor in averting a war, but they were a significant one. A political operative as savvy as Dorothy Detzer would have understood that the battles within the Senate and between Congress and the White House, and especially the influence of the banking lobby, played no small part in the resolution of the crisis. She also recognized—and welcomed—Coolidge's appointment of Dwight Morrow as U.S. ambassador to Mexico in July as a significant shift in the administration's diplomatic approach. But as Detzer herself said, she had been "on the inside of the situation from the beginning." Even if Coolidge, Kellogg, or senators like William Borah did not acknowledge it publicly, Detzer knew they had been swayed in part by the mobilization of the Peace with Mexico campaign.

When combined with other factors like the influence of U.S. bankers and the temporary resolution of the situation in Nicaragua, public pressure from peace activists helped to dissuade the Coolidge administration from considering military intervention. Over the course of several months, the newspaper editorials, the letters to Congress and to the president, and the public appeals for arbitration combined to persuade Coolidge and Kellogg that a war against Mexico would not enjoy popular support. Women like Detzer and Morgan were central to this mobilization of public opinion. The efforts of the Peace with Mexico campaign brought information to state and local affiliates that might not otherwise have reached them. U.S. women internationalists helped to articulate an attitude that was already prevalent among the U.S. public in general. With memories of World War I less than a decade old, most people in the United States were not prepared to support another war, particularly one whose justification was unclear at best. Women like Morgan and Detzer marshalled that sentiment and put it to use.

The Peace with Mexico campaign marked a significant point of transition in U.S. women's internationalism. The campaign witnessed the emergence of sophisticated, modern strategies to exert influence on policy makers and to harness public opinion in support of their agenda. Gone was the apolitical spirituality of human internationalism. Orchestrating a mobilization of public opinion on this level gave women like Morgan and Detzer practical experience in working with other organizations, with newspaper editors, and with public officials. It sharpened their mechanisms for communication and coordination—mechanisms they would employ again in the 1930s in their efforts to raise awareness of fascism in Europe. Indeed, it helped transform Detzer into one of the most effective peace lobbyists of the decade. She used her contacts and knowledge of Capitol Hill acquired during 1926 and 1927 to establish ties with members of Congress who also opposed armed intervention in Latin America, and then called on them again just a few years later during her efforts to end the U.S. occupation of Nicaragua. Finally, the campaign also further

developed women's political consciousness, and brought a new sophistication to their understanding of the myriad factors that went into shaping
foreign policy.

The impact of the campaign on U.S. women's relationships with Mexican women is less clear. In contrast to U.S. women's internationalist organizing methods in the early 1920s, during the 1927 crisis most U.S. women
made no attempts to bring Mexican or Latin American women into their
peace campaigns. Carrie Chapman Catt, Laura Puffer Morgan, or Dorothy
Detzer never suggested pointing to earlier internationalist endeavors like
the Pan American Conference of Women in order to support their claims
that the broader American public did not want war. The one exception was
the Women's Peace Union, the most radically pacifist of the women's peace
organizations, which believed in complete nonresistance to violence. On
January 20, 1927, at a small luncheon in honor of a Women's Peace Union
representative visiting Mexico City, Mexican members passed a resolution
condemning the U.S. oil companies that had not complied with the oil
law.[75] But the union struggled to gather support among Mexican women
for nonresistance. Another U.S. member, traveling in Mexico in late 1926,
reported that many women with whom she spoke feared that preaching
nonresistance was just a ploy by U.S. interests to seize even more Mexican
land and property, and perhaps even to take over the government itself.
According to historian Harriet Hyman Alonso, since the WPU did not concern itself with other issues concerning women, it never found much success in Mexico.[76] More prominent activists, such as Catt and members of
the U.S. section of WILPF, who had tried to organize and recruit Mexican
women into international organizations, do not appear even to have considered that Mexican women might have played a role in their campaign to
avert war with Mexico in 1927. Whatever potential benefit there was to be
gained from opposing U.S. imperialism in Mexico was thus never directly
realized.

As a result of the resolution of the crisis, however, U.S. women internationalists renewed their efforts in Mexico over the next few years. WILPF
in particular revived its attempts to organize a section in Mexico City, relying in part on the momentum generated by the peace campaign to secure
interest and support from within the United States. Despite the lack of
Mexican involvement in the campaign, U.S. women internationalists had
positioned themselves well for a new round of efforts to promote inter-
American cooperation. They could claim to have played a significant role

7 new method for collaboration

not only in forestalling U.S. military intervention but in attempts to lessen the extent of U.S. financial dominance and exploitation in Mexico. Over the next several years, Dorothy Detzer and WILPF in particular tried to take advantage of the abatement of the crisis to renew their internationalist work in Mexico City.

Chapter 5

Politicizing Internationalism

"International feminism was born," according to U.S. feminist Doris Stevens, at the Sixth International Conference of American States in Havana, Cuba, in January 1928.[1] Stevens, a longtime member of the U.S. National Woman's Party (NWP) and a veteran of the U.S. suffrage campaign, had traveled to Havana with three other women to pressure the Pan American Union to create a greater role for women in inter-American affairs. Along with hundreds of Cuban women, Stevens and her colleagues protested the absence of women delegates to the conference and demanded permanent representation in the form of a special commission devoted to women's rights. "We want no more laws written for our good and without our consent," she declared in a speech to the conference delegates. "We must have the right to direct our own destiny jointly with you. . . . Our subjection is world-wide. The abolition of our subjection will be accomplished by the world-wide solidarity of women."[2] Their approach worked; by the end of the conference the delegates had established the Inter-American Commission of Women. Three months later the Pan American Union appointed Stevens as the commission's first chair. Over the next two years, all American countries named commissioners to represent them. In February 1930, the Mexican government appointed Margarita Robles de Mendoza to such a position. Robles de Mendoza had strong ties to the NWP, and was enthusiastic about working with Stevens.

Stevens's self-serving claim that international feminism began only in 1928 excluded significant precedents, but she was correct that the kind of women's internationalism she envisioned represented a departure from what had come before. Both in its connection to an official intergovernmental organization and in its exclusive focus on studying and advancing women's civil and political status, the Inter-American Commission was a different type of organization from the Women's International League for Peace and Freedom or the League of Women Voters. This was not the human internationalism of Jane Addams, premised on personal exchanges and mutual appreciation. Doris Stevens did not subscribe to the notion that women, as the "world's mothers," should or could enact internationalism in gendered ways. She saw women as political actors, no different from men in their ability to organize and enact change. Like the human internationalists, Stevens and her colleagues established contacts and exchanged information, but their overarching purpose was to study and to change national laws concerning women's status, and they worked through government channels to do so. In their first five years of work they made exhaustive studies of statutes pertaining to women in every American country. Their primary goal throughout the 1930s was the passage of hemispheric agreements to standardize legal equality between men and women. Ironically, this legalistic approach harkened back to the very methods of internationalism Addams had criticized—the days of formal treaties arranged through governments. But Stevens and her colleagues believed in the power of international agreements, and the recognition that accompanied them, to change the status of women throughout the Americas.

The Inter-American Commission of Women represented the epitome of the more politicized women's internationalism that Dorothy Detzer and others forged during the Peace with Mexico campaign. Although the commission grew from very different roots than WILPF, the former was the group that followed most closely the model of sophisticated organizing, information gathering, and lobbying established by WILPF in the mid-1920s. The commission took that model one step further by using internationalism as a mirror to press for change on domestic issues. U.S. members of the IACW hoped their organizing strategies on the hemispheric level would bring pressure on the United States to enact new legislation on the national level. The changes with which they were most concerned related to women's civil and political status, namely equal nationality for married women and equal rights for all women.[3]

Theirs was not the only approach at work in the late 1920s, however. Despite myriad failures among its adherents earlier in the decade, Addams's human internationalism was not yet defunct. At the same time that Stevens was addressing the delegates in Havana, the Women's International League and the Young Women's Christian Association were renewing their programs in Mexico in the wake of the 1926–1927 diplomatic crisis. Both groups followed methods similar to those they had established earlier in the decade, and both encountered challenges that echoed previous ones. Not least was Mexican women's frustration with U.S. women's imperialist internationalism and with U.S. foreign policies. But that frustration had shifted in nature by the early 1930s. The impact of the Great Depression and U.S. efforts to remove hundreds of thousands of Mexicans and Mexican Americans from the U.S. to create jobs for whites created resentment not just in that region but throughout Mexico, including among Mexican feminists in the capital. Citing U.S. women's failure to address discrimination against Mexicans along the border, Mexican feminists questioned U.S. women's commitment to internationalism as a whole.

Both U.S. and Mexican women thus began using internationalism as a tool to advance other agendas. Although many of them were still interested in the same goals that had driven earlier internationalists—such as peace and hemispheric cooperation—they had grown politically savvy enough to understand how to leverage the idea of internationalism to achieve other goals, such as women's equal rights in the United States and an end to U.S. discrimination against Mexican Americans. The politicization of women's internationalism that had begun during the crisis of 1926–1927 expanded during the late 1920s and early 1930s not only to other groups of U.S. women but to Mexican women as well. While WILPF and the YWCA continued their work in Mexico City, the IACW brought that politicized internationalism into the realm of formal diplomacy, most notably at the Seventh International Conference of American States in Montevideo, Uruguay, in 1933.

Internationalizing Domestic Agendas

The Inter-American Commission of Women was born from three different initiatives that coalesced in early 1928. The first was intergovernmental. At the Fifth International Conference of American States, held in Santiago in 1923, the Pan American Union for the first time allowed social issues like labor and education onto the agenda. The delegates planned to discuss women's rights at the Havana meeting, and a handful of them even went so far as to recommend that women be invited as official representatives. The second originated in the United States. When no women were in fact named as delegates to the Sixth Conference, four women from the U.S. National Woman's Party, led by Doris Stevens, planned a series of events to protest their exclusion. The third initiative was activism among Cuban and Latin American women for legal equality and an end to women's subjugation in all areas of life.[4] Stevens and the other NWP members joined Cuban women who were already planning a parade and a mass demonstration outside the conference. These events were very successful. On January 28, the birthday of Cuban hero José Martí, 700 women from throughout the Americas joined a procession of the Cuban flag through the streets of Havana. Several hundred more Cuban women followed, carrying banners decorated with Martí's proclamations on social justice.[5] Ten days later, on February 7, almost 2,000 women attended a series of speeches by Cuban feminist leaders and the NWP representatives, including Stevens. Stevens had tried to get on the program of the conference itself, but when she was denied she and her colleagues used the mass meeting to propose a treaty securing equal rights for women throughout the Americas. Few official delegates attended, but it was to all of them that Stevens and the other speakers directed their remarks.

This was the gathering Stevens believed represented the birth of international feminism. The eight women who took the podium were from four countries: Cuba, the United States, Puerto Rico, and the Dominican Republic. All addressed the need for equality between the sexes and for women's permanent representation in the Pan American Union. They also each argued that women best represented the ideal of Pan American unity, since, unlike men, women were not constantly battling for power over one another.[6]

Stevens's own speech focused on the legal aspects of equality. First, she argued that recognizing women's equality was a matter of restoring equilibrium in gender relations, not a matter of "granting" rights to women to make them equal to men: "For you see, no group of men, no government, no nation, no group of nations ever had the right to withhold from us the rights we ask today. We ask to have restored rights which have been usurped. These are our human rights." Second, she maintained that an international treaty was the most dignified, easiest, and most permanent method of guaranteeing equal status for men and women: "It will not only abolish existing national and international inequalities, it will prevent new ones from being written." She challenged the male delegates not to be timid, to dare to "establish great precedents," to "adventure in unknown paths." She also argued for the expediency of an equal rights treaty. It would do away with "piecemeal" conventions on prostitution, women workers, pregnancy and childbirth, and nationality of married women.

Finally, Stevens denounced the suggestion that equal rights were "all right for the women of North America" but not for their Latin American counterparts—hence the need for "world-wide solidarity of women," represented by an official international organization.[7]

Stevens and the other members of the National Woman's Party brought to Havana a draft of an Equal Rights Treaty that institutionalized legal equality between the sexes throughout the Americas. Despite support from a handful of Latin American nations, including Cuba, the treaty was never formally brought before the delegates in Havana. But the women who spoke on February 7 did accomplish another important goal. The Havana delegates agreed to establish the Inter-American Commission of Women on a temporary basis "to prepare the juridical information necessary for a proper consideration at the Seventh Conference of the civil and political equality of women."[8] Over the next five years, the members of the commission would survey the legal and civil codes of every American nation in order to make recommendations to the Seventh Conference for "international action on the status of women."[9]

The Pan American Union officially established the Inter-American Commission of Women on April 4. Stevens, who was named the first chair, applauded the move. The Pan American Union had grown up, she announced. Like a boy growing into a man, it had become aware of women. Wherever the road led, men and women would travel it together. "We do not guarantee an easy partnership," she cautioned. "We do, however, most profoundly believe that man and woman in the Americas have undertaken a new international life together from which will flow mutual understanding, greater mutual benefit, confidence and esteem and a greater mutual love."[10]

The commission's official task was to carry out a study of women's status throughout the Americas, and to prepare a report for the Seventh International Conference of American States, to be held in Montevideo in 1933. To that end members spent their first few years compiling a survey of laws pertaining to women's civil and political rights. They also established a committee on married women's nationality. Whether women should lose their citizenship status if they married foreign nationals had long been an important question for the National Woman's Party, and was due to come before the League of Nations in 1929. Stevens and the commission wanted to be in a position to make a recommendation to the League based on existing laws in Western Hemisphere nations.[11] This approach—working within intergovernmental organizations like the Pan American Union and the League of Nations—was what marked Stevens's and the commission's departure most sharply from earlier forms of women's internationalism.

The IACW also marked a significant departure from the days of Jane Addams because internationalism per se was not the only or even the primary goal of the women behind it. Later in her life Stevens expounded on the fact that she and her colleagues in the National Woman's Party hoped the commission would help bring international pressure to bear on the United States to pass the Equal Rights Amendment to the U.S. Constitution. Stevens claimed that despite the passion she and her friends displayed in Havana, neither she nor the NWP had originally set out to lead an inter-American feminist movement. The party in the 1920s was under the control of its charismatic leader, Alice Paul, whose primary concern was the Equal Rights Amendment. In 1926 the NWP formed a Committee on International Action, which Paul convinced Stevens to chair, although Stevens had at that time no international experience. She had spent the 1910s by Paul's side, using militant tactics to argue for women's suffrage and spending several weeks in jail for her trouble. The committee had no members aside from Stevens, and recorded no accomplishments, but the nominal position was enough for Paul to appoint Stevens to attend the Havana Conference two years later, after a Cuban woman approached the NWP for help in getting the status of women on the conference agenda. Stevens felt though that Paul's willingness to collaborate with Cuban women was another means to her own end. Reflecting in 1960, Stevens wrote, "It is only honest to say that, at this time, the Inter-American Commission of Women was a round-about device for enabling the National Woman's Party to have a new Amendment enacted. It was, to begin with an obvious way to get up interest, and get newspaper discussion, of the subject. Then, too, it formed a way of raising the subject each time a Conference would be held. The United States would have to formulate an official position on Women's Rights."[12] The IACW thus became for the NWP a mirror on the status of women in the United States.

Stevens was ambivalent about chairing the Commission, in part because she felt she lacked the requisite experience. Born in Omaha in 1892, she graduated from Oberlin College in 1911, where she studied sociology, labor problems, and modern languages. A meeting at Oberlin with Emmeline Pankhurst and her daughter Sylvia, both militant British suffragists, converted Stevens to the cause, and she eventually became a leading member of the Congressional Union for Woman Suffrage, the precursor to the NWP. During the 1920s she held several prominent positions on the

NWP's executive committee, including political chair and legislative chair.[13] She did not need to be convinced of the significance of international organizing, but the size of the task facing her after Havana was overwhelming. To Stevens it "seemed like a stone mountain which I had to claw open with my bare hands." Driven primarily by her own conscientiousness and an "intense dislike of failing," she regularly put in fourteen- to sixteen-hour days at her job. "The chairmanship of the IACW," she recalled later, "at that time, represented a chore which I would never have chosen of my own accord. It did not then seem like anything in which I would take any other satisfaction than that of doing a disagreeable job well."[14]

Their stance on equal rights further distanced the leading members of the IACW from earlier women internationalists. The NWP position on the need for a constitutional amendment guaranteeing full equal rights to women put Doris Stevens in the minority of U.S. women in the 1920s. Soon after the passage of the Nineteenth Amendment, former suffragists divided on the question whether women should campaign for an equal rights amendment like the one favored by Alice Paul, or whether women's biological and social capacities as mothers necessitated special legislation, for example to protect them from unsafe working conditions. The majority of politically active women, led by the League of Women Voters, favored the latter position. This debate, over whether women's *equality* with men or *difference* from men should take priority in securing their rights, characterized much of U.S. women's activism in the 1920s and 1930s, and came to play a central role in debates over the course and direction of the IACW.[15]

The friction created by these debates over domestic policy spilled over into the international arena, not only in the Pan American Union but in the League of Nations as well, where NWP representatives and their allies were also trying to advance equal rights. Throughout Stevens's tenure as chair, the IACW faced a constant stream of criticism from other U.S. women who disagreed with the NWP position. For many Latin American women, however, the issue of equal rights was not as polarizing. Throughout most of the Latin America there was no dichotomy between "equal rights feminism" and what is generally called "social feminism." Many women saw no inherent conflict between demanding equal civil and political status and preserving their socially protected roles as wives and mothers.[16] The disjuncture between the U.S. debate and the Latin American perspective would lead to problems in the coming years over whether and how to prioritize full equal rights for women.

Figure 6. Doris Stevens.
Schlesinger Library, Radcliffe Institute, Harvard University.

Renewing Human Internationalism

While the IACW and its members were exploring political and legal approaches to internationalism, both the YWCA and WILPF worked to reinvigorate human internationalism in Mexico. In the wake of the 1926–1927 crisis between the United States and Mexico, both organizations felt that strengthening their branches in Mexico City might go a long way toward repairing whatever damage had resulted from the widespread pro-war rhetoric in the United States. Both groups sent new representatives to

Mexico City to establish new contacts and reconnect with old ones, and both made efforts to tailor their programs for peace and service to women according to Mexican women's own perceptions of their needs. But while the groups faced similar challenges—not least of which was trying to revive this work during the first few years of the Great Depression—they did not emerge from this period with comparable standing among Mexican women. The most significant challenge, particularly for WILPF, was how to contend with challenges from Mexican women who had grown even more frustrated with the United States than Elena Torres and Elena Landázuri had been in the early 1920s. Changes in U.S.-Mexican relations and implementation of repatriation programs in the United States cast new light on old prejudices, which Mexican women protested vociferously.

In the wake of the diplomatic crisis, and in light of the progress that had been made since its founding, in 1927 the Foreign Division of the YWCA made the Mexican branch a priority. Even before the crisis, the board declared that the Mexican association fell "under the heading of groups that should get assistance before new ones are created."[17] After the worst of the crisis had passed in mid-1927, several U.S. members familiar with the Mexican situation believed that supporting the YWCA could go a long way toward restoring cordial feelings in Mexico. A U.S. observer reported in April that in the YWCA she had "not found antagonisms towards foreigners who have an interest in Mexico and are sympathetic with their problems."[18] Elizabeth Curtiss, who took over as U.S. foreign secretary in 1927, found that "the Association has won a very real place in the community and that it has the enthusiastic cooperation of a large number of girls who find it meeting the needs of their present-day life. It has the love and devotion of a few committee women who are invaluable to the future life and development of the Association."[19] By early 1928 she was able to report to Sarah Lyon, who was still in charge of the Foreign Division, that businessmen in Mexico City saw good reason to be hopeful about Mexico's political and economic recovery, both of which would benefit the YWCA. "It may prove to be just optimism," she cautioned, "but I don't think so."[20]

Curtiss focused during her tenure on strengthening the YWCA health and physical education programs. A recreational club of Mexican girls was so enthusiastic about gymnastics and other physical activities that they had employed a dancer to teach them and coordinated classes for more than 400 girls. Curtiss desperately wanted to get them a real teacher and better facilities, since they were forced to conduct their gymnastics classes on the patio of the boarding home. The president of the board, Antonia Ursua, was a medical doctor who was anxious to expand the YWCA role as a source of medical care and health education for women and girls, but she lacked the funds and facilities to realize her goals. Curtiss drew attention to these issues in her reports to the Foreign Division.[21] She noted that physical education stimulated girls' characters as well as their bodies; they learned promptness, fairness, and cooperation: "We can honestly say in Mexico that directly as a result of the contacts and stimulated interest through the department, the whole purpose of the YWCA in Mexico is being accomplished in the lives of many girls."[22] Largely in response to Curtiss's pleas, the Foreign Division in 1929 sent a Mexican woman to Boston for four weeks to be trained in physical education, and sent another U.S. woman to Mexico City for six months as a physical education coordinator. By 1930, when Curtiss left Mexico, the physical education program was a success, and the health department was providing 900 examinations to women and children every year.[23] An outside observer remarked, "I cannot speak too highly of the Health Education Department," noting that the classes offered in Mexico City were as good as any she had attended in the United States.[24]

Both Curtiss and other members of the Foreign Division continuously stressed the need to recruit and train Mexican leadership in the YWCA, but this was easier said than done. Leona Scott, who spent several months in Mexico City as an interim U.S. representative, recommended that the Foreign Division make staffing its highest priority. She urged Sarah Lyon and other members to send a second foreign secretary to Mexico City to aid Curtiss, and to concentrate on training Mexican women, both in Mexico City and as sponsored visitors in the United States. Scott felt this kind of support was the most valuable help U.S. women could give Mexico.[25]

Both Scott and Curtiss acknowledged, however, that the primary obstacle to full-scale "Mexicanization" of the association lay in its own board of directors. They remarked repeatedly on the difficulties they faced convincing the non-Mexican members of the board to support the Mexican staff and the program for Mexican leadership. These members, who were mostly U.S. women living in Mexico City, and not regular members of the U.S. YWCA, made up only about 25 percent of the board, but they wielded disproportionate power. According to Scott, they felt that Mexicans were unreliable and disorganized, and feared that "'Mexican rule' might hurt the prestige of the Association."[26] In 1930 another observer characterized the foreign members of the board as "conservative and imperialistic."[27] But the association relied heavily on these board members—and on other U.S. and European women in Mexico City—for its fund-raising. In 1930 fully 90 percent of the funds raised in Mexico came from foreign women.[28]

Despite this impediment, both the Foreign Division and the U.S. secretaries in Mexico continued to pursue Mexicanization. A field report commissioned jointly by the YMCA and YWCA in the late 1920s backed them up. While acknowledging the myriad difficulties facing the associations in Latin America, including suspicion of U.S. Americans and the influence of the Catholic Church, the report argued that expanding the YWCA's influence was not only possible but desirable. The authors noted that the upheaval of the Mexican Revolution carried the potential for promising changes in that country. "Already in Mexico City something new and vital is in the air," they observed. Increased interest in "social education"—education geared toward solving social problems—among women represented a particular opportunity for the association.[29] This fact made it crucial that the YWCA adapt itself to its environment, both in Mexico and in the rest of Latin America—in other words, that they pursue Mexicanization. "The question of *attitude* toward program development," the report concluded, "is of major significance." If a group of U.S. members went to a new country with a predetermined program and course of action, they would encounter resistance and even defeat. "If, however, the attitude of the Association is one of enquiry as to need and of response as far as possible to needs as they are presented, the normal human response can hardly fail to be one of progressive co-operation. Even from the standpoint of the Association, not to build it up for its own sake, but to meet a recognized need is the approach which will bring to the YWCA itself the best results."[30] The association accordingly continued to pursue "Mexicanization," even in the face of less-than-enthusiastic support from a handful of board members.

Determination alone might not have been enough, but the association was assisted in 1930 by a bequest of $100,000 from a wealthy U.S. donor. The board used the funds to purchase a new building, large enough to accommodate the boarding house and expand the physical education program considerably. This legacy allowed the Mexican association to capitalize on its recent successes by increasing the number of women who could be accommodated as boarders along with the number of women and children who could use the new swimming pool. The new U.S. foreign secretary, Sue Perry, arrived in fall 1930, and oversaw the purchase of the new building and the transfer of the headquarters to their new location.[31]

The U.S. section of WILPF, meanwhile, concentrated its energies on reviving the section in Mexico City that had disintegrated in the mid-1920s. Interest in Mexico on the part of the international office and the U.S. section had waned during the mid-1920s, but after the crisis of 1927 the U.S. section once again organized a Mexican Committee to coordinate visitors to Mexico, try to reestablish contacts, and ultimately revive the Mexican section. The first U.S. woman to take on this task was Mildred Scott Olmsted, a social worker and executive secretary of the Pennsylvania WILPF, who traveled to Mexico in summer 1928. Her primary goal was to drum up support for a conference of U.S. and Mexican women, to be held near the U.S.-Mexican border. Her expectations were low, based on her correspondence with several people who had told her that "Mexican women wouldn't go anywhere, that they wouldn't sign their names to anything, that they were either too conservative or too radical, that they weren't interested in international matters, etc., etc." But Olmsted was pleased to find most of the women with whom she spoke "delightfully and surprisingly responsive."[32]

Olmsted's brief visit left her very optimistic. The original Mexican section was gone, but she had formed a new group of nine women. This group was not yet "active," but she expressed "hope that it may be made to function, especially if it can be nursed along at this time."[33] Her most important insights concerned the effects of the Mexican Revolution on the women she encountered. The experience had had a deep impact on all of them, Olmsted argued, but left them divided over the best method of national reconstruction, and the role women should play in it. Some had renounced war and become conscientious objectors; others wanted to retain their ideas of "honorable fighting." Some felt Mexican women needed to assert their independence in the national context; others believed they had to work with women in other countries to help Mexico "take her place among the nations." With regard to the latter opinion, Olmsted pointed out that "knowledge of international problems in any general sense is limited to a very few." She admitted that organizing women with such diverse perspectives would be challenging: "They will work with us, but will they work with each other?" In addition, the ongoing tensions between Catholics and anticlericals ran so deep as to make any kind of cooperation difficult, though Olmsted was pleased to report that women from both sides were represented in the new WILPF group. In the end she proposed sending another U.S. representative to continue nurturing the nascent section, one who would be able to stay in the country for many months and establish lasting connections among Mexican women.[34]

Encouraged by Olmsted's report, the U.S. executive board asked Sybil Jane Moore, formerly of the American Friends Service Committee, to visit Mexico City in 1929 to bolster the new section. The board's choice did not augur well for its commitment to Mexican women. Moore was dedicated to the cause of peace, but she had little experience in the country, spoke no Spanish, and admitted she knew "little of the work or its needs." The board decided to send her despite her protests, believing she could do "useful work" in Mexico.[35] Her mandate was twofold. First, she was to make contact with the women Olmsted had organized the year before and, if possible, work with them to communicate with the Geneva office about becoming recognized as an official section. Her second task was less concrete. The U.S. section leadership conceived of Moore's role as a goodwill ambassador, whose task was to foster relationships with Mexican women and encourage them to press their own government for an end to the violence that was still prevalent in early 1929. "We are profoundly hopeful," Emily Greene Balch wrote to Moore in March, "that the fact that you are in Mexico on our behalf at this critical time may prove really useful. . . . There may be opportunities to convey to Mexicans a sense of the sympathy we feel for Mexico, our profound regret that Mexicans should have invoked violence to effect a change, and our desire to be of use in any way that we can."[36] Dorothy Detzer, meanwhile, wrote to the Mexican ambassador to the United States to inform him of Moore's visit. "The WILPF cannot express how deeply we deplore and regret the unhappy situation which your country is suffering now," she wrote. "[Miss Moore is] planning to live in Mexico for some time in a hope of creating a closer relationship between the women of your country and ours."[37] WILPF based its agenda for Moore in Mexico on a desire to do good and to be flexible, but the U.S. section's failure to give her specific and concrete instructions was surprising given her inexperience in the country.

By the end of May, Moore was finally able to report to Detzer that she had reestablished a section, but its existence was tenuous. She had persuaded Clemencia de Kiel, a Mexican teacher whose German husband worked in the Secretariat of Public Education, to accept the chair, but only on a temporary basis. All the members seemed enthusiastic, but Moore worried about their ability to follow through on their commitment to the group. "The ladies are delightful—gracious and hospitable," she wrote to

Detzer, "but babes in the woods when it comes to organizing action."[38] She distributed literature on WILPF's mission and the guidelines for becoming an official section, but worried that the group would not continue with the preliminary work she had done. Kiel only confirmed Moore's uncertainty by observing that "conditions are so unsettled that no one wants to undertake anything new."[39] Moore could not deny the truth of the observation, but time and money constraints forced her to leave while the group was still being formed. She urged the U.S. board to send more representatives in the coming months and years to continue to encourage the Mexican section's progress.

In the interest of sustaining the Mexican section, the executive board of the U.S. section adopted a proposal in 1929 to organize a conference on peace in Mexico City. They hoped it would be a way to introduce Mexican women to as many U.S. women as possible, and to make them feel part of the international organization.[40] The bulk of the work to organize the conference fell to Kathleen Jennison Lowrie, a member from Michigan. She tried hard to let Mexican women take the lead in planning the conference, but ran into communication problems reminiscent of WILPF's early years in the country. Lowrie reported in late March that Kiel was "really interested" in the conference, and that her group was taking "real initiative" in organizing it.[41] But Kiel's correspondence with the international office in Geneva evinced a much lower level of enthusiasm and involvement. In May, less than two months before the conference, Kiel mentioned in a letter to Mary Sheepshanks, the outgoing executive secretary, that the Mexican section had nominated one of its members to represent them at the conference. Kiel implied that was the extent of her personal participation in the matter.[42] A few weeks later she reported to Sheepshanks that the Mexican women were looking forward to meeting with U.S. women to discuss "specific problems that are of great importance to us," but again she did not mention anything about having organized the conference herself.[43] This discrepancy between U.S. members' understanding of Kiel's level of activity and the latter's real actions would become a recurring theme over the next several years.

The theme of the conference was Education for Peace. The three-day meeting took place July 10–12 at the Teatro Hidalgo in Mexico City, and included speeches on "Women's Responsibility to the Peace Movement," "Cultural Relations," and "Economic and Political Relations."[44] Over 150 women attended, including Mexican women from Tampico and Yucatán, three women from Cuba, Camille Drevet, the executive secretary of the international WILPF in Geneva, and twenty-five women from the United States. Lowrie reported that in addition to the scheduled talks on selected topics and a standard WILPF meeting about goals and agenda, the delegates had been careful to allot a separate time just for discussion. Had only members been present it would have gone smoothly, she believed, but "there were present also some communists, nationalists and syndicalists who had not worked with the Mexican Section and who were especially anxious to express their philosophy." Nonetheless, the discussions were "lively and interesting." There was also significant time built in to the program for socializing, in the hopes that it would allow the U.S. and Mexican women to get to know each other personally. The day before the conference opened the Mexican women hosted a tea for the U.S. women. The next evening featured a musical concert to celebrate all the attendees. Lowrie reported the Mexican section had also "arranged for a peace exhibit prepared in our honor by twelve secondary schools showing how the teaching of geography, history, manual training and art, tends to make pupils appreciate the contribution of other nations."[45]

Lowrie felt the meeting was a success. She was pleased with the attendance, which she attributed in large part to the thorough job the Mexican women had done in advertising the conference. She felt the discussions reflected a broad range of issues concerning U.S.-Mexican relations, education, and women's roles in peace activism. Lowrie was also satisfied with the resolutions passed by the conference attendees. They pledged support for the Kellogg-Briand Pact, and invoked it in their calls to both the U.S. and Mexican governments to reduce troop numbers along the border, and to conduct their diplomatic relations fairly. They also opposed the vestiges of the U.S. policy of Dollar Diplomacy, by calling on their governments "to enact legislation to prevent the use of the army for the collection of public or private debts." Finally, they encouraged both countries to appoint more women to positions in embassies and consulates, in the interest of allowing them to "take their place" in the work of promoting peace. The Mexican section, Lowrie noted, deserved credit for arranging such a large event while such a new group. She also hoped the meeting would encourage greater openness on their part. "It was not that they were not articulate before, but there is strong anti-U.S.A. feeling in Mexico . . . and they did not really visualize there a group they could be frank with and expect some help from."[46]

Lowrie argued that for the Mexico City conference to help sustain the Mexican section, some provision had to be made for continued contact between U.S., European, and Mexican members. In her report to the U.S. executive board in October 1930 she predicted that the Mexicans would feel the same: "In Mexican ideology these is little interest in a conference which results only in expressions of common purpose. There is a directness and realism and urgency about this new group and a willingness to go to an endless amount of work if there is to be a plan for continuing work toward more understanding relations between the United States and Mexico." Lowrie proposed reforming the committee that had planned the Mexican conference into a group dedicated to inter-American relations more broadly. The board enthusiastically approved; they appointed Lowrie chair of a new Inter-American Committee, and named Mildred Scott Olmsted, Sybil Jane Moore, and four other women to serve on it. Lowrie proposed a program for the committee based on the resolutions that came out of the Mexican conference. Members would apply themselves to lobbying for the reduction of troops along the border and diplomatic cooperation, and to studying the "depressed standards of living in connection with peaceful economic penetration." The last question, Lowrie noted, seemed to Mexicans "more dangerous than armed intervention." In addition, she suggested a study of immigration relations and a study of the tariff in both countries.[47]

By summer 1930, then, both the Foreign Division of the YWCA and the U.S. section of WILPF had cause for optimism. The association's Mexican branch had taken strong enough hold within its community to find support for the expansion of the health and physical education programs, and to be assured of good attendance at its classes and clinics. WILPF's conference in Mexico City, meanwhile, had been successful among its attendees, and had garnered attention and interest for the Mexican section. The extent to which both organizations could capitalize on the progress they had made thus far in rebuilding their respective programs would determine their future success—and perhaps more significantly, would determine how well they would weather the depletion of financial support for their work as the first effects of the Depression began to sink in over the next few years.

Mexican Women's Resistance

Both groups, however, encountered a similar challenge to implementing their new programs, one that had shadowed U.S. women's internationalist agendas in Mexico since 1915, but crystallized in a new way in the late 1920s and early 1930s. The organizational culture and habits that most U.S. women took for granted could not be grafted on to Mexican women who did not have the same experience with mass mobilization that so many U.S. women had gained from the abolition, temperance, suffrage, and other movements. And throughout the 1920s more and more Mexican women had been politicized by the ongoing battles over the meaning of the Revolution. U.S. internationalists encountered women who resisted human internationalism both passively, by not attending meetings and not responding to correspondence, and actively, by challenging U.S. women directly. As in the early 1920s, if the mechanics of human internationalism did not work—attending meetings, setting agendas, discussing items on that agenda, following up on those discussions with related actions—then all that was left was rhetoric about friendship and cooperation.

Both YWCA and WILPF representatives remarked on this challenge. YWCA secretary Elizabeth Curtiss noted the difficulties in getting women to come to meetings: "The person is very rare who can be depended upon to come to a meeting on time no matter how important the meeting may be, and very often they seem to feel no responsibility for it whatsoever, coming if their time permits."[48] Sybil Jane Moore reported to Emily Greene Balch that all the women with whom she spoke were interested in peace, but when it came time to act on that interest she could not pin them down. She scheduled meetings and conversations only to have no one show up. Mexican women were busy with other activities, she acknowledged, and had many demands on their time, but they were also not in the habit of being members of organizations. When Moore was finally able to call a meeting in late April, three of the women who had helped her plan it never appeared, with no explanation. One woman who did attend was Guadalupe Ramirez, now also president of the board of the Mexican YWCA. Noticing Moore's frustration, Ramirez told her that it had taken five years to "train" local members of the board to go to meetings, and when there, to discuss association matters. "I feel myself quite helpless," Moore admitted.[49]

As they had during the earlier period, a handful of U.S. women fell back on racialized assumptions about the lack of education and motivation among Latin American women to explain challenges like this. Non-Mexican members of the YWCA board occasionally attributed their reluctance to embrace Mexicanization to their sense that Latin women could not be trusted to run the association as efficiently and effectively as U.S. women or European women. In response to Sybil Jane Moore, Emily Greene Balch asked, "Are Latin women *organizable* in our sense?" Her impression of the Mexican WILPF section was "that it is, like so many Latin groups, entirely outside the European-North American code as to keeping up correspondence, reporting, etc."[50] This observation echoed an exchange Balch had had with Elena Landázuri several years earlier, in which Balch expressed her belief that "Latin women" should "follow their own natural lines," despite their "natural" affinity for businesslike habits.[51] Again, her assumptions about what was "natural" to one race or another influenced the way she measured her expectations for the Mexican section, and the way she counseled its leaders.

Other U.S. women attributed the difficulties to a different kind of cultural divide. Myra Smith, a representative of the YWCA Foreign Division who visited Mexico City briefly in 1930, saw shortcomings on both sides. She described the Mexicans as too idealistic and the U.S. Americans as too practical in their approaches to the association. The association had been held in high esteem in the city a few years earlier, Smith felt, even though "our book-keeping and our records were nil. But now our business methods are efficient and the spirit is unsatisfactory." In her view what the association needed was a U.S. leader who could train Mexican women in organizational habits while harnessing their ideas for YWCA work. Smith also remarked that the personal habits of some members of the American colony in Mexico City were not to the liking of Mexican women: "Many of the common practices of the American colony are in complete contrast to Mexican ideas of conduct, and our secretary must avoid cocktail drinking and cigarette smoking, at least in public."[52] Smith's assumption was somewhat outdated; there were Mexicans for whom the "flapperista" represented immorality and the dangers of U.S. influence, but for others, especially young Mexicans, drinking and smoking were behavior associated with fashion and modernity.[53] The latter though were not among the clientele typically attracted to the association.

Whatever the underlying reasons, both the YWCA and WILPF had difficulty transplanting their organizational culture to Mexico City in ways that ensured the productivity they sought. But given its financial and personnel resources, and its more concrete plans of action, the YWCA was better able to move forward, despite the Foreign Division's ongoing frustrations about the difficulties of Mexicanization. Securing the new building was the largest, but not the only task Perry undertook during the early

1930s. She also expanded the membership rolls and helped to found a camp for girls and adolescents in Cuernavaca, all despite having her budget reduced by half between 1931 and 1934.[54] Though these efforts were not initiated or implemented by Mexican members of the association, collectively they helped to ensure a stable, long-term basis for membership and activity among Mexican women in the association.

WILPF's continued presence in Mexico City, by contrast, was much more tenuous. In addition to the long-standing difficulties the group had been facing for years, like the contrast in organizational cultures between the United States and Mexico, given its explicitly political mission the league had to contend with other hurdles that did not vex the YWCA. The challenges WILPF members encountered were twofold: they faced Mexican constituents who feared or mistrusted the United States, and therefore often hesitated to trust any U.S. Americans, and they faced women who had specific topics they wanted the U.S. section to address—topics that did not always coincide with U.S. women's own agendas. Unlike in the early 1920s, however, changes in the relationship between the two countries—brought on in large part by the Depression—colored both Mexican women's frustrations with the United States and the demands they made of U.S. women.

Dorothy Detzer was a particularly astute observer of Mexican attitudes toward the United States. She had been heavily involved in the 1927 U.S.-Mexican crisis as well as the WILPF protests against U.S. intervention in Nicaragua, and knew better than many of her colleagues that resentment of the United States in Latin America was widespread. But at the 1930 WILPF conference in Mexico City, Detzer found herself "quite unprepared for the fear which lie in the hearts of most Mexicans; the fear that some day we might take from them their freedom; the fear that we might make Mexico a part of the United States." Both during the conference proceedings and in her private conversations with Mexican women, Detzer discovered a pervasive belief in the possibility of further U.S. imperialism: "It was almost impossible to make these Mexican friends understand that in our America there is not a popular, deliberate, conscious plan of annexation. Our economic control of great portions of Mexican land has made them feel that they were being strangled by a force too big for them." Detzer hoped that she had conveyed the "sense of responsibility" she felt to "these delightful neighbors," and that she and her colleagues had "left them the consciousness of oneness." But she warned the U.S. section to act resolutely in its pursuit of demilitarization along the U.S.-Mexican border: "If we are to have gardens and not guns between us, there is much to be done in removing the fear on their part by checking the imperialistic designs of some American nationals, and building in their place such political and economic arrangements as will change the fear to security and confidence."[55]

Other Mexican women expressed less fear and more frustration, both with U.S. policies in particular and with U.S. mindsets in general. At a WILPF meeting in April 1929, Sybil Jane Moore read a message from Emily Greene Balch, encouraging Mexican women to speak out against the violence in their country. It was met with silence. Finally Elena Landázuri, the only member of the original group in attendance, spoke up. "I have never been able to make my American friends," she said to Moore, "not even [Jane] Addams, see that, in our present stage of development, violence is inevitable." Until the "common man" was allowed full participation in government, she argued, he would "follow any leader who offers a respite from his deadening toil. As long as he must die tomorrow, why not risk dying today, with the fun of fighting and looting thrown in?"[56] Landázuri's frustration with U.S. women's continued lack of understanding of what she saw as the situation in Mexico—even after over ten years of exchanges with Addams and Balch—not only signaled the difficulties WILPF faced in trying to apply its peace ideals in other national and local contexts without any adaptation or modification, but called its entire mission into question. Given Landázuri's perspective, it was not clear that appeals to "peace" even had a place in a country whose inhabitants felt their revolution had been denied.

Even more pointed was the encounter between a group of Mexican students and another WILPF representative, Ellen Starr Brinton, in which the students proposed several topics they wanted the U.S. section to address. Brinton's irritation with these suggestions—"hatred of Mexicans for the U.S.," "student segregation of Mexicans in U.S. schools," and "appropriation by residents of the U.S. of the terms 'Americans, or North Americans'"—was quite revealing.[57] Like Detzer and Moore, she was at a loss to know how to address the hostility toward the United States that she encountered in Mexico City. She had traveled there to try to help bolster the Mexican section of WILPF, but found her offers resented. Despite years of U.S. military interventions and economic exploitation, she seemed surprised to find that Mexicans resented the attitude of individuals from the

United States. The second topic may have been the most unexpected for Brinton. WILPF members prided themselves on their inclusiveness and acceptance, although throughout the 1910s and 1920s nonwhite women in the United States were frequently marginalized in the U.S. section.[58] Most U.S. women like Brinton who visited Mexico from Washington, D.C., and the northeastern United States were also unaware of the realities of life between U.S. Americans and Mexicans in the Southwest and elsewhere. The women with whom Brinton met were not the only ones to make such demands. The Mexican section told Moore they wanted WILPF to protest continued U.S. economic imperialism in Mexico as well as the "lack of liberty" enjoyed by Mexican women.[59] The attendees at the 1930 conference resolved to work for the demilitarization of the U.S.-Mexican border, but the U.S. executive board took little action on the subject over the next several years.

Clemencia de Kiel also made several requests in the early 1930s to have the U.S. section protest the repatriation and forced deportation of Mexican Americans taking place throughout the country. By 1929, at least 1.5 million Mexican Americans were living in the United States, some Mexican-born, some U.S.-born. The overwhelming majority lived and worked in the border region, most doing agricultural labor in Southern California. After the stock market collapse in October 1929, unemployment began rising dramatically, and many people in the United States began to blame Mexican laborers for stealing jobs from white Americans. Local, state, and federal government officials saw a solution in the deportation of thousands of these workers back to Mexico. From 1929 to 1935, somewhere between 500,000 and 1 million people, many of whom had been born in the United States, were repatriated. This forced movement destabilized communities in both countries, and created widespread anger over the limitation of economic opportunities and racist attitudes of the United States.[60] A few U.S. WILPF members in California tried to bring this issue to the attention of the executive board. In October 1931 a member from Los Angeles wrote to Detzer, detailing the "objectionable" program and requesting that WILPF make a statement opposing it. Despite her impassioned pleas, there is no record of any action having been taken on this issue by the executive board.[61]

As it had in the mid-1920s, WILPF again struggled to implement a successful program in Mexico. Its program was too inflexible, too inadaptable to Mexican women's demands and desires. And sending representatives who knew little about Mexico and spoke no Spanish did not help. Just as they had not capitalized on their success in helping to resolve the diplomatic crisis in 1927, U.S. WILPF officials did not transfer the political experience they gained during that crisis to their work with women in Mexico City. As a result, they were ill-prepared to respond to Mexican women's demands regarding repatriation and discrimination. The YWCA flourished by comparison, even as the early years of the Depression led to shrinking budgets and diminishing resources. In part this was due to the generosity of its main patron, and it part it was because Elizabeth Curtiss, Sue Perry, and their colleagues had tangible goals and concrete plans for achieving them. But ultimately the YWCA adherence to Mexicanization not only allowed it to adapt to the needs of its constituents but also allowed it to sidestep any potentially thorny political discourse. Focusing on buildings, classes, and activities left little room on the agenda for debates over U.S. policies or economic imperialism. Once again, the YWCA found success by focusing on the local, to the exclusion of the international.

The International Equal Rights Campaign

WILPF's experience showed that Mexican women were prepared to use internationalism to advance their own agendas in much the same way the Inter-American Commission was trying to do in the late 1920s with the National Woman's Party agenda on equal rights. Women such as Doris Stevens, chair of the commission, and Margarita Robles de Mendoza, the Mexican representative, took advantage of the commission's international platform to further equal rights and equal nationality, and to improve women's status in their own countries. But neither Stevens nor Robles de Mendoza represented a unanimous position on equal rights among their countrywomen. Especially for Stevens, the trouble stirred by domestic debates among equal rights feminists and social feminists spread rapidly and publicly into the international arena. First in Europe, and then in Montevideo, Uruguay, U.S. women fought their national battles on the international stage.

The Inter-American Commission's campaign to secure equal nationality for married women began not in the Western Hemisphere but at The Hague. In 1930 the League of Nations convened an International Conference for the Codification of Law, in part to address the upheavals in nationality caused by the fall of old empires and creation of nation-states after

World War I. Stevens led a delegation of commissioners to press for uniform legal codes that treated men and women equally when it came to determining their nationality and citizenship status. Despite weeks of work, the convention eventually produced at the conference represented a significant setback for married women's nationality rights by stipulating that all family members' status would be determined by that of the husband or father, thus denying women independent citizenship. The only small victory for Stevens and her colleagues came when the United States voted against the treaty. While Stevens worked in Europe, Alice Paul and other NWP members had taken full advantage of isolationist sentiment in the United States to convince the Hoover administration not to support an international agreement on equal nationality.[62] Their frustrations at The Hague galvanized Stevens and the IACW to bring the issue of equal nationality before another intergovernmental body—the Pan American Union.[63] Between The Hague conference in 1930 and the Seventh International Conference of American States in 1933, the commission prepared to mount again its campaign for equal nationality and equal rights.

Like Doris Stevens, the Mexican commissioner Margarita Robles de Mendoza saw the Inter-American Commission as an opportunity to use an international platform to advance Mexican women's rights. Robles de Mendoza was a teacher from Morelos who had spent four years in California, representing the Mexican Department of Education and attending the University of Southern California.[64] She later moved to New York in order to enroll in the master's program in sociology at Columbia University. Self-described as a psychologist, sociologist, educator, author, labor organizer, peace advocate, and feminist, she was characterized upon her appointment to the commission as "a women of boundless energy" and "an indefatigable worker against oppression of all sorts."[65] Over her years with the commission she evinced sincere passion for its work, but she was also unreliable and—like Stevens—clashed with other women in her country who felt she did not represent their interests.

Throughout the early 1930s, Robles de Mendoza played a key role in the Mexican women's suffrage movement, which had gained momentum in no small part through Mexican women's participation in international conferences throughout the 1910s and 1920s. Like the delegates to the 1923 conference in Mexico City, Robles de Mendoza believed that improving women's economic and social status was key to their emancipation, and

Figure 7. Margarita Robles de Mendoza.
Schlesinger Library, Radcliffe Institute, Harvard University.

that the vote was the best method of securing it. Mexican feminists' interactions with U.S. and other women allowed them to pressure their own government by comparing their status to that of women in other countries.[66] Focusing on the ambiguity of Article 34 of the 1917 Mexican Constitution, which defined citizens as those over twenty-one years of age and having "an honest and legal mode of living" but did not specify whether women could be included in the category, Robles de Mendoza made an equal rights argument for suffrage. In an open letter to President Calles in 1932, she demanded equal opportunity, equal access to education and health care, and an equal voice in government. "The new nations of Europe have conceded equal civil and political rights to men and women," she pointed out.

"What will the Mexican revolutionary government do for the women of this country? We need the vote which is the legal personality and voice of the free citizen, so that we can address public affairs. So that we can address OUR AFFAIRS!"[67] Throughout the 1930s, Robles de Mendoza played a leadership role in various campaigns to secure Mexican women's status as full citizens, including their right to vote.[68]

Also like Stevens, however, Robles de Mendoza occasionally found herself at odds with other Mexican women. Her model of feminist activism was the U.S. National Woman's Party, and she tended to hold other Mexican women to standards set by Alice Paul, Doris Stevens, and their associates.[69] In 1932 she told a colleague that Mexican women should show up to vote in the next election, and should be prepared to go to jail if they were not allowed to cast a ballot: "Think what women have done to win suffrage in other parts of the world, they have suffered hunger, mockery, and prison before reaching victory."[70] Robles de Mendoza measured Mexican women's progress by U.S. standards. When Stevens expressed her surprise that the Mexican delegate to the Hague codification conference had rejected the treaty on equal nationality for married women, Robles de Mendoza reminded her that "in some aspects of progress and mainly in this concerning rights of women, your country is in the 'xyz' while mine is just starting with the 'abc.'"[71] Sometimes she berated her countrywomen publicly. In January 1932, Robles de Mendoza gave an interview in the *Washington Post* in which she stated her belief that Mexican women were in an "awkward stage" in which they had not yet learned to "handle themselves" publicly, and were at a loss when an occasion required "poise, self-confidence, and quick wits." When her statement was misinterpreted by the *Post* as being directed toward U.S. women, Robles de Mendoza reiterated that she was referring to Mexican women; she had nothing but admiration for "American women and their marvelous achievements."[72] Robles de Mendoza told Stevens that she felt more affinity for her "new country" than for her old one. "In my heart I sometimes consider this land more mine than the other," she admitted, adding, "I have more points of contact with the women of this side of the border."[73] This admiring attitude toward U.S. women became increasingly problematic for Robles de Mendoza over the course of the 1930s.[74]

After the setbacks at The Hague in 1930, the next significant test of the IACW efforts to use the international stage to advance women's rights came at the Seventh International Conference of American States. Stevens hoped to use the information gathered over the previous five years to push for two measures: an Equal Nationality Treaty, and an Equal Rights Treaty. To that end, the commission submitted its extensive report on women's civil and political status, as it had been officially charged with doing at the Sixth Conference in Havana. But while Stevens and the commission achieved some important successes in Montevideo, events there also demonstrated the extent to which Stevens faced opposition from other U.S. women.

In addition to submitting their official report, members of the commission took advantage of several opportunities at the conference to press their case for the treaties. A subcommittee of official conference delegates considered the commission's report and met on December 15 and 16 to debate both measures and to consider whether to continue the commission, now that its original task had been completed. The Equal Nationality Treaty in particular found considerable support among the Latin American representatives. Between the subcommittee's discussion and that of the general conference, several members of the IACW had an opportunity to address all the conference delegates. They all spoke of the need to have women take their place alongside men as full and equal citizens, able to exercise their abilities in politics no less than in society and the family. Ana Rosa Tornero of Bolivia declared, "We want to win the rights of women in the community and be dignified, not through the lyrics of the poets, but through the laws of the country in every domain of life." Minerva Bernadino of the Dominican Republic drew attention to the gathering storm in Europe: "We women, conscious of our responsibilities, demand the participation which belongs to us, not only in the arduous tasks of saving the world from the shame of a new universal conflagration, but also in acting with our brothers in all domains of life."[75]

Margarita Robles de Mendoza gave a particularly impassioned speech in favor of equal rights. She argued there was no more important task before the delegates "than that half of the inhabitants of America pass from the category of slaves to that of human beings." The same rationales were used to deny liberty to women as were once used to justify slave-owning, she protested. All she and her colleagues were demanding was that laws be made for individuals and not for the sexes. Equal treatment, equal opportunity, equal privilege and obligation should be given to women not because they were superior to men—"We can offer nothing in exchange for the granting of our rights," she declared; "we are no better nor worse than our brothers"—but because they were human: "We demand our rights because they are ours, and you should give them to us only to save a principle of justice and integrity." Robles de Mendoza did though promise benefits to society if these demands were met. Marriages and families would be stronger, because they would be made up of equals. "A woman slave can create only conscientious slaves," she contended. Children would be stronger and more patriotic if they were raised by strong, free women. This strength in turn would flow to the nation, and "raise the level of our countries."[76]

In the end, the Inter-American Commission won two battles in Montevideo and lost a third. First, the conference delegates enthusiastically endorsed the commission's endeavors; by a wide margin they passed a resolution acknowledging the commission's work with "a vote of warm applause and appreciation . . . for the painstaking and outstanding work it has accomplished in support of the ideals which it upholds." They also extended their support for the commission for five more years, until the next International Conference of American States in 1938.[77] Second, the delegates overwhelmingly approved the Equal Nationality Treaty, which declared, "There shall be no distinction based on sex as regards nationality, in their legislation or in their practice."[78] This marked a major victory for Doris Stevens and the commission, as well as for Alice Paul and the U.S. National Woman's Party. They had accomplished in Montevideo what they had failed to do three years earlier at The Hague. However, neither measure was without controversy; the United States notably abstained from both votes. Alexander Weddell, U.S. ambassador to Argentina and a leader of the U.S. delegation, declared that the United States would not support either measure because it no longer supported the commission itself. His country championed all efforts to advance women's rights, he announced carefully, but believed the best way to do so was on the national level, and on an issue-by-issue basis, rather than through international measures.[79] The United States was almost entirely isolated in its views; only one other country abstained from the nationality vote, and the rest voted yes to both continuing the commission and endorsing equal nationality.

But the Equal Rights Treaty never came to a vote. The subcommittee reviewing the commission's report ultimately decided not to bring this resolution before the whole conference, concluding that diverse social and cultural contexts in each nation necessitated national, rather than international, implementation of equal rights. The delegates did vote on a resolution urging all nations to "endeavor, so far as the peculiar circumstances of each country will conveniently permit, to establish the maximum of equality between men and women in all matters pertaining to the possession, enjoyment and exercise of civil and political rights." This passed as well; the United States abstained at first, but later approved, with the reservation that any equal rights legislation would have to win congressional approval.[80]

Most of the difficulties the commission encountered in Montevideo stemmed from the opposition of other U.S. women to its approach in general and to Stevens in particular. The official U.S. delegation to the conference was co-led by Sophonisba Breckinridge, one of the most prominent and accomplished social feminists in the United States, and a longtime adversary of the NWP and Alice Paul. Members of the League of Women Voters, the Women's Trade Union League, and other groups that endorsed protective legislation for women were in favor of equal nationality for married women, but they opposed the "treaty method" of securing it. Leading social feminists equated the treaty method of securing equal nationality with the amendment method of securing equal rights—they feared a blanket approach would destroy protective laws.[81] Breckinridge and her allies also disliked Stevens personally. In a confidential memo to the State Department, Weddell and Breckinridge reported, "It is not an overstatement to remark that the general conduct of the Stevens group has been characterized by a lack of dignity and a tone which is to be deplored. Miss Stevens herself is [a] highly nervous, overwrought and fanatical type, and her determination to carry her program through to the end leads her to an extravagance of conduct and language which have caused astonishment in Conference circles."[82] Stevens largely refrained from refuting such attacks directly. Reflecting on the conference in the 1950s, Stevens tied the Commission's success to the larger political context of the U.S. position in the hemisphere: "Whereas two or three U.S. delegates were attributing this manifestation of support for our proposals to some mysterious political power in her own right held over delegates by what they called the 'leader' of a militant minority in the U.S., a more perceptive student of political science would have understood that this was the result of the United States' own loss of support."[83] The protests at home notwithstanding, Stevens remained in her position as the IACW was made a permanent body at Montevideo.

The Inter-American Commission was fighting two interrelated campaigns in Montevideo: the first was to use its international platform to advance women's rights, and the second was against its opponents in the

United States. In the first they found a measure of success, especially on the issue of married women's nationality. Conference delegates endorsed the Equal Nationality Treaty, and over the next three years it was ratified by seven American countries, including the United States and Mexico. While Stevens emerged victorious from the second battle, that war was far from over. Her conflicts with social feminists during the conference provided additional fodder for confrontations between the National Woman's Party and the League of Women Voters and their supporters over the course of the 1930s.

The politicization of women's internationalism that began during the crisis of 1926–1927 continued and expanded over the next few years, embraced both by the Inter-American Commission of Women and by Mexican women. Both groups used internationalism as a mirror on their domestic agendas. Mexican women pressured the Women's International League to recognize and speak out on repatriation and discrimination against Mexicans and Mexican Americans in the United States. Doris Stevens and other members of the IACW hoped to use hemispheric treaties on equal rights and equal nationality to pressure the United States and to bolster the NWP's Equal Rights Amendment. But the difficulties Stevens encountered in Montevideo proved that the domestic battles among feminist factions would only become more entrenched by fighting them on the international stage.

The status of human internationalist endeavors, meanwhile, was uncertain. The YWCA managed to weather the onset of the Depression and forge ahead with a new building and expanded programming, but their emphasis on internationalism itself continued to decline. The Mexican section of WILPF, though reestablished, met with little more success in the early 1930s than it had several years earlier. Once again, the nature of human internationalism made it vulnerable to interpersonal frustrations and miscommunications. The contrast here with the Inter-American Commission is significant. Like WILPF, the commission relied on personal contacts and shared information. But in their case, that human interaction was in service to the end goal of securing hemispheric treaties and national legislation. For WILPF, the means were integral to the ends. Human internationalism was predicated on the belief that greater transnational and cross-cultural knowledge would bring an end to armed conflicts. If those personal interactions stalled, it jeopardized the entire project.

For the rest of the 1930s, U.S. women's internationalism in Mexico would be shaped by a transformation in U.S. foreign policy toward Latin America. Both WILPF and the YWCA's human internationalist approach and the IACW's more legalistic one stood to benefit from Franklin Roosevelt's open declaration that the United States and Latin America were "good neighbors." But U.S. women still had much work to do to translate that opportunity into success for their endeavors.

Chapter 6

Not Such Good Neighbors

In his 1933 inaugural address, U.S. President Franklin Roosevelt declared, "In the field of world policy I would dedicate this Nation to the policy of the good neighbor—the neighbor who resolutely respects himself and, because he does so, respects the rights of others—the neighbor who respects his obligations and respects the sanctity of his agreements in and with a world of neighbors."[1] That year the United States abrogated the Platt Amendment, which had established Cuba as a U.S. protectorate in 1901. In 1934 Roosevelt withdrew U.S. marines from Haiti, ending the nineteen-year occupation of that country, and restructured the U.S. agreement with Panama, scaling back the extent of U.S. control over the Panama Canal. The United States did not scale back its economic investments and loan programs, nor did it attempt to reduce its political influence, but the Good Neighbor Policy symbolized a commitment to hemispheric solidarity and to more egalitarian relations throughout the Americas.[2]

The election of Mexican President Lázaro Cárdenas in 1934 disrupted the improvement of U.S.-Mexican relations that had begun after the crisis of 1926–1927. Cárdenas's ability to mobilize the popular masses had propelled him into office, where he was determined to make good on the Revolution's promises. He redistributed forty-four million acres of land, established new credit systems to finance agricultural production, and implemented a nationwide education program designed to instill a "shared language" of culture, identity, and values.[3] As U.S. bankers and oilmen cringed, Cárdenas became immensely popular among Mexican peasants and workers. His support was built on mass organizations composed primarily of these two groups. Most were dominated by men, but almost all encouraged women's participation, albeit in marginalized and limited ways. Cárdenas's intense nationalism, particularly as evidenced by his land redistribution, made many U.S. observers wary. His land programs evoked strong memories of the crises over Article 27 in the 1920s, and foreshadowed another showdown with the United States over oil in 1938.[4]

Both of these developments represented opportunities for U.S. women internationalists. First, heightened rhetoric about "neighborliness" clearly fit with the personal interactions and shared experiences that practitioners of human internationalism had been promoting for almost two decades. Not coincidentally, both the Mexican YWCA and the Mexican section of WILPF experienced something of a renaissance during the second half of the 1930s, as they capitalized on the United States' willingness to soften both its policies and its tone. In doing so, the human internationalists evinced more of the sophisticated, politicized internationalism that Dorothy Detzer and others had pioneered in the mid-1920s. Second, Cárdenas's willingness to consider women as revolutionary citizens opened the door to the legal advancements the Inter-American Commission of Women sought through the Equal Nationality and Equal Rights Treaties. Both Doris Stevens and Margarita Robles de Mendoza hoped that Cárdenas's support for equal nationality, and for the woman suffrage campaign that gathered strength during the 1930s, heralded significant advancements for Mexican women.

At the same time, however, Cardenismo—renewed revolutionary nationalism—belied much of the rhetoric about "good neighbors." Mexican women who cooperated too closely with U.S. women became open targets for accusations of disloyalty. Ultimately, Mexican women's activism developed during the 1930s in conjunction with Cardenismo, not with U.S. women's internationalism or with prevailing trends in "Western" feminism. This left little opportunity for U.S. women to secure their long-term endeavors in Mexico before the outbreak of war in Europe commandeered their attention. Ironically, Mexican women had finally developed political machinery that would have impressed Carrie Chapman Catt, the woman who had once written them off as fat and lazy. But they put that machinery to use for their own ends, not the ends U.S. women like Catt had envisioned for them.

Women Internationalists Are Good Neighbors

The human internationalist organizations, the Women's International League for Peace and Freedom and the Young Women's Christian Association, were best positioned to take advantage of rhetoric about "neighborliness." WILPF in particular desperately needed it. The U.S. section had established an internal Inter-American Committee to coordinate sections, correspondence, visits, and programs throughout the Western Hemisphere, but it had suffered throughout the first half of the 1930s from a lack of leadership and direction. In 1934, Ellen Starr Brinton began work on a project to establish and maintain correspondence with women peace activists in every Latin American country. By October she was able to report that she had compiled a list of 170 names in twenty-one countries, but she soon realized there was no plan for what to do with that information. "I believe this contact work will serve a useful purpose," she reported to the executive committee, "but something concrete is needed besides exchange of conventional pleasantries. We must investigate the information given us and take some action that can be definitely reported to the writers in other countries."[5] Brinton recognized one of the limitations that had dogged human internationalism from the beginning—without some definite action, endless professions of friendship only went so far. With regard to the moribund Mexican section in particular, Brinton recommended circumventing Clemencia de Kiel, its ineffectual and temperamental leader, by appointing a different Mexican woman to the Inter-American Committee. Her hope was that the committee could revive the section without confronting Kiel directly.[6]

It took time, but WILPF did not give up on its inter-American project. In 1935 the U.S. section signaled its rededication to the committee by choosing a new woman to lead it. The executive board had struggled to find a chair for the Inter-American Committee; they did not want Brinton, and no one else could spare the time. In June one member suggested asking Heloise Brainerd to consider taking the job. Brainerd had just retired as chief of the Division of Intellectual Cooperation at the Pan American Union, had extensive knowledge of Latin America, and—unlike Lowrie, Moore, or Brinton—spoke fluent Spanish. She was also a longtime member of WILPF.[7] Brainerd accepted the job in summer 1935, though she did not officially start her duties until November. In the interim, several members of the U.S. executive board worked to secure formal recognition of the committee from the international office in Geneva.[8] The U.S. section would still oversee its activities, but officially it would be a committee of WILPF International.

Brainerd seemed the ideal person to lead a renewed inter-American effort. After graduating from Smith College in 1904, she spent four years living in Mexico City, working as a secretary in a law firm and living with Mexican families. This made her the first WILPF representative to Latin

America who spoke Spanish and knew something about the country. She worked at the Pan American Union for twenty-six years before her retirement, first as private secretary to the assistant director, and later as the head of the education division. When the Division of Intellectual Cooperation was created in 1929, Brainerd was named its first chief. The division's responsibilities were to promote educational and cultural exchanges throughout the Americas. In that capacity Brainerd developed an extensive correspondence with men and women in every Latin American country, and traveled to nearly every nation at least once.[9]

Brainerd quickly followed through on Ellen Starr Brinton's call for concrete action. She started her tenure in early 1936 by making contact with WILPF supporters in Latin America, and by planning an initial trip to Mexico and Central America. She also organized an advisory committee, made up of U.S. and Latin American women living in the United States. In her first report to the U.S. executive board she outlined what she hoped to do in the future: organize more official sections, consolidate peace forces in Latin America and formulate concrete plans of action, recruit as many women as possible into leadership positions in the peace movement, and encourage mediation of various border disputes.[10] This agenda reflected both the goals of human internationalism and the need to make it work in practice.

Brainerd also demonstrated her understanding of the need to employ "neighborly" rhetoric as much as possible. Eager to counter the impression of "North American dominance" of the Western Hemisphere, Brainerd argued that the U.S. section was coordinating inter-American work because it had been asked to do so explicitly by the Geneva office, not because U.S. women felt possessive about their "sphere." She also acknowledged that her previous association with the Pan American Union, which some Latin Americans felt was an agent of U.S. imperialism, was a potential mark against her. "I can only say," she concluded her first committee report, "that I shall endeavor to follow in the footsteps of Ambassador [to Mexico Dwight] Morrow, who when asked rather scornfully by someone what *he* could do for the Mexicans, replied, 'I can love them.' "[11] Her invocation of Morrow was shrewd; he had replaced the obstinate and racist James Sheffield in 1927, and his role in diffusing the oil crisis earned him respect from many Mexicans.

Brainerd's trip to Mexico City was by far the most successful any member of the Inter-American Committee had undertaken since its inception.

She made contact with every woman who had registered as a member of the Mexican section, including Clemencia de Kiel. She gave interviews to local newspapers, spoke in front of several local groups interested in peace, and met with both U.S. and Mexican officials about WILPF's agenda.[12] Brainerd encouraged Mexican women's focus on peace education, and urged them to work with other groups dedicated to social reform. In her report to the U.S. executive board, she noted that even resentment of the United States seemed to be receding, and she did what she could to further the process. "I always carefully explained that our *people* are not imperialistic," she wrote, "and that the imperialistic interests are being curbed by the government, whose 'good neighbor' policy is sincere." Finally, Brainerd recommended strengthening the ties between the U.S. section and the Mexican section by encouraging local branches in the United States to develop their own contacts in Mexico, and by organizing another inter-American conference similar to the one held in 1930.[13] Brainerd's arrival revived the Inter-American Committee. She brought fresh energy and a new perspective to WILPF's potential role in Latin America.

Brainerd argued it was the duty of the U.S. section, not the international office, to organize Latin American women. To that end she proposed nationwide fund-raising for future trips to the region, and encouraged local U.S. sections to develop their own contacts. She also proposed encouraging Latin American women to develop programs for peace education, and to incorporate peace work into their existing social programs. "As internal peace," she noted, "there as well as here, depends on improving the condition of the masses, it seems wise to direct their efforts that way."[14] In Mexico, Brainerd's visit poured new life into the struggling section. She found Kiel a "lovely person," who "worked very hard."[15] All the members, Brainerd reported, had worked with "considerable calm and abnegation" in the face of opposition and even ridicule.[16] Less than three weeks after she left Mexico City, the international office received fifty francs as back payment on the section's dues, allowing them to retain their status as a section.[17]

The YWCA was even more deliberate than WILPF about harnessing the rhetoric of neighborliness toward the cause of human internationalism. After several years of curtailed budgets and shrinking staff, the Foreign Division decided in the mid-1930s to focus its efforts on six countries in particular: China, Japan, Syria, the Philippines, Argentina, and Mexico. As the closest "good neighbor," the board noted, Mexico was strategically important not only for the YWCA but for the United States as a whole.[18]

The association's main goals in Mexico during these years remained the same: to advance women's status and to educate Mexican women for leadership in community affairs.[19]

In a self-study conducted by the Foreign Division, board members reiterated several underlying principles guiding YWCA work abroad during the 1930s, including "cooperation" and "person-to-person contact." Cooperation among women in particular, they noted, was still necessary: "As a preparatory step to the cooperation of nations, organizations cooperating on a world scale across national boundary lines may be significant. Nor is it improbable that women, uninhibited by past experience in the old forms of diplomacy, may find it easier than men would to lead out in this realm. . . . Not *for* but *with* the leaders of other countries can the World's Association and the world community be built."[20] Interactions among people, likewise—as opposed to the exchange of funds and resources only—were still crucial. Quoting a report from the World YWCA, the Foreign Division noted, "We are likely to forget that we have a distinctive task, which differentiates our work from that of some other women's movements; namely, the slow silent building of international relationships on the basis of personal contacts. . . . International understanding is achieved not as an end in itself, but as the inevitable result of the personal association of individual women and girls of different nations."[21] Over twenty years after Jane Addams's address to the Women's Auxiliary Conference, the YWCA was advocating for human internationalism just as strongly as she had done, and arguing again that women were uniquely suited to practice it.

The Foreign Division's commitment to Mexico bore fruit in the popularity of YWCA classes, activities, and facilities among the women and girls of Mexico City. The active membership remained steady at between 300 and 350 throughout the second half of the decade, while the number of people taking classes, using the swimming pool and gymnasium, boarding in the residence, and taking advantage of the free health care reached almost 3,000 per year by 1940. The swimming pool and the medical care were the most popular offerings, largely because the YWCA was the only place in Mexico City to provide facilities and doctors exclusively for the use of women and girls. Every U.S. visitor noted the significance of the new building in bringing about these changes. In order to accommodate the expanding section, the Foreign Division sent a second secretary to Mexico City in 1935 to assist Sue Perry. Katharine Briggs concentrated her efforts on coordinating the community activities of the YWCA, leaving to Perry the work of overseeing the active members and finances of the group. Briggs sent her own regular reports to the Foreign Division, frequently noting that the association had more demand for classes and services than it could supply.[22]

Both Perry and Briggs reported regularly on the ongoing violence in Mexico City, and on the tensions created occasionally by the United States, but gave no indication that these events had a direct impact on them or their ability to do their work. The Cárdenas government was well disposed to the YWCA, much as earlier regimes had been under Calles.[23] Perry noted that any remaining tensions between the YWCA and prominent Catholics were gradually subsiding. More and more Catholic mothers were sending their children to play and learn at the association.[24] When U.S. senator William Borah began agitating for military intervention in Mexico to protect U.S. American Catholics in 1935, Sue Perry and Sarah Lyon debated the efficacy of denouncing such an intervention. Perry thought it might earn them some credit with the Mexican government; "Mexicans in general," she reported to Lyon, "think Borah absurd and illogical." Further, they did not see how the United States could refuse to take part in the World Court and then "turn round and interfere with Mexico." But in the end, Perry counseled Lyon against a protest, on the grounds that "None of it all, so far, seems to affect us as an organization here."[25]

U.S. YWCA members frequently cited and praised the degree to which the association in Mexico City had been "Mexicanized." In early 1935 sixteen of the twenty board members were Mexican. One U.S. traveler was struck by how many of the activities and programs carried out by the association originated with Mexican members. "The program does seem indigenous," she noted. In the dining room, for instance, "at all times one heard lively discussions of politics, religion, et cetera." The same observer credited Sue Perry for establishing an atmosphere of cooperation and collaboration: "She has the confidence of the foreign and Mexican constituency to a marked degree. It seemed to me that her attitude toward people of another race is exceptional. She has not a trace of that 'Nordic superiority.'"[26] Briggs, for her part, discovered on her arrival that her lack of Spanish language skills, rather than being seen as an impediment born of ignorance, endeared her to the Mexican members and made them feel they were playing an important role in the life of the association: "A secretary arriving without facility in the Spanish language, finds it helpful in that it creates a personal 'give and take.' She is 'being taught' instead of "teaching."[27] In

Briggs's case, her lack of Spanish helped facilitate this little bit of human internationalism, rather than hindering it.

Both Perry and Briggs though, along with other U.S. observers, expressed frustration with what they saw as the slow development of real Mexican leadership. Most felt that while Mexican women were enthusiastic about the association and its programs, they were not ready or not willing to assume leadership responsibilities for those activities. In Margaret Forsyth's words, "the stage has not been reached in Mexico where the Mexican women 'get down underneath' the burden of the Association." She recounted one exchange with a Mexican member who, when Forsyth asked for a suggestion of a person who could do some educational work, replied, "Send for a worker from the United States to draft a plan and carry it out."[28] Several other reports concluded that the Mexican members were too apt to rely on the U.S. secretaries for the execution of their ideas. These concerns echoed those of WILPF leaders who worried about Mexican women's experience with and willingness to shoulder the burden of organizational leadership.

The YWCA did not have much direct contact with other women's organizations in Mexico City, but many of its members belonged to other groups, particularly groups that also had some affiliation with the United States. There was significant overlap, for example, in the membership rolls of the YWCA and WILPF. Others belonged to the Association of University Women, or to the Pan American Round Table. These organizations were made up almost exclusively of middle-class and professional women, noted one YWCA observer, and wielded little influence beyond their own circle. Among the groups that were purely Mexican in origin and focus, the same observer continued, there was not much room or opportunity for women's involvement. "Women's organizations have up to date been rather slow in their growth," she reported. "One correspondent told me of his experience in attending a women's conference here last year which aimed to unite existing organizations. The women were very limited in their outlook and organizational ability. There was no leadership of the group and the whole thing petered out. Women rarely organize separately from men and only in a few radical political organizations is there any attempt to train women leaders in these organizations."[29]

YWCA president Guadalupe Ramirez echoed this sentiment in her evaluation of the social constraints facing Mexican women. The average Mexican woman was shamed out of civic activity, she argued, by the pressures of self-abnegation and by arguments that her first and only duty was to her family: "She has been told, in the first place, that the Mexican mother is the best in the world because she sacrifices herself unconditionally for the sake of her children and her husband, and she is made to believe that outside of the home, there is nothing worthy of the attention of a good mother. In this way, she is estranged from all the political and social problems, which should receive her support just because she is a woman and a mother." Ramirez argued that women needed better education in all matters, ranging from sex education to professional training, and that they needed the vote: "Many believe that woman's suffrage will not be of much weight, but the fact that they do obtain recognition, in a legal sense, is to them of great significance."[30] The confidence that came with that legal recognition, Ramirez believed, would make women work harder to educate themselves on social and political questions.

Cardenismo Ascendant

Under Cárdenas, some of these political and legal changes seemed like real possibilities. His election in 1934 ushered in a period of intense nationalism and a renewed effort to institutionalize the goals of the Mexican Revolution, led by the president himself. Along with workers, peasants, and other major sectors of the population, Mexican feminists hitched their wagons to Cardenismo. They spent the 1930s trying to stake a claim for themselves as revolutionary citizens at a time when the meanings of both citizenship and womanhood were contested.[31] There was no unified feminist movement in Mexico, just as there was none in the United States. Since the early 1930s most women activists had allied either with the government party—the National Revolutionary Party (PNR)—or with the Mexican Communist Party. In 1935, however, these two strands came together in the Frente Único Pro-Derechos de la Mujer, or the Sole Front for Women's Rights (FUPDM). Together, they fought for an equal share in the promises of the Revolution, acknowledgment of their significance in the concept of the Mexican nation, and recognition as political actors.

The problem for WILPF and the YWCA was that these were feminist impulses, not internationalist ones. Any increase in Mexican women's political activism occurred under the banner of Cardenismo, not inter-American cooperation. Although in theory the branches of WILPF and the

YWCA in Mexico City could have benefited from greater civic and political involvement of Mexican women, in practice whatever organizing occurred in the early to mid-1930s drove those women further away from international groups and from women of other nations.

The Inter-American Commission of Women, on the other hand, seemed ideally poised to capitalize on the promise of revolutionary citizenship for Mexican women. On the surface, both the Equal Nationality Treaty and the Equal Rights Treaty offered mechanisms for the Mexican government to start expanding the benefits of revolutionary citizenship to women, especially given that the divide between "social feminism" and "equal rights feminism" was negligible in Latin America. After the Montevideo conference, Doris Stevens's and Margarita Robles de Mendoza's primary focus was on securing ratification of the Equal Nationality Treaty. Even though the Equal Rights Treaty had not been adopted, they also worked to ensure that every American country adhered to the resolution passed at the conference encouraging nations "to establish the maximum of equality between men and women."[32] Stevens had survived the attempt by her opponents in the United States to remove her from office, for which Robles de Mendoza was grateful, but Stevens's position as chair was far from secure. Back in the United States, she publicized the commission's achievements, and lauded the conference delegates for their action. "Women all over the world . . . decided to demand that government set up a world law that inequality for women should no longer be permitted anywhere," she proclaimed in a nationwide broadcast. "The first step toward setting up this rule of civilized conduct for the world has been taken."[33] But Stevens also reiterated the necessity of adopting the Equal Rights Treaty. The protective legislation that existed in the United States and other countries did not protect women, she argued, it harmed them. "Legal handicaps" prevented every woman from exercising "her maximum inherent capacities in politics, the professions, commerce, industry, or almost any other department of life."[34] If the American nations were in fact based on the principle of liberty, she pointed out, they could hardly deny women the same basic freedoms enjoyed by men, and could not impose restrictions on the opportunities available to them.

The first and biggest victory for the IACW after the Montevideo conference came in May 1934, when the U.S. Senate ratified the Equal Nationality Treaty.[35] Nine months later, Mexico became the third country to grant women equal nationality, after the United States and Chile. The IACW also

tried to make inroads with the Equal Rights Treaty. Four countries—
Uruguay, Paraguay, Ecuador, and Cuba—had signed that treaty in Montevideo, but it had not been accepted by the conference as a whole. Several
members of the commission spent much of their time before the 1938
conference compiling a report on the status of women's political and civil
rights, to be presented at Lima in support of the Equal Rights Treaty. Stevens spent most of her time between 1933 and 1938 lobbying for both
treaties, and fending off the ongoing attacks from opponents of the
National Woman's Party in the United States. The League of Women Voters
and other prominent supporters of protective legislation for women,
including Eleanor Roosevelt, were still determined to redirect the work of
the commission away from a strict equal rights approach, and to remove
Stevens as chair. As the Eighth International Conference approached, the
fight became more and more heated.

But it was not only in the United States that the Stevens and the commission encountered hurdles. Mexican commissioner Margarita Robles de
Mendoza continued to behave erratically, frustrating Stevens and alienating
other U.S. women working with the commission. In 1936 she was named
secretary of women's affairs for the PNR, a move calculated by party leaders
to pacify women's groups, who wanted a woman in the post.[36] Their choice
was odd, however, given that dozens of prominent women activists immediately placed notices in major newspapers denouncing Robles de Mendoza's selection.[37] Robles de Mendoza was dissatisfied with her position in any
case, particularly after Cárdenas and other party leaders ignored her
repeated demands that Mexico ratify the Equal Rights Treaty. She resigned
from the PNR in May, just three months after her appointment was first
announced.[38] Robles de Mendoza had many acquaintances among the radical factions of the suffrage movement like the FUPDM, but she did not
respond to repeated requests from Stevens that she provide their contact
information to the Inter-American Commission. In 1937, when Heloise
Brainerd was advising a U.S. WILPF member on the women she was likely
to encounter during a visit to Mexico City, Brainerd warned her to be wary
of Robles de Mendoza. "She is a dynamic person, but very ill-bred and I
don't think has much reputation."[39]

All three organizations thus worked to take advantage of the opportunities offered by the Good Neighbor Policy and by Cárdenas's support for
women's rights, but they also understood they would have to act quickly
and smartly to overcome the various obstacles posed by Mexican women's

nationalism and their reluctance to fully engage with U.S. women's interna-tionalism. Perhaps their best chance came in 1936, at the Inter-American Conference of Peace in Buenos Aires. Proposed by Franklin Roosevelt as an opportunity to reaffirm hemispheric solidarity in the face of German, Soviet, Italian, and Japanese advances, the conference in many ways seemed an ideal way to bring together the different strands of women's internation-alism that had been forming throughout the 1930s.[40] The official delegates discussed trade, intellectual cooperation, disarmament, and the need for neutrality and hemispheric solidarity in the face of the growing threat of a European war. President Roosevelt traveled to the conference in person to declare, "In this determination to live at peace among ourselves we in the Americas make it at the same time clear that we stand shoulder to shoulder in our final determination that others who, driven by war madness or land hunger, might seek to commit acts of aggression against us will find a Hemisphere wholly prepared to consult together for our mutual safety and our mutual good."[41] The speech had little impact in Europe, at which it was mainly directed, but it did help reinforce the Good Neighbor Policy in the Americas.[42]

WILPF celebrated the theme of the conference, while the IACW sought to use it to further their efforts on the Equal Rights Treaty. Brainerd felt the time was propitious to establish lasting inter-American peace. "Now," she argued, "it is the task of peace workers in all the Americas to cement this friendship and assure the ratification of the peace treaties, so that the Western Hemisphere may be both a safeguard—a solid neutral unit—and an object lesson to the rest of the world." She urged all Americans to learn more about Latin America by organizing study groups and acquiring mate-rial from the Pan American Union. WILPF in particular needed to take seriously Roosevelt's dream of a "sisterhood of twenty-one nations strongly united in sympathy and mutual helpfulness." The future of inter-American relations, she argued, would be largely what women in the United States made it.[43]

The issue of women's status was not originally on the program for dis-cussion in Buenos Aires, because it was already on the agenda of the Eighth International Conference of American States in 1938. But when Bolivia added the topic, the United States could not remove it without being accused of betraying its professed neutrality. In July Stevens, who had not expected the IACW would participate in the conference but was pleased with Bolivia's action, learned from a confidential source that several U.S.

women's organizations, including the League of Women Voters and the Women's Trade Union League, were petitioning the State Department to remove the question of women from the agenda. "This is more than human flesh can bear," she wrote to Dorothy Detzer. "We do not know who started this but presumably organizations who fear we may repeat another Montevideo victory."[44] As Stevens's correspondence with Detzer indicates, the two organizations kept in touch, and in fact the U.S. section of WILPF was one of the commission's steadiest supporters throughout the 1930s.

Stevens rallied significant support from Detzer and other allies, most of whom urged the State Department to keep women on the agenda precisely because of the close relationship between international peace and the status of women. The commission issued a statement arguing that "An unequal status of men and women is a cause of internal irritation, which affects stability, which, in turn, disturbs the peace."[45] Hannah Clothier Hull, president of the U.S. section of WILPF, wrote U.S. secretary of state Cordell Hull (no relation) that "our organization considers the political rights of women are very closely allied to the subject of Peace and Freedom and therefore we are of the opinion that the subject belongs on the agenda for this Inter American Conference."[46] The issue stayed on the agenda, and Stevens and the IACW celebrated a resolution passed by the delegates encouraging all nations to adhere to the Equal Rights Treaty.[47]

The following summer, Stevens elaborated on the close relationship between the status of women and peaceful inter-American relations. She compared the governance of the nation-state to that of a family, arguing that both functioned best when run according to a stable constitutional order in which both men and women shared power. The United States was making progress toward this model, but too many Latin American countries and families alike, Stevens contended, perpetuated a "father-rule, which . . . gives an inferior position to women and denies wholesome self-direction to young people." She characterized the commission's undertaking as a fight for greater equality in state and in family rule. The same principles held true for international relations, she went on. "It is generally accepted that the most-favored-nation doctrine in international commerce is essential to peace," she pointed out. "What we stand for is the family in which neither men nor women have preferential treatment, where all enjoy the advantages of a most-favored-individual clause." Stevens acknowledged that guaranteeing equality before the law did not guarantee a perfect system, either in families or in states, but doing away with special privileges was essential, she argued: "In our scrutiny of roads to harmony, security, stability and peace, which is our common aim during these deliberations, it is essential that the leaders of opinion acquaint themselves with the problem of removing irritations at the root, the family, in order to remove them from the State. When we acknowledge the importance of this and act upon it, the problem of inter-State relations will be settled with less pain and more beauty. For peace is but a by-product of stability within and of good relations without our several homelands."[48] For Stevens and the commission, good neighbors were equal neighbors. Moreover, equality between the sexes would lead to more equitable relations among nations. The IACW seemed ready, then, not only to capitalize on the opportunity to advance women's rights but to play an important role in promoting hemispheric peace.

Neighborliness Is Not Enough

But while the promise of the Buenos Aires conference lingered in other countries, within six months whatever potential positive impact it had on the relationships between U.S. and Mexican women had been reversed. While the Inter-American Commission tried to help Mexican women with their suffrage campaign, members of WILPF tried to keep the Mexican section afloat. But both encountered resistance from Mexican women that effectively ended their efforts. Meanwhile, Cárdenas's decision in 1938 to nationalize the Mexican oil industry threatened his "neighborly" relations with the United States. At the Eighth International Conference of American States, held in Lima in December 1938, official diplomats tried to restore equilibrium, while women internationalists supported the search for peace and furthered their work for equal rights. But before the end of the decade it was clear that all hemispheric concerns would be subsumed beneath the threat of the new war in Europe.

Both WILPF and the IACW encountered a new round of difficulties in summer 1937, when representatives of both organizations visited Mexico City in conjunction with the Third Inter-American Conference on Education. As teachers and educators, many Mexican feminists were eager to take part in it, including Margarita Robles de Mendoza. The Inter-American

Commission was invited to send a representative, but as Robles de Mendoza was in New York, Stevens decided to send Hazel Moore, a member of the National Woman's Party and prominent birth control activist. Stevens also empowered Maria Refugio ("Cuca") García, president of the Frente Único Pro-Derechos de la Mujer, and a few other women, chosen on Robles de Mendoza's recommendation, to act with Moore on behalf of the commission. Stevens sent Robles de Mendoza a copy of the resolution the IACW planned to submit, citing women's long service to the cause of education in the Americas and demanding equal pay for teachers as well as general woman suffrage, and asked her to rally support for it among her Mexican colleagues.[49]

On her arrival in Mexico City, however, Moore found that all the Mexican women with whom she spoke were strongly opposed to including a demand for suffrage in the IACW resolution. In her report to Stevens, Moore indicated that their opposition stemmed from their fear of bold action: "I have tried to answer their arguments about the church controlling women etc., and tried to convince them you cannot expect people to learn to swim when they are not in the water etc., but they are still so afraid of Suffrage for women, it is pathetic."[50] Stevens advised Moore to introduce the resolution anyway, and explain to the Mexican women present that it was not binding, and that other inter-American conferences had already expressed support for woman suffrage. She also wrote immediately to Robles de Mendoza, to ask why the delegates Robles de Mendoza had suggested to work with the IACW did not support the commission's stance on suffrage. Robles de Mendoza defended her colleagues' decision to oppose the suffrage clause, noting they probably felt they could not support a "political" demand at an educational conference, and had been instructed by other organizations to which they belonged to prioritize the resolutions they supported. Robles de Mendoza's explanations had no effect on the conference; Moore managed to get the resolution concerning equal pay passed by the delegates, although the suffrage clause was omitted.[51] The whole incident troubled Stevens; she assumed that Robles de Mendoza was misrepresenting Mexican woman's readiness to demand suffrage.

But a better explanation for why Mexican women did not want to support the commission's resolution on suffrage can be found in an exchange between Cuca García and another IACW supporter that took place a few months before the education conference. In May 1937, Anna Kelton Wiley, a prominent member of the General Federation of Women's Clubs as well as the National Woman's Party, traveled to Mexico City. During her week-long visit, Wiley toured the city and surrounding area, met with the U.S. ambassador to Mexico, and addressed a meeting of the FUPDM. The latter had been arranged by Robles de Mendoza, who was in Mexico City during Wiley's visit and spent several days with her. Wiley's speech outlined the history of the suffrage battle in the United States, and noted that delegates from all the American countries had supported full citizenship for women the year before in Buenos Aires.[52]

Cuca García issued a response to Wiley's speech that she addressed to "all the women of North America." Mexican women were "deeply inter-ested in getting our political rights," she acknowledged. But García rejected Wiley's implication that Mexican women should follow in the footsteps of U.S. women in their strategic political battle for suffrage. She pointed out that Mexican women had "helped to make the Revolution" and then been denied a share the victory: "The smoke of the powder from the battlefields passed through our hair many times without making us turn back, but the Government of our country, when the Revolution was ended and they had taken advantage of our services, sent us back home." García was grateful for what she had learned from the women of the United States, but pointedly reminded them that since the FUPDM's struggles took place in a "semi-colonial country," Mexican women would have to find their own path to suffrage.[53] Thus it was not suffrage itself that García rejected, it was what she saw as the imperialist feminism of the IACW. Mexican women were more than ready to demand suffrage, but they wanted to do it as Mexicans, as revolutionary citizens, not as mouthpieces of the Inter-American Commission.

The U.S. section of WILPF heard the same message from a different set of Mexican women. Two members, Frances Benedict Stewart and Esther Crooks, also traveled to Mexico City to attend the education conference. Heloise Brainerd asked them to call a meeting of the Mexican section and see whether Clemencia de Kiel was still dominating the group. As a result of her inactivity, the Mexican group had lost its official standing, although the international secretary remained hopeful that WILPF could retain some ties to individual women in Mexico City, and perhaps eventually organize a new section.[54] Brainerd wanted Crooks and Stewart to gauge whether this would be possible. Kiel's participation at the education conference was not a propitious sign. Stewart reported to Brainerd that not only had Kiel given a speech in support of her husband's native Germany—a speech roundly booed by the audience—but she had also proposed a resolution in the name of WILPF to prevent anyone from the United States from using the name "Americans." "Needless to say," Stewart told Brainerd, "she and her proposal were ridiculed and utterly thrown out."[55] In the context of WILPF's history in Mexico and Mexican women's interactions with Ellen Starr Brinton in 1931, however, Kiel's comments were not so ridiculous.

After the conference, Kiel refused to call a meeting of the Mexican section. When Stewart and Crooks finally managed to organize one themselves, they focused on encouraging Mexican women to revive their section by recruiting new members, formally adopting the WILPF constitution, and collecting dues. Crooks also updated the women present on other recent WILPF activities. In response, Kiel flew into a rage, accusing both U.S. women of trying to undermine her authority and "stir up trouble." She declared herself and her group publicly insulted, and said she was not interested in peace work suggested by "foreigners—especially North Americans!"[56] Other Mexican women at the meeting tried to calm her, and later assured Crooks and Stewart that they did not agree with Kiel's interpretation of their remarks. They felt unable to confront her though because they were indebted to her for their jobs. Many of the women were teachers, and while her husband was affiliated with a normal school in Mexico City Kiel had persuaded him to secure employment for several of the women.[57] Crooks managed to pacify Kiel enough to finish the meeting, but after that incident Brainerd took definite steps to dissociate Kiel from WILPF and encourage other women to organize a new section. "Advantage must be taken now," she resolved, "of the situation created by the 'explosion' to organize a real Mexican peace society, which can become a national section of the WILPF."[58] Yet over the next few years this did not happen. One woman told Brainerd Kiel had gone to considerable trouble to discredit other women who might have been expected to take her place. Brainerd's correspondent assured Brainerd that she and her friends would continue to campaign for peace within other organizations, but "women of action" were more concerned with other issues.[59]

The IACW and WILPF reliance on Margarita Robles de Mendoza and Clemencia de Kiel respectively proved how difficult it was for them not only to appreciate the direction of Mexican feminism in the 1930s but to find women who could help them bridge the gaps between their agendas and those of Mexican women activists. Neither woman could be counted on to foster relationships between U.S. and Mexican women that would be constructive to the Inter-American Commission and the Women's International League. But more significantly, as Cuca García's address shows, Robles de Mendoza's associations with the National Woman's Party and with U.S. women in general hurt her with Mexican women more than they helped. The majority of Mexican feminists in the 1930s framed their claims for political rights within the revolutionary conception of citizenship, which meant positioning themselves *as women* within a revitalized nationalistic polity. Both the IACW and WILPF, however, adhered to more liberal conceptions of citizenship in which women were political individuals in the same way as men. Unlike in the 1920s, therefore, it was not imperialist internationalism that was the problem, it was imperialist feminism. The friendly rhetoric of the Good Neighbor Policy was no match for these underlying divisions between U.S. and Mexican women.

Over the following year, as the IACW and WILPF networks in Mexico City disintegrated, so did diplomatic relations between Mexico and the United States. In May 1937, Mexican workers at U.S. oil companies in Mexico went on strike, demanding higher wages and greater job security. Several rulings of the Mexican Supreme Court favored the workers, but the companies did not comply with the court's directives, arguing that pay increases would bankrupt them. Citing this failure to follow the legal ruling, Cárdenas nationalized the entire Mexican petroleum industry in March 1938.[60] The move stemmed from two deeper, persistent trends: lingering Mexican resentment over U.S. limitations on the implementation of Article 27, and Cárdenas's drive to modernize Mexico's economy. He also knew that the previous five years' worth of treaties and agreements under the Good Neighbor Policy would make it difficult for the United States to justify the use of force to protect the oil companies.[61] U.S. concerns over the move were not only financial. They were also stoked by a cable from an American financier in Mexico, who claimed the takeover of U.S. properties had "been fomented by the representatives of Japan, Italy, and Germany, particularly the last named."[62] Secretary of State Hull wanted Roosevelt to threaten military intervention if Cárdenas did not back down. Roosevelt recognized the danger; the issue for the United States was not the oil itself but the precedent of allowing a foreign government to seize U.S. holdings, and the threat of German influence in the Western Hemisphere. But he could not use force, nor was he willing to try to depose Cárdenas by fueling Mexican opposition to him. Nor was Hull ever able to prove the connection to any other hostile government. Economic pressure and diplomacy were the only avenues open to Roosevelt, and by 1939 the oil companies had entered into the long process of negotiation with the Mexican government for compensation.

The IACW and the YWCA assumed a neutral stance on the expropriation. The commission could not afford to antagonize either government; they were preoccupied with the upcoming inter-American conference in Lima, at which members hoped to reintroduce a resolution on equal rights for women. In response to a letter from Cuca García, asking the IACW to send messages throughout Latin America in support of the Mexican government, Stevens expressed the commission's sympathy for Mexico, but claimed she could not offer to do more than provide contact information for affiliated organizations.[63] Though neither woman likely would have realized it, this exchange echoed those between the Consejo Feminista Mexicano and the League of Women Voters more than fifteen years earlier. Once again, U.S. women did not respond when Mexican women asked them to take action.

U.S. YWCA members in Mexico were more affected, both emotionally and practically, but refrained from taking sides on the issue. Katherine Briggs wrote to a member of the Foreign Division that in the wake of the expropriation "the manifestation in favor of Cárdenas was so huge that practically no one was left to see it from the sidelines. Naturally, the foreign employees of the petroleum companies are passing through hard times. Always some group or persons have to suffer. However, it appears as if Mexican economic independence has been expressed and for the first time, Mexico is emerging from the so-called Colonial Status. . . . Being right in it and hearing so many different slants and reactions makes one realize how involved it all is. The air is charged and people talk and think nothing but this."[64] Briggs's reaction simultaneously encompassed a clear recognition of U.S. economic imperialism in Mexico and a neutral, almost impersonal perspective on its effects. She did not take personally Mexicans' frustration toward the United States, but neither did she see herself or the YWCA as a potential target of that frustration.

WILPF took a much more active approach to the situation, displaying once again the political sophistication they had developed over the previous decade. In April, U.S. executive secretary Dorothy Detzer paid visits to the Mexican ambassador to the United States and to Sumner Welles, U.S. under-secretary of state for Latin American affairs. Neither was very forthcoming about potential solutions to the problem.[65] In October the U.S.

national board passed a resolution urging members to study the issue and exert pressure on the State Department for a just and peaceful settlement.[66] Brainerd commended the U.S. government for conceding Mexico's right to expropriate U.S.-owned properties at fair value, but opposed its subsequent cessation of silver purchases as a form of economic coercion.[67] "Mexico is fighting for the economic freedom of its people," she argued, "but by over-great speed is strangling instead of recovering the goose that lays the golden eggs, while our Government is fearful lest leniency here may ruin American investment elsewhere." WILPF's responsibility was to urge both sides toward compromise to forestall the acceleration of tensions while drawing attention to Latin American hostility to economic imperialism.[68]

Another U.S. WILPF member spoke even more strongly on behalf of Mexico. Blanca Saunders, a member of Brainerd's committee and head of the California section's own inter-American committee, gave a radio address in October 1938 titled "Mexico and Her Good Neighbor." She characterized the conflict over oil expropriation as "a problem between an overwhelming native population and a modern form of white invasion." The promises of the Mexican Revolution, she argued, had not been carried out by revolutionary leaders—until Cárdenas. His program of land redistribution and the beginnings of irrigation projects and school systems had brought "new hope for a better life to thousands of isolated, backward and illiterate peasant communities." As with any reform that benefited a large number of people, there were a small number who were dispossessed of their privileges. Among the dispossessed this time, she noted, were "a few American citizens who had abandoned their own country in search of an easier life somewhere else." They bought the land for nothing, made enormous fortunes on it at the expense of Mexican peasants and laborers, and then cried injustice when it was taken away from them. Saunders disputed the oil companies' claim that their investments had brought development and economic modernization to Mexico. "Foreign investors have taken out of Mexico from 1901 to 1936 over three billions and a half of Mexican dollars from petroleum," she argued. "What has been left in Mexico in return? A few dollars for salaries to underpaid laborers, over a smaller amount for taxes, and a few holes in the ground." The time had come for Mexicans to share in the wealth. Mexico's failure to provide compensation was due to its inability, not its unwillingness. If the United States did not account for that and take steps to reach a compromise, Mexico would out of necessity turn to Germany and Japan for markets. The least the United

States could do, Saunders argued, was to treat Mexico financially the same way it had treated its European allies in the matter of paying back war debts: "Is it sporting of a wealthy nation like ours to pin to the wall our weak, poor, and defenseless neighbors at the most critical period in their struggle for national development?"[69] Unlike other U.S. Americans and most U.S. investors, who saw Cárdenas's actions as part of a long history of threats to U.S. security, Saunders linked them to a long history of U.S. oppression and imperialism.

Both U.S. and Mexican officials used the Eighth International Conference of American States at Lima in December 1938 as an opportunity to calm the furor over expropriation. Secretary of State Hull relieved some of his government's pressure on Mexico, and Mexican foreign minister Eduardo Hay publicly voiced his government's support for the Good Neighbor Policy.[70] U.S. women attending the conference were pleased with these developments, and with renewed discussions among the delegates about the need for inter-American peace and solidarity. Mabel Vernon, a prominent U.S. WILPF member and director of the People's Mandate Committee, addressed the delegates on December 17. The committee had been working since 1935 to gather signatures for the People's Mandate to Governments to End War, a joint venture among several U.S. women's organizations. They had gathered over three million signatures worldwide by 1938, a significant portion of them from Latin America. At Lima, Vernon presented herself as "the voice of that multitude of signers, who in every country are hoping and praying for peace. . . . It is the voice of mothers, of fathers, of wives, of sisters, pleading that the great statesmen here assembled further banish war from this part of the world, and give strength and permanence to the peace that now exists on this continent." Women, Vernon argued, had a unique part to play in this work. They were not "animated by selfish motives," and had "no axes to grind," but desired only "to do the things that will be for the welfare and advancement of the people of the world."[71]

Members of the Inter-American Commission of Women, meanwhile, spent their time and energy in Lima much as they had in Montevideo, fighting for their Equal Nationality and Equal Rights Treaties, and fending off attacks on Stevens. Stevens presented a report to the conference delegates on women's civil and political status in each of the twenty-one American republics, including a list of those countries that had ratified or voiced support for the treaties. The commission recommended to the delegates that their governments adopt a convention on the political rights of women, stipulating "the right of women to vote and be elected shall not be denied or abridged on account of sex."[72] As they had five years earlier, the delegates approved some but not all of the measures the IACW sought. The "Lima Declaration in favor of Women's Rights" declared "that women have the right . . . to political treatment on the basis of equality with men, [and] to the enjoyment of equality as to civil status." So far Stevens was happy, but the statement went on to declare women's right "to full protection in and opportunity for work, [and] to the most ample protection as mothers."[73]

The last two clauses were evidence of the powerful influence that social feminists in the United States still wielded over the issue of equal rights. Before the conference resolutions had been officially proposed, word reached the office of the League of Women Voters in Washington that the IACW recommendations included equal political and civil rights for women. LWV members, along with women from the Women's Trade Union League and other protectionist organizations, flooded Secretary Hull's office with letters and telegrams opposing the adoption of such recommendations.[74] Whether the United States would have supported full equality for women on IACW terms is doubtful, but the social feminists' influence did not stop with the declaration. Although the commission itself was made in Lima a permanent body of the Pan American Union, Stevens was effectively ousted as chair. She had gained a significant measure of support for women's political and civil status, but lost her own position in the process.[75]

Between the two major inter-American conferences in 1936 and 1938, the Good Neighbor Policy was put to a significant test in Mexico with Cárdenas's decision to nationalize the Mexican oil industry. Whereas the YWCA remained interested but noncommittal, the U.S. section of WILPF was more sympathetic to Mexico's economic plight. Having spent most of the 1920s protesting U.S. economic imperialism in Central America and the Caribbean Basin, WILPF was alarmed at the possibility of a return to the contentious climate of the 1920s. But although the exertions of various members in defense of Mexico's right to control its own natural resources underscored WILPF's opposition to economic imperialism, by 1938 it was too late to save the Mexican section. The IACW focus on the Equal Nationality and Equal Rights Treaties, meanwhile, paid off in Lima. Since 1923, when the demand for female delegates first appeared as a resolution at the

Fifth Conference in Santiago, U.S. women had been an integral part of the effort both to secure equal rights for women and to ensure peace throughout the Americas. Fifteen years later, they had helped to secure major statements of support for equal nationality as well as women's civil and political rights, and a permanent place for women within the Pan American Union. As the first official intergovernmental organization dedicated to women's advocacy, the IACW set a precedent that future international bodies would have no choice but to follow. They did it without the help, however, of Margarita Robles de Mendoza or any other Mexican representatives. While Stevens retained an active interest in the progress of the women's suffrage battle in Mexico, the IACW does not seem to have received any support from Mexican women for its work in Lima.

The year 1939 was a critical one for both U.S. women internationalists and Mexican women. The beginning of World War II in September changed the global landscape irrevocably, and for most of the war years inter-American women's cooperation either ceased altogether or focused exclusively on the war in Europe and the Pacific. After supporting Franklin Roosevelt's public stance on neutrality for most of the 1930s, and protesting any U.S. involvement between 1939 and 1941, members of WILPF and other U.S. women peace activists accepted the U.S. declaration of war in December 1941 with regret, and focused on rebuilding their agendas as soon as the war was over.[76] In the Western Hemisphere, the solidarity evoked by the Good Neighbor Policy became more strategically important than ever in 1939. The outbreak of war in Europe gave both the United States and Mexico a strong impetus to resolve the issue of oil expropriations. Cárdenas, who knew the Roosevelt administration feared the potential for Nazi influence in Mexico, used the threat of a German alliance to force the U.S. government to agree to compensation for the land and oil the major companies had lost. Roosevelt, whose relationship with the oil companies was never as close as Calvin Coolidge's had been, accepted, and the issue was largely resolved by 1941.[77]

The work of the IACW, the U.S. section of the WILPF, and the YWCA in Mexico had either dissipated or changed dramatically by 1939. By the time World War II started, the WILPF section in Mexico City had collapsed, and showed no signs of imminent revival. Membership levels were holding steady in the Mexican YWCA, but the approach of the U.S. Foreign Division to international work was already changing by the time the outbreak of war demanded their resources in Europe and Asia. Over the course of the 1940s, the U.S. YWCA shifted away from starting new associations in foreign countries, choosing to leave that work exclusively to the World YWCA. The Foreign Division focused instead on offering support to fledging or struggling associations "as comrades in a world organization. . . . The old idea had been to send and receive; the new was to cooperate."[78] The U.S. association continued to support the Mexican association under this new policy, but took a less and less active role in maintaining it between 1940 and the mid-1950s, when Mexico formally joined the World YWCA.

The IACW underwent a tectonic shift in 1939. When it was made permanent at Lima, all countries were asked to appoint commissioners. Implicit in the request was the expectation that each country would name the woman already serving as commissioner.[79] But under pressure from U.S. women who opposed Doris Stevens, the National Woman's Party, and the Equal Rights Amendment, Franklin Roosevelt appointed Mary Winslow as U.S. commissioner. Winslow was an outspoken supporter of protective labor legislation for women. Stevens's supporters in the United States immediately rallied to her defense, forming the Doris Stevens Membership Committee to protest her removal. They argued her replacement had been illegal, and accused First Lady Eleanor Roosevelt and Secretary of Labor Frances Perkins of intervening on behalf of the League of Women Voters and other protectionist organizations. Elinor Byrns, original founder of the Women's Peace Society, condemned the "obvious effort to transform the commission into a welfare agency."[80] Roosevelt and Perkins denied the charges, though neither was sorry to see Stevens go.[81] Latin American women, for their part, were grateful for the work Stevens had done over the previous ten years, but they also favored rotating the position of chair among other nations to avoid U.S. dominance of the commission. One unqualified letter of support came from Robles de Mendoza in Mexico, who wrote to Stevens offering her sympathy and support.[82] Many U.S. women hoped Winslow would be able to exercise the same degree of control over the commission that Stevens had, but the Pan American Union, heeding the wishes of Latin American members, named an Argentinean woman as chair in November 1939 and moved the commission's headquarters to Buenos Aires.[83]

As U.S. women's internationalist efforts in Mexico faltered, Mexican feminists themselves suffered a major setback. Led by the FUPDM, organized Mexican women continued to agitate for greater participation in the political machinery of their country, especially through the ballot. Cárdenas initially seemed receptive to the idea. In September 1937 he called on the Mexican Congress to amend the 1917 Constitution to provide for women's suffrage. The amendment passed both houses of Congress, and by November 1938 it had been ratified by the requisite majority of states. Congressional leaders, however, adjourned without publishing the amendment in the congressional record, effectively exploiting a procedural loophole to avoid legalizing women's suffrage.[84] The historical record remains "eerily silent" on the reasons for Congress's failure to publish the amendment.[85] The argument at the time, that women were more likely to support conservative political candidates, thereby jeopardizing the ruling party's status, rings hollow, since by 1939 the Mexican Revolutionary Party (formerly the National Revolutionary Party) was already drifting rightward. Mexican women did not win the right to vote at the national level until 1953.[86]

Though it might be reasonable to assume that after over two decades of involvement in Mexico—to say nothing of a seven-decade suffrage battle of their own—U.S. women played some part in the Mexican women's suffrage movement, that was in fact not the case. U.S. women played no direct role in Mexican women's campaign for the ballot in the late 1930s, and there is little evidence that many U.S. women even knew much about it. Stevens and other members of the IACW were aware of it, but after 1937 it was not a central concern for the commission as a whole. Anna Kelton Wiley's visit to Mexico City was the only such visit by a U.S. woman who had worked extensively for women's suffrage in the United States. In this respect the battle for the ballot in Mexico was not only nationalist in ideology, but national in scope. U.S. women internationalists had little to do with it.

Overall, U.S. women's internationalism in Mexico grew less imperialistic in tone and approach over the course of the 1930s—the IACW efforts on behalf of Mexican suffrage notwithstanding. Both the United States and Mexico signed the Equal Nationality Treaty, protecting the rights of women who married husbands of a different nationality. Heloise Brainerd almost singlehandedly revived the WILPF inter-American project. Her visit to Mexico City in 1936 set a much more friendly and cooperative tone than the visits of other members such as Ellen Starr Brinton in the early 1930s. Most important perhaps, for the first time since 1916 U.S. women internationalists were no longer hampered by interventionist U.S. policies in Latin America. They took advantage of improved U.S.-Latin American relations after 1928 to establish more genuine connections with Latin American women than they had been able to do in the 1910s and 1920s.

But although the Good Neighbor Policy served its purpose in presenting a unified face against German and Japanese influence, it could not make U.S. and Mexican women better neighbors. The impact of the policy was lessened in Mexico by political changes, and the resurgence of revolutionary nationalism under Lázaro Cárdenas revived resentment of U.S. policies, particularly concerning oil. U.S. women, even members of anti-imperialist peace organizations such as WILPF, were still tainted by their own national affiliations. The one organization that could be considered a success during this period, the Mexican YWCA, had withdrawn almost completely from any political discussion or activism. Both WILPF and the IACW struggled, as had other women internationalists before them, to adapt their programs and goals in ways that resonated with Mexican women. The commission in particular, because it operated throughout the 1930s according to the equal rights model of the National Woman's Party, focusing almost exclusively on legal reform to achieve its goals, found little sympathy for its agenda beyond the Mexican commissioner Robles de Mendoza. By the time World War II erupted in Europe, demanding the full attention of internationalists everywhere, little remained of over two decades' worth of work in Mexico.

U.S. women originally became internationalists in order to promote peace and hemispheric cooperation by forging gendered ties with women in other countries. Their vision was based on notions of a universal womanhood exempt from politics, a "spiritual" connection they shared with women around the globe. Over the course of their interactions with Mexican women in the 1920s and 1930s, U.S. women learned to play politics, to harness and adapt to broader changes and sentiments within the U.S. government and between the U.S. and Mexico. By the late 1930s, when the stakes of playing politics heightened, they were good at it. Their successes did not come in time to preserve their internationalist programs in Mexico, which had largely disintegrated by the time World War II broke out in 1939. But the newly politicized internationalism reflected much more closely the changes in women's international and transnational activism that would come after 1945.

Epilogue

The image on the cover of this book is from a mural by Diego Rivera entitled "Marriage of the Artistic Expression of the North and South on This Continent" but more commonly known as "Pan American Unity." Commissioned for the 1940 Golden Gate International Exposition in San Francisco, it is one of the largest murals Rivera ever created, twenty-two feet high and seventy-four feet across. This section of the mural shows Helen Crlenkovich, a diver from the City College of San Francisco, suspended above a crowd of onlookers and an artisan carving the image of Quetzalcoatl, the plumed serpent frequently used by Mexican muralists as a representation of pre-Hispanic indigenous culture and identity. Rivera's principal themes in the mural centered on the blending of art and industry. Of this panel in particular, he wrote, "The conquest of time and space was symbolized by a woman diving and the Golden Gate Bridge spanning San Francisco Bay."[1] Though neither Rivera nor his wife, Frida Kahlo, plays a part in this story, most U.S. women internationalists would have been aware of their art and their transnational careers.[2] The "marriage" Rivera evoked in this entire mural was a true blending, a meeting of equals, not simply a new iteration of U.S. dominance over Mexico and Latin America. In 1940 it stood in marked contrast to the state of inter-American cooperation among women.

This story is more about failure than about success. It is more about obstacles than about overcoming them. By 1939 there were not many more institutional and organizational connections between U.S. and Mexican women than there had been in 1915. Many of the groups formed in Mexico City during this period either were no longer in existence by the time World War II started or died out shortly thereafter. Some of these internationalist initiatives did record significant achievements. The Pan American Conference of Women was the largest hemispheric gathering of women at that time. Doris Stevens and the Inter-American Commission helped secure the right of married women in the United States and Mexico to retain their nationality. But accomplishments like these were rare, and many of them proved ephemeral. Ultimately, U.S. women internationalists were their own worst enemy. Their imperialistic approaches to both internationalism and feminism served neither cause. Their conviction of the superiority of their own ideas and methods, and their lack of knowledge about Mexican nationalism and feminism, hindered their attempts to establish lasting connections with Mexican women. U.S. women assumed that the bonds of gender would prove stronger in the end than the bonds of nation. When they were proved wrong, U.S. women were at a loss.

As disheartening as it may be at times, this is still an important story to tell. Failure is illuminating. The ways U.S. women internationalists tried to organize Mexican women reveal how they thought about themselves as citizens of the world. Most saw themselves as first among equals, ready to teach and to guide Mexican women down whatever path U.S. women thought they should take. Even as their methods grew more politically sophisticated, U.S. women still assumed that Mexicans both needed and wanted their help. But that confidence in their experience and sense of superiority limited their effectiveness. Conversely, the limitations of U.S. women's internationalism in Mexico reveal the strength and vitality of the feminist movement in Latin America. Mexican women had their own agendas and desires; they were not blank slates on which U.S. women could write. Many of their goals may have been similar to U.S. women's: suffrage, economic equality, access to education and health care, and so forth. But though they may have appreciated guidance on occasion, they were determined to follow their own paths to advancement.

Not all the larger organizations examined here survived the upheaval of World War II. Both the Pan American International Women's Committee and the Pan American Association for the Advancement of Women were defunct by the late 1920s, due primarily to a lack of interest, leadership, and resources. Carrie Chapman Catt's National Committee on the Cause and Cure of War held annual conferences until 1941. The committee was reorganized twice over the next four years, but after Catt's death in 1947 it disbanded completely.[3] The National Council for the Prevention of War held out slightly longer. Frederick Libby, who had formed the organization in 1921, essentially became the organization by 1945. He had thrown all his efforts into keeping the United States neutral, and struggled to maintain morale within the council after Pearl Harbor. After his retirement in 1954, the group slowly dissolved.[4]

World War II had a significant impact on women's internationalism and on many of the organizations that did survive it, including the League of Women Voters, the Women's International League for Peace and Freedom, the Young Women's Christian Association, and the Inter-American Commission of Women. The outbreak of war in 1939, and U.S. entry into it two years later, discouraged and depleted many women's peace organizations like WILPF, but they regrouped and dove eagerly into the work of postwar reconstruction. Noticeably, however, many postwar efforts of women internationalists reanimated old patterns of imperialist internationalism and feminism. The LWV, for example, took part in cooperative efforts between the U.S. government and voluntary organizations to promote democracy and "the American way of life" in wartorn Europe, especially what became West Germany.[5] Other women were active in Japan, which the United States occupied from 1945 to 1952. Women involved in reconstruction efforts in Japan sought to "liberate" Japanese women by implementing a feminist agenda modeled on that of the National Woman's Party. Particularly in light of entrenched U.S. stereotypes of Asia dating back to the war in the Philippines, Mire Koikari argues, "it comes as no surprise that the two major gender reforms—women's suffrage and an Equal Rights Amendment in the new constitution—were granted to Japan with little involvement of the Japanese themselves."[6] The onset of the Cold War also drew U.S. women into the international arena, both as anticommunist activists and as "Cold Warriors." WILPF and the IACW were especially targeted as communist sympathizers for their peace work and their campaigns against nuclear weapons.[7]

The primary focal point for women's international nongovernmental organizations in the postwar period, and especially after 1970, was the United Nations. Women and women's NGOs played integral roles in developing the UN Declaration on Human Rights in 1948, and in securing the establishment of the UN Commission on the Status of Women. But the UN's biggest contribution came with the declaration of International Women's Year in 1975, the Decade for Women from 1975 to 1985, and the four major Conferences on Women in Mexico City (1975), Copenhagen (1980), Nairobi (1985), and Beijing (1995). Together these efforts helped institutionalize attention to women and to questions of political, economic, and social equity and justice on a global scale. The conferences in particular, and the NGO forums that accompanied them, also presented opportunities for women from around the world to interact and mobilize. In many ways the UN forums—and the conflicts they engendered—helped give rise to what have become truly transnational feminist movements, to cooperative efforts among women from different nations that are not dominated by one group or another, or by one nation or another. The UN, in turn, is able to exert pressure on governments to enact and enforce legislation, making it, in Margaret Snyder's words, the "unlikely godmother" of the global women's movement.[8]

But the UN has also been a site of tension and conflict as well as opportunity for transnational solidarity. Charges of imperialist feminism reverberated throughout the years of decolonization and independence in the 1940s, 1950s, and 1960s, and grew even stronger amid the clashes surrounding the UN Decade for Women and the UN conferences in Mexico City, Copenhagen, and Nairobi. Dominated initially by "Western" women, the UN conferences focused disproportionately on their concerns, such as economic opportunity, access to democratic politics, freedom from sexual harassment, gay rights, and equality. Women from the "Third World" challenged the dominant assumptions of "Western" women that essentialized all women, erased differences among them, and privileged the voices and experiences of the few over the many. They demanded room on the UN agendas for issues such as easing the transition from subsistence agriculture to agribusiness, combating the spread of epidemic disease, and dealing with the impact of civil wars and political instability. These conflicts have been fruitful as well as difficult; transnational feminist movements today encompass broad efforts to claim and protect women's human rights, to promote equity and justice in all aspects of life, and to secure global peace.[9]

The tensions between U.S. women's internationalist ideals and Mexican women's nationalist aspirations thus not only mirrored encounters between other Euro-American women and non-"Western" women in the nineteenth and early twentieth centuries, but foreshadowed those that came after 1945. The tendency of U.S. women toward imperialist internationalism and feminism was not unique to the interwar period. It began amid the height of European colonialism and the formation of the first international women's organizations in the nineteenth century. It continued into the period of postwar reconstruction in Germany and Japan. I can only hope that it culminated in the conflicts that grew from the UN conferences, and that the story of the future will be the growth and development of additional transnationalist feminist initiatives.

Notes

Introduction

1. Ellen Starr Brinton, "Co-operation Between U.S. and Mexican W.I.L.," August 18, 1931, Series C, Box 12, Folder 24, Women's International League for Peace and Freedom Records, United States Section (WILPF U.S. Records), Swarthmore College Peace Collection, Swarthmore, Pennsylvania (SCPC) (emphases in original). The word Brinton heard but did not understand was probably *estadounidenses*, or "United Statesians."

2. Leila J. Rupp, *Worlds of Women: The Making of an International Women's Movement* (Princeton, N.J: Princeton University Press, 1997).

3. Rupp, *Worlds of Women*. On the period roughly between 1870 and 1945, see also Patricia Ward D'Itri, *Cross Currents in the International Women's Movement, 1848–1948* (Bowling Green, Ohio: Bowling Green State University Popular Press, 1999); Mrinalini Sinha, Donna J. Guy, and Angela Woollacott, eds., *Feminisms and Internationalism* (Oxford: Blackwell, 1999); Caroline Daley and Melanie Nolan, eds., *Suffrage and Beyond: International Feminist Perspectives* (New York: New York University Press, 1994); Pernilla Jonsson, Silke Neunsinger, and Joan Sangster, eds., *Crossing Boundaries: Women's Organizing in Europe and the Americas, 1880s–1940s* (Uppsala: Uppsala Universitet, 2007); Ellen Carol DuBois and Katie Oliviero, eds., special issue of *Women's Studies International Forum* 32, 1 (January 2009); Karen Garner, *Shaping a Global Women's Agenda: Women's NGOs and Global Governance, 1925–85* (Manchester: Manchester University Press, 2010); Kimberly Jensen and Erika Kuhlman, eds., *Women and Transnational Activism in Historical Perspective* (Dordrecht: Republic of Letters, 2010); Karen Offen, ed., *Globalizing Feminisms, 1789–1945* (London: Routledge, 2010); Ann Taylor Allen, Anne Cova, and June Purvis, eds., special issue of *Women's History Review* 19, 4 (September 2010).

4. Rupp, *Worlds of Women*, 108.

5. For recent perspectives on Wilsonian internationalism, see John Milton Cooper, ed., *Reconsidering Woodrow Wilson: Progressivism, Internationalism, War, and Peace* (Washington, D.C.: Woodrow Wilson Center Press, 2008).

6. Akira Iriye, *Global Community: The Role of International Organizations in the Making of the Contemporary World* (Berkeley: University of California Press, 2002), 9–10. See also Iriye, *Cultural Internationalism and World Order* (Baltimore: Johns

Hopkins University Press, 1997); Frank A. Ninkovich, *Global Dawn: The Cultural Foundation of American Internationalism, 1865–1890* (Cambridge, Mass: Harvard University Press, 2009).

7. Iriye, *Global Community*, 9–10.

8. Ian Tyrrell, *Reforming the World: The Creation of America's Moral Empire* (Princeton, N.J.: Princeton University Press, 2010), 6–7; see also Ian Tyrrell, "Reflections on the Transnational Turn in United States History: Theory and Practice," *Journal of Global History* 4, 3 (November 2009): 453–74; "AHR Conversation: On Transnational History," *American Historical Review* 111, 5 (December 2006): 1440–64; several relevant entries in Akira Iriye and Pierre-Yves Saunier, eds., *The Palgrave Dictionary of Transnational History* (Basingstoke: Palgrave Macmillan, 2009).

9. Ellen Carol DuBois and Katie Oliviero, "Circling the Globe: International Feminism Reconsidered, 1920 to 1975," *Women's Studies International Forum* 32, 1 (2009): 1.

10. Kimberly Jensen, Erika Kuhlman, and I made similar distinctions in 2010. See Jensen and Kuhlman, "Introduction," and Megan Threlkeld, "How to 'Make This Pan American Thing Go?' Interwar Debates on U.S. Women's Activism in the Western Hemisphere," in Jensen and Kuhlman, *Women and Transnational Activism in Historical Perspective*, 1–2, 173–74.

11. Jane Addams, "Toward Internationalism," in *Report on the Women's Auxiliary Conference, held in the city of Washington, D.C., in connection with The Second Pan American Scientific Congress, December 28, 1915–January 7, 1916*, ed. Emma Bain Swiggett (Washington, D.C.: Government Printing Office, 1916), 59–60.

12. International Congress of Women, *Report: International Congress of Women, The Hague, 28th April–May 1st, 1915* (Amsterdam: Internationales Frauenkomitee für dauernden Frieden, 1915), 225; see also Nitza Berkovitch, *From Motherhood to Citizenship: Women's Rights and International Organizations* (Baltimore: Johns Hopkins University Press, 1999); Seth Koven and Sonya Michel, eds., *Mothers of a New World: Maternalist Politics and the Origins of Welfare States* (New York: Routledge, 1993).

13. Not all the women or organizations considered here supported women's rights, which is why I do not use the term "feminist" to characterize these internationalists as a whole.

14. See, for example, Erez Manela, *The Wilsonian Moment: Self-Determination and the International Origins of Anticolonial Nationalism* (New York: Oxford University Press, 2007).

15. Deborah J. Baldwin, *Protestants and the Mexican Revolution: Missionaries, Ministers, and Social Change* (Urbana: University of Illinois Press, 1990).

16. Bonnie Anderson, *Joyous Greetings: The First International Women's Movement, 1830–1860* (Oxford: Oxford University Press, 2000); Margaret McFadden, *Golden Cables of Sympathy: The Transatlantic Sources of Nineteenth-Century Feminism* (Lexington: University Press of Kentucky, 1999).

17. Rupp, *Worlds of Women*; Ian Tyrrell, *Woman's World/Woman's Empire: The Woman's Christian Temperance Union in International Perspective, 1880–1930* (Chapel Hill: University of North Carolina Press, 1991); Harriet Hyman Alonso, *Peace as a Women's Issue: A History of the U.S. Movement for World Peace and Women's Rights* (Syracuse, N.Y.: Syracuse University Press, 1993).

18. On mobilization during World War I, see Frances H. Early, *A World Without War: How U.S. Feminists and Pacifists Resisted World War I* (Syracuse, N.Y.: Syracuse University Press, 1997); David S. Patterson, *The Search for Negotiated Peace: Women's Activism and Citizen Diplomacy in World War I* (New York: Routledge, 2008).

19. International Congress of Women, *Report*, 19.

20. Tyrrell, *Woman's World/Woman's Empire*. See also Jane Hunter, *The Gospel of Gentility: American Women Missionaries in Turn-of-the-Century China* (New Haven, Conn.: Yale University Press, 1984); Patricia Hill, *The World Their Household: The American Woman's Foreign Mission Movement and Cultural Transformation, 1870–1920* (Ann Arbor: University of Michigan Press, 1985).

21. On this phenomenon among women from the United States, see Louise Michele Newman, *White Women's Rights: The Racial Origins of Feminism in the United States* (New York: Oxford University Press, 1999); Tracey Jean Boisseau, *White Queen: May French-Sheldon and the Imperial Origins of American Feminist Identity* (Bloomington: Indiana University Press, 2004); Nancie Caraway, *Segregated Sisterhood: Racism and the Politics of American Feminism* (Knoxville: University of Tennessee Press, 1991); Ruth Frankenberg, *White Women, Race Matters: The Social Construction of Whiteness* (Minneapolis: University of Minnesota Press, 1993). Many scholars have also examined this dynamic among European women. See Nupur Chaudhuri and Margaret Strobel, eds., *Western Women and Imperialism: Complicity and Resistance* (Bloomington: Indiana University Press, 1992); Antoinette M. Burton, *Burdens of History: British Feminists, Indian Women, and Imperial Culture, 1865–1915* (Chapel Hill: University of North Carolina Press, 1994); Kumari Jayawardena, *The White Woman's Other Burden: Western Women and South Asia During British Colonial Rule* (New York: Routledge, 1995); Vron Ware, *Beyond the Pale: White Women, Racism, and History* (London: Verso, 1992); Jane Haggis, "White Women and Colonialism: Towards a Non-Recuperative History," in *Gender and Imperialism*, ed. Clare Midgley (Manchester: Manchester University Press, 1998), 45–78.

22. Joyce Zonana originally coined the term "feminist orientalism" in "The Sultan and the Slave: Feminist Orientalism and the Structure of 'Jane Eyre,'" *Signs* 18, 3 (Spring 1993): 592–617. See also Charlotte Weber, "Unveiling Scheherazade: Feminist Orientalism in the International Alliance of Women, 1911–1950," *Feminist Studies* 27, 1 (Spring 2001): 125–57. On imperial feminism, see especially Leila Rupp, "Challenging Imperialism in International Women's Organizations, 1888–1945," *NWSA Journal* 8, 1 (April 1, 1996): 8–27; also Chaudhuri and Strobel, *Western Women and Imperialism*; Valerie Amos and Pratibha Parmar, "Challenging Imperial Feminism," *Feminist Review* 17 (Autumn 1984): 3–19; Chandra Talpade Mohanty, "Under Western Eyes:

Feminist Scholarship and Colonial Discourses," *Feminist Review* 30 (Autumn 1988): 61–88.

23. Leila Rupp has used this phrase as well, while sociologist Nitza Berkovitch uses the term "colonial-style internationalism." Rupp, "Challenging Imperialism," 9; Berkovitch, *From Motherhood to Citizenship*, 19.

24. Progressive U.S. senators like William Borah, Lynn Frazier, and Gerald Nye worked closely with the U.S. Section of WILPF and often championed WILPF causes in Congress. See Robert Johnson, *The Peace Progressives and American Foreign Relations* (Cambridge, Mass.: Harvard University Press, 1995); Alonso, *Peace as a Women's Issue*.

25. Rupp, "Challenging Imperialism."

26. On this phenomenon outside the Western Hemisphere during the first decades of the twentieth century, see Weber, "Unveiling Scheherazade"; Rumi Yasutake, *Transnational Women's Activism: The United States, Japan, and Japanese Immigrant Communities in California, 1859–1920* (New York: New York University Press, 2004); Fiona Paisley, *Glamour in the Pacific: Cultural Internationalism and Race Politics in the Women's Pan-Pacific* (Honolulu: University of Hawai'i Press, 2009); Mina Roces and Louise P. Edwards, eds., *Women's Movements in Asia: Feminisms and Transnational Activism* (New York: Routledge, 2010); Elizabeth Littell-Lamb, "Caught in the Crossfire: Women's Internationalism and the YWCA Child Labor Campaign in Shanghai, 1921–1925," *Frontiers: A Journal of Women's Studies* 32, 3 (2011): 134–66; Motoe Sasaki, "American New Women Encountering China: The Politics of Temporality and Paradoxes of Imperialism, 1898–1927," *Journal of Colonialism & Colonial History* 10, 1 (Spring 2009).

27. Mark T. Gilderhus, *Pan American Visions: Woodrow Wilson in the Western Hemisphere, 1913–1921* (Tucson: University of Arizona Press, 1986), x.

28. See David Sheinin, ed., *Beyond the Ideal: Pan Americanism in Inter-American Affairs* (Westport, Conn: Praeger, 2000).

29. Emily S. Rosenberg, *Financial Missionaries to the World: The Politics and Culture of Dollar Diplomacy, 1900–1930* (Cambridge, Mass: Harvard University Press, 1999); Benjamin T. Harrison, *Dollar Diplomat: Chandler Anderson and American Diplomacy in Mexico and Nicaragua, 1913–1928* (Pullman: Washington State University Press, 1988). For good general surveys of U.S. foreign relations during this period, see Emily Rosenberg, *Spreading the American Dream: American Economic and Cultural Expansion, 1890–1945* (New York: Hill and Wang, 1982); Akira Iriye, *The Globalizing of America, 1913–1945*, vol. 3 of *The Cambridge History of American Foreign Relations*, ed. Warren I. Cohen (New York: Cambridge University Press, 1993); Warren I. Cohen, *Empire Without Tears: American Foreign Relations, 1921–1933* (Philadelphia: Temple University Press, 1987); Thomas O'Brien, *The Revolutionary Mission: American Enterprise in Latin America, 1900–1945* (Cambridge: Cambridge University Press, 1996).

30. K. Lynn Stoner, "'In Four Languages But with One Voice': Division and Solidarity Within Pan American Feminism, 1923–1933," in Sheinin, *Beyond the Ideal*,

80. Francesca Miller, Donna Guy, and others have also highlighted the constructive possibilities of hemispheric cooperation. See Francesca Miller, "The International Relations of Women of the Americas, 1890–1928," *Américas* 43, 2 (1986): 171–82; Donna J. Guy, "The Politics of Pan-American Cooperation: Maternalist Feminism and the Child Rights Movement, 1913–1960," *Gender & History* 10, 3 (November 1998): 449–69; E. Sue Wamsley, "Constructing Feminism Across Borders: The Pan American Women's Movements and the Founding of the Inter-American Commission of Women," in Jonsson, Neunsinger, and Sangster, *Crossing Boundaries*, 51–71; Ellen DuBois and Lauren Derby, "The Strange Case of Minerva Bernardino: Pan American and United Nations Women's Rights Activist," *Women's Studies International Forum* 32, 1 (2009): 43–50.

31. See Amy Kaplan and Donald E. Pease, eds., *Cultures of United States Imperialism* (Durham, N.C.: Duke University Press, 1993); Gilbert M. Joseph, Catherine LeGrand, and Ricardo Donato Salvatore, eds., *Close Encounters of Empire: Writing the Cultural History of U.S.-Latin American Relations* (Durham, N.C.: Duke University Press, 1998). To compare U.S. imperialism in Puerto Rico and Haiti, see Eileen J. Suárez Findlay, *Imposing Decency: The Politics of Sexuality and Race in Puerto Rico, 1870–1920* (Durham, N.C.: Duke University Press, 1999); Laura Briggs, *Reproducing Empire: Race, Sex, Science, and U.S. Imperialism in Puerto Rico* (Berkeley: University of California Press, 2002); Mary A. Renda, *Taking Haiti: Military Occupation and the Culture of U.S. Imperialism, 1915–1940* (Chapel Hill: University of North Carolina Press, 2001).

32. Rosalyn Terborg-Penn, "Enfranchising Women of Color: Woman Suffragists as Agents of Imperialism," in *Nation, Empire, Colony: Historicizing Gender and Race*, ed. Ruth Roach Pierson and Nupur Chaudhuri (Bloomington: Indiana University Press, 1998), 41–56; Gladys M. Jiménez-Muñoz, "Deconstructing Colonialist Discourse: Links Between the Women's Suffrage Movement in the United States and Puerto Rico," *Phoebe: An Interdisciplinary Journal of Feminist Scholarship, Theory, and Aesthetics* 5 (Spring 1993): 9–34; Kristin Hoganson, "'As Badly Off as the Filipinos': U.S. Women's Suffragists and the Imperial Issue at the Turn of the Twentieth Century," *Journal of Women's History* 13, 2 (2001): 9–33; Allison Sneider, *Suffragists in an Imperial Age: U.S. Expansion and the Woman Question, 1870–1929* (New York: Oxford University Press, 2008).

33. See Terborg-Penn, "Enfranchising Women of Color"; Christine Ehrick, "Madrinas and Missionaries: Uruguay and the Pan-American Women's Movement," *Gender & History* 10, 3 (November 1998): 406–24; Corinne A. Pernet, "Chilean Feminists, the International Women's Movement, and Suffrage, 1915–1950," *Pacific Historical Review* 69, 4 (November 2000): 663–88.

34. Ehrick, "Madrinas and Missionaries," 419.

35. Jean Meyer, "Mexico: Revolution and Reconstruction in the 1920s," in *Mexico Since Independence*, ed. Leslie Bethell (Cambridge: Cambridge University Press, 1991), 8.

36. John M. Hart, *Empire and Revolution: The Americans in Mexico Since the Civil War* (Berkeley: University of California Press, 2002), 260; Alan Knight, *U.S.-Mexican Relations, 1910–1940: An Interpretation* (La Jolla: University of California, San Diego, 1987), 21. See also Josefina Zoraida Vázquez and Lorenzo Meyer, *The United States and Mexico* (Chicago: University of Chicago Press, 1985).

37. For a good overview, see Michael Gonzales, *The Mexican Revolution, 1910–1940* (Albuquerque: University of New Mexico Press, 2002). See also John Mason Hart, *Revolutionary Mexico: The Coming and Progress of the Mexican Revolution* (Berkeley: University of California Press, 1987); Alan Knight, *The Mexican Revolution* (Cambridge: Cambridge University Press, 1986); Thomas Benjamin, *La Revolución: Mexico's Great Revolution as Memory, Myth, and History* (Austin: University of Texas Press, 2000); Mary Kay Vaughan and Stephen E. Lewis, *The Eagle and the Virgin: Nation and Cultural Revolution in Mexico, 1920–1940* (Durham, N.C.: Duke University Press, 2006).

38. For an introduction to U.S.-Mexican relations during the Revolution, see Lorenzo Meyer, *Mexico and the United States in the Oil Controversy, 1917–1942* (Austin: University of Texas Press, 1977); Friedrich Katz, *The Secret War in Mexico: Europe, the United States, and the Mexican Revolution* (Chicago: University of Chicago Press, 1981); Daniela Spenser, *The Impossible Triangle: Mexico, Soviet Russia, and the United States in the 1920s* (Durham, N.C.: Duke University Press, 1999); Robert Freeman Smith, *The United States and Revolutionary Nationalism in Mexico, 1916–1932* (Chicago: University of Chicago Press, 1972); Linda B. Hall, *Oil, Banks, and Politics: The United States and Postrevolutionary Mexico, 1917–1924* (Austin: University of Texas Press, 1995); Mark T. Gilderhus, *Diplomacy and Revolution: U.S.-Mexican Relations under Wilson and Carranza* (Tucson: University of Arizona Press, 1977); Gilbert M. Joseph, *Revolution from Without: Yucatan, Mexico, and the United States, 1880–1924* (Cambridge: Cambridge University Press, 1982); Daniel Nugent, ed., *Rural Revolt in Mexico: U.S. Intervention and the Domain of Subaltern Politics* (Durham, N.C.: Duke University Press, 1998); Julie Moreno, *Yankee Don't Go Home! Mexican Nationalism, American Business Culture, and the Shaping of Modern Mexico, 1920–1950* (Chapel Hill: University of North Carolina Press, 2003). On U.S. Americans' cultural perceptions of Mexico, see Helen Delpar, *The Enormous Vogue of Things Mexican: Cultural Relations Between the United States and Mexico, 1920–1935* (Tuscaloosa: University of Alabama Press, 1992); Allen L. Woll, *The Latin Image in American Film* (Los Angeles: UCLA Latin American Publications, 1980); Molly M. Wood, "A Diplomat's Wife in Mexico: Creating Professional, Political, and National Identities in the Early Twentieth Century," *Frontiers: A Journal of Women's Studies* 25, 3 (2004): 104–33.

39. On the emergence of Mexican feminism, see Anna Macías, *Against All Odds: The Feminist Movement in Mexico to 1940* (Westport, Conn.: Greenwood Press, 1982); Shirlene Ann Soto, *Emergence of the Modern Mexican Woman: Her Participation in the Revolution and Struggle for Equality, 1910–1940* (Denver: Arden Press, 1990); Gabriela Cano, "The Porfiriato and the Mexican Revolution: Constructions of Feminism and

Nationalism," in Pierson and Chaudhuri, *Nation, Empire, Colony*, 106–20; Jocelyn Olcott, *Revolutionary Women in Postrevolutionary Mexico* (Durham, N.C.: Duke University Press, 2005); Gabriela Cano, "Revolución, Feminismo, y Ciudadanía en México (1915–1940)," in *Historia de las mujeres en occidente*, ed. Georges Duby and Michelle Perrot (Madrid: Taurus, 1993), 685–95; Jocelyn Olcott, Mary K. Vaughan, and Gabriela Cano, eds., *Sex in Revolution: Gender, Politics, and Power in Modern Mexico* (Durham, N.C.: Duke University Press, 2006); Stephanie Mitchell and Patience A. Schell, eds., *The Women's Revolution in Mexico, 1910–1953* (Lanham, Md.: Rowman & Littlefield, 2007); Sarah Anne Buck, "Activists and Mothers: Feminist and Maternalist Politics in Mexico, 1923–1953," Ph.D. dissertation, Rutgers University, 2002; Stephanie J. Smith, *Gender and the Mexican Revolution: Yucatán Women and the Realities of Patriarchy* (Chapel Hill: University of North Carolina Press, 2009). For important comparisons to the emergence of feminism elsewhere in Latin America during the same period, see K. Lynn Stoner, *From the House to the Streets: The Cuban Woman's Movement for Legal Reform, 1898–1940* (Durham, N.C.: Duke University Press, 1991); Asunción Lavrin, *Women, Feminism, and Social Change in Argentina, Chile, and Uruguay, 1890–1940* (Lincoln: University of Nebraska Press, 1995); Donna Guy, *Women Build the Welfare State: Performing Charity and Creating Rights in Argentina, 1880–1955* (Durham, N.C.: Duke University Press, 2009); Christine Ehrick, *The Shield of the Weak: Feminism and the State in Uruguay, 1903–1933* (Albuquerque: University of New Mexico Press, 2005); June Edith Hahner, *Emancipating the Female Sex: The Struggle for Women's Rights in Brazil, 1850–1940* (Durham, N.C.: Duke University Press, 1990).

Chapter 1. The Best Kind of Internationalism

1. Addams, "Toward Internationalism," 59–60 (emphasis mine). On Addams's critiques of traditional internationalism, see Addams, *Newer Ideals of Peace* (London: Macmillan, 1907); Kathryn Kish Sklar, "'Some of Us Who Deal with the Social Fabric': Jane Addams Blends Peace and Social Justice, 1907–1919" *Journal of the Gilded Age and Progressive Era* 2, 1 (January 2003): 80–96. Addams's conception of human internationalism is reminiscent of what Beth Kraig has called "the activism of 'little interactions.'" Beth Kraig, "The Activism of 'Little Interactions': A Historical Case Study," *Peace & Change* 37, 1 (January 2012): 37–63.

2. Patterson, *The Search for Negotiated Peace*, 6.

3. Quoted in Patterson, *The Search for Negotiated Peace*, 6. Ironically, Addams and Butler shared the Nobel Prize for Peace in 1931.

4. Sklar, "'Some of Us Who Deal with the Social Fabric.'"

5. Jane Addams, *Democracy and Social Ethics* (London: Macmillan, 1902), 11–12; Addams, *Newer Ideals of Peace*; Sklar, "'Some of Us Who Deal with the Social Fabric'"; Wendy Sarvasy, "A Global 'Common Table': Jane Addams's Theory of Democratic Cosmopolitanism and World Social Citizenship," in *Jane Addams and the Practice of Democracy*, ed. Marilyn Fischer, Carol Nackenoff, and Wendy Chmielewski (Urbana: University of Illinois Press, 2009), 183–202.

6. Addams, "Toward Internationalism," 60.

7. International Congress of Women, *Report*, 225.

8. Rupp, *Worlds of Women*, 108.

9. Rupp, *Worlds of Women*, 208.

10. Rupp, *Worlds of Women*, 99–100.

11. On U.S. women and World War I, see Kimberly Jensen, *Mobilizing Minerva: American Women in the First World War* (Urbana: University of Illinois Press, 2008); Erika A. Kuhlman, *Petticoats and White Feathers: Gender Conformity, Race, the Progressive Peace Movement, and the Debate over War, 1895–1919* (Westport, Conn: Greenwood Press, 1997); Early, *A World Without War*; Patterson, *The Search for Negotiated Peace.*

12. There are several good histories of WILPF. See Rupp, *Worlds of Women*; Carrie A. Foster, *The Women and the Warriors: The U.S. Section of the Women's International League for Peace and Freedom, 1915–1946* (Syracuse, N.Y.: Syracuse University Press, 1995); Linda K. Schott, *Reconstructing Women's Thoughts: The Women's International League for Peace and Freedom Before World War II* (Stanford, Calif.: Stanford University Press, 1997); Jo Vellacott, "A Place for Pacifism and Transnationalism in Feminist Theory: The Early Work of the Women's International League for Peace and Freedom," *Women's History Review* 2, 1 (1993): 23–56. For more on the post-World War I period in particular, see Erika A. Kuhlman, *Reconstructing Patriarchy After the Great War: Women, Gender, and Postwar Reconciliation Between Nations* (New York: Palgrave Macmillan, 2008).

13. On Addams, see Louise Knight, *Citizen: Jane Addams and the Struggle for Democracy* (Chicago: University of Chicago Press, 2005); Victoria Bissell Brown, *The Education of Jane Addams* (Philadelphia: University of Pennsylvania Press, 2004); Jean Bethke Elshtain, *Jane Addams and the Dream of American Democracy: A Life* (New York: Basic Books, 2002); Anne Firor Scott, "Jane Addams," in *Notable American Women, 1607–1950: A Biographical Dictionary*, ed. Edward T. James, Janet Wilson James, and Paul Boyer (Cambridge, Mass.: Belknap Press of Harvard University Press, 1971), 16–22. On Balch, see Kristen Gwinn, *Emily Greene Balch: The Long Road to Internationalism* (Urbana: University of Illinois Press, 2010); Barbara Miller Solomon, "Emily Greene Balch," in *Notable American Women: The Modern Period: A Biographical Dictionary*, ed. Barbara Sicherman and Carol Hurd Green (Cambridge, Mass.: Belknap Press of Harvard University Press, 1980), 41–45; Harriet Hyman Alonso, "Introduction," in Jane Addams, *Women at The Hague: The International Congress of Women and Its Results*, ed. Harriet Hyman Alonso (Urbana: University of Illinois Press, 2003).

14. Alonso, *Peace as a Women's Issue*, 93–95.

15. Nancy F. Cott, *The Grounding of Modern Feminism* (New Haven, Conn.: Yale University Press, 1987), 60–61.

16. Cott, *The Grounding of Modern Feminism*, 60–61.

17. Nancy Marie Robertson, *Christian Sisterhood, Race Relations, and the YWCA, 1906–46* (Urbana: University of Illinois Press, 2007), 48–49. On the YWCA, see also Nancy Boyd, *Emissaries, the Overseas Work of the American YWCA 1895–1970* (New York: Woman's Press, 1986); Daphne Spain, *How Women Saved the City* (Minneapolis: University of Minnesota Press, 2001); Nina Mjagkij and Margaret Spratt, eds., *Men and Women Adrift: The YMCA and the YWCA in the City* (New York: New York University Press, 1997); Karen Garner, "Global Feminism and Postwar Reconstruction: The World YWCA Visitation to Occupied Japan, 1947," *Journal of World History* 15, 2 (June 2004): 191–227; Littell-Lamb, "Caught in the Crossfire"; Dorothea Browder, "A 'Christian Solution of the Labor Situation': How Workingwomen Reshaped the YWCA's Religious Mission and Politics," *Journal of Women's History* 19, 2 (Summer 2007): 85–110.

18. Boyd, *Emissaries*; see also Littell-Lamb, "Caught in the Crossfire"; Sasaki, "American New Women Encountering China."

19. Browder, "A 'Christian Solution of the Labor Situation'"; Boyd, *Emissaries*, 78–79.

20. Boyd, *Emissaries*, 82, 111; Caroline Duval Smith, "Report to the Foreign Division," Reel 61, Microdex 6, YWCA of the U.S.A. Records (YWCA Records), Record Group 5: International Work, Sophia Smith Collection, Smith College, Northampton, Massachusetts.

21. Hereafter, unless otherwise indicated, "YWCA" refers to the YWCA of the U.S.A. The Mexican branch of the YWCA did not affiliate with the World YWCA until 1955.

22. "Biographical Note," Sarah Scudder Lyon Papers, Sophia Smith Collection, http://asteria.fivecolleges.edu/findaids/sophiasmith/mnsss418.html.

23. Boyd, *Emissaries*, 88–91.

24. "Emma Bain Weds Glenn Swiggett," *Bloomington Republican*, November 30, 1892, 3.

25. Swiggett to "newspapers," October 1, 1917, Box 2, Pan American International Women's Committee Papers (PAIWC Papers), Manuscript Division, Library of Congress, Washington, D.C.

26. "Quotations," Box 3, PAIWC Papers.

27. Gilderhus, *Pan American Visions*, 81. There is very little secondary literature on the committee; see Miller, "The International Relations of Women in the Americas," and Wamsley, "Constructing Feminism Across Borders." Both, however, overstate the connections between the PAIWC and the later Inter-American Commission of Women.

28. International Congress of Women, *Report*, 19.

29. Emily Greene Balch to Elena Torres, September 14, 1921, Reel 80, Women's International League for Peace and Freedom Papers, International Office (WILPF International Papers), University Library, University of Colorado at Boulder.

30. On these U.S. interventions, see Gilderhus, *Diplomacy and Revolution*; John S. D. Eisenhower, *Intervention! The United States and the Mexican Revolution, 1913–1917* (New York: Norton, 1993); Linda B. Hall and Don M. Coerver, *Revolution on the Border: The United States and Mexico, 1910–1920* (Albuquerque: University of New Mexico Press, 1988).

31. Gilderhus, *Pan American Visions*, 88.

32. Barry Carr, *Marxism and Communism in Twentieth-Century Mexico* (Lincoln: University of Nebraska Press, 1992), 16–29; see also Donald L. Herman, *The Comintern in Mexico* (Washington, D.C.: Public Affairs Press, 1974); Spenser, *The Impossible Triangle*.

33. John Womack, "The Mexican Revolution, 1910–1920," in *Mexico Since Independence*, ed. Leslie Bethell (New York: Cambridge University Press, 1991), 79–153; Vázquez and Meyer, *United States and Mexico*, 132–35.

34. See Ana Lau and Carmen Ramos-Escandón, *Mujeres y revolución, 1900–1917* (México, D.F.: Instituto Nacional de Estudios Históricos de la Revolución Mexicana, 1993); Olcott, *Revolutionary Women in Post-Revolutionary Mexico*; Mitchell and Schell, *The Women's Revolution in Mexico*; Macías, *Against All Odds*; Soto, *Emergence of the Modern Mexican Woman*.

35. Olcott, *Revolutionary Women in Post-Revolutionary Mexico*, 28–29; Macías, *Against All Odds*, 70.

36. For more on Alvarado and the Yucatán, see Joseph, *Revolution from Without*; Smith, *Gender and the Mexican Revolution*.

37. *El primer congreso feminista de Yucatán: Anales de esa memorable asamblea* (Mérida: Talleres Tipograficos del Ateneo Peninsular, 1916), 90–96.

38. "La Mujer en el porvenir: Discurso de la Srita. Hermila Galindo," in *El primer congreso feminista de Yucatán*, 195–200; Alaide Foppa, "The First Feminist Congress in Mexico, 1916," *Signs* 5, 1 (Autumn 1979): 192–99; Olcott, *Revolutionary Women in Postrevolutionary Mexico*, 30–31.

39. Francesca Miller, *Latin American Women and the Search for Social Justice* (Hanover, N.H.: University Press of New England, 1991): 76–77.

40. Macías, *Against All Odds*, 76.

41. Martha Eva Rocha, "The Faces of Rebellion: From Revolutionaries to Veterans in Nationalist Mexico," in *The Women's Revolution in Mexico*, 24–25; Macías, *Against All Odds*, 106–7.

42. Macías, *Against All Odds*, 96.

43. Cano, "Porfiriato and the Mexican Revolution," 115.

44. Torres to Byrns, 7 December 1919; [Torres], "Invitación del Consejo Feminista Mexicano, a todas las Mujeres," [December 1919], Box 1, Folder 4, Women's Peace Society Papers (WPS Papers), SCPC.

45. "Invitación del Consejo Feminista Mexicano, a todas las Mujeres," Folder 4, Box 1, WPS Papers.

46. Torres to Byrns, December 7, 1919.

47. "Invitación del Consejo Feminista Mexicano, a todas las Mujeres."

48. Torres to Byrns, December 7, 1919.

49. Swiggett to Eva Perry Moore, January 31, 1919, Box 1, PAIWC Papers.

50. Elisa Cortes, "War Work Done Among Mexican People on the Border, Sept. 12–Dec. 10," 2 January 1919, Reel 62, Microdex 1, YWCA Records.

51. Rosa Manus to Salvador Alvarado, 4 March 1917; Governor's aide to Manus, May 28, 1917,; Alvarado to Manus, eptember 6, 1917; Torres to Manus, November 11, 1917; all Reel 80, WILPF International Papers.

52. Torres to Byrns, December 7, 1919.

53. Manus to Alvarado, March 4, 1917; Swiggett to Adelia Palacios, February 9, 1917, Box 1, PAIWC Papers; Torres to Byrns, December 7, 1919.

54. Balch to Torres, January 24, 1922, Reel 80; Torres to Balch, April 9, 1922; both Reel 80, WILPF International Papers.

55. Palacios to Swiggett, April 30, 1921, Box 1, PAIWC Papers; "Report of Elena Landázuri to Foreign Division," Reel 61, Microdex 5, YWCA Records.

56. Rose Standish Nichols to Balch, May 18, 1920, Reel 80, WILPF International Papers.

57. Harriet Taylor and Caroline Duval Smith, "Report to Foreign and Overseas Committee of the National Board of the Young Women's Christian Association on a Study of the Situation of Women in Mexico," May–June 1921, Reel 61, Microdex 4, YWCA Records; Minutes of the Foreign and Overseas Department, June 9, 1921, Folder 7, Box 308A, YWCA Records.

58. Swiggett, *Report*, 7–13.

59. Swiggett, *Report*, 7.

60. Swiggett, *Report*, 23–25.

61. Catherine Allgor, *Parlor Politics: In Which the Ladies of Washington Help Rebuild a City and a Government* (Charlottesville: University Press of Virginia, 2000), 1.

62. Swiggett, *Report*, 27–28, 42–43.

63. Swiggett to Palacios, May 30, 1918, Box 1, PAIWC Papers.

64. *Bulletin of the Women's Auxiliary Conference of the Second Pan American Scientific Congress*, February 1921, Box 2, PAIWC Papers. Neither Swiggett nor many other members of the committee seem to have put this information to much use. They did not, for example, participate in a significant way in the Pan American Child Congresses. On the antagonisms between the PAIWC and the Child Congress, see Guy, "The Politics of Pan-American Cooperation."

65. Taylor and Smith, "Report."

66. Balch to Landázuri, January 23, 1922, Reel 80, WILPF International Papers.

67. Landázuri to Balch, March 7, 1922, Reel 80, WILPF International Papers.

68. Swiggett to Palacios, June 30, 1921, Box 1, PAIWC Papers.

69. Taylor and Smith, "Report"; Minutes of the Foreign and Overseas Department, June 9, 1921; Minutes of the Foreign Division, January 18, 1922, Folder 9, Box 308A, YWCA Records.

70. Torres to Balch, April 9, 1922.

71. Torres to Byrns, December 7, 1919.

72. Copy found in Landázuri to E. R. Freyman, August 1921, Reel 80, WILPF International Papers.

73. Palacios to Swiggett, January 7, 1918; Palacios to Swiggett, July 30, 1918; Palacios to Swiggett, March 6, 1920; all Box 1, PAIWC Papers.

74. Torres to Byrns, December 7, 1919.

75. Landázuri to Freyman, August 1921.

76. Charlotte Weber, "Between Nationalism and Feminism: The Eastern Women's Congresses of 1930 and 1932," *Journal of Middle East Women's Studies* 4, 1 (Winter 2008): 83–106; Rupp, *Worlds of Women*, 199–203.

77. Torres to Byrns, December 7, 1919.

78. Torres to Byrns, February 19, 1921.

79. Landázuri to Freyman, August 1921.

80. Torres to Villard, August 10, 1921.

81. Torres to Fanny Garrison Villard, August 10, 1921, Folder 4, Box 1, WPS Papers.

82. Byrns to Torres, April 4, 1921.

83. Bulletin, 1 September 1920, Series E, WILPF U.S. Records.

Chapter 2. The Pan American Conference of Women

1. "Call to Conference," Series I, Box 64, League of Women Voters Papers (LWV Papers), Manuscript Division, Library of Congress.

2. For a general history of the first fifty years of the league, see Louise M. Young, *In the Public Interest: The League of Women Voters, 1920–1970* (New York: Greenwood Press, 1989).

3. Secretary of State Charles Evans Hughes agreed to issue invitations to Latin American delegates through official State Department channels, even though the invitations made clear that the conference was not officially sponsored by the U.S. government.

4. Lavinia Engle to Maud Wood Park, [1921], Series II, Box 16, LWV Papers.

5. Carrie Chapman Catt to Park, August 8, 1921, Series II, Box 3, LWV Papers.

6. Judith N. McArthur and Harold L. Smith, *Minnie Fisher Cunningham: A Suffragist's Life in Politics* (New York: Oxford University Press, 2003).

7. Park to Charles Evans Hughes, July 8, 1921, Series II, Box 16, LWV Papers.

8. Park to Hughes, June 27, 1921, Series II, Box 16, LWV Papers; Park to Hughes, July 8, 1921.

9. Minnie Fisher Cunningham to Caroline Slade, October 1, 1921, Series I, Box 33, LWV Papers; Park to Hughes, October 5, 1921, Series I, Box 29, LWV Papers; Hughes to Park, 6 October 6, 1921, Series II, Box 16, LWV Papers.

10. Cunningham to Park, 13 October 1921, Series I, Box 29, LWV Papers.

11. Kristi Andersen, *After Suffrage: Women in Partisan and Electoral Politics Before the New Deal* (Chicago: University of Chicago Press, 1996): 36–37; Alonso, *Peace as a Women's Issue*, 85; Christine K. Erickson, "'So Much for Men': Conservative Women and National Defense in the 1920s and 1930s," *American Studies* 45, 1 (Spring 2004): 85–102.

12. "Two Great Conferences," *San Antonio Express*, April 22, 1922.

13. "An Event of the First Magnitude," *Baltimore Sun*, April 20, 1922. The Washington Naval Conference took place from November 1921 to February 1922; one of its results was a treaty limiting the naval armaments of the United States, Japan, Britain, France, and Italy.

14. Edwards to Drexel, February 27, 1922, Series I, Box 26, LWV Papers.

15. See Rupp, *Worlds of Women*, 85–86; Alonso, *Peace as a Women's Issue*, 10–12.

16. "Abridged Minutes of the Convention Proceedings: Third Annual Convention and the Pan American Conference of Women, Baltimore, April 20–30, 1922" (Baltimore: League of Women Voters, 1922), 8.

17. Marie Stewart Edwards to Constance Drexel, February 27, 1922.

18. Park to Carrie Chapman Catt, October 1, 1921, Series II, Box 3, LWV Papers.

19. P. L. Bell to Philip Smith, November 25, 1921, Series II, Box 16, LWV Papers.

20. "Obregón Finds Harding Friendly," *New York Times*, March 23, 1922.

21. Vázquez and Meyer, *The United States and Mexico*, 127–28.

22. Bell to Smith, January 26, 1922, Series II, Box 16, LWV Papers.

23. Bell to Smith, January 26, 1922; "Women Citizens at Work," *Woman Citizen*, April 8, 1922.

24. Dorothy Hubert to Elena Torres, January 3, 1922, Series II, Box 17, LWV Papers; Hubert to Smith, January 17, 1922, Series II, Box 16, LWV Papers; Elena Torres [to LWV], January 31, 1922, Series II, Box 17, LWV Papers.

25. Elena Landázuri to Jane Addams, April 3, 1922, Reel 14, Frame 1198, *The Jane Addams Papers, 1860–1960*, ed. Mary Lynn McCree Bryan (Ann Arbor: University Microfilms International, 1984) (Addams Papers).

26. "Women Citizens at Work"; "Flag Made by Mexican Women is Presented to Sisters of U.S.," *Baltimore Sun*, April 21, 1922.

27. "[Women] Accept a Mexican Flag," *New York Times*, April 28, 1922.

28. Park to Hughes, July 8, 1921.

29. Engle to Park, October 8, 1921, Series II, Box 16, LWV Papers.

30. Cunningham to Park, October 13, 1921.

31. Rosenberg, *Financial Missionaries to the World*, 122–50. On opposition to Dollar Diplomacy, see also Akira Iriye, *The Globalizing of America, 1913–1945*, Cambridge History of American Foreign Relations 3 (New York: Cambridge University Press, 1993); Joseph et al., *Close Encounters of Empire*; Warren Cohen, *Empire Without Tears: America's Foreign Relations, 1921–1933* (Philadelphia: Temple University Press, 1987).

32. In 1925 the LWV joined Carrie Chapman Catt's National Committee on the Cause and Cure of War, which criticized U.S. economic imperialism, but even then the LWV refrained from any strong statements on pacifism or military intervention. See Cott, *The Grounding of Modern Feminism*, 259–60.

33. Torres to LWV, February 16, 1922, Series II, Box 17, LWV Papers.

34. Hubert to Torres, March 16, 1922, Series II, Box 17, LWV Papers.

35. Lily T. Joseph, "Our Neighbor on the South," *Woman Citizen*, February 11, 1922, 16–17 (emphasis in original).

36. Joseph, "Our Neighbor on the South," 7, 16–17.

37. "National League of Women Voters Third Annual Convention and Pan American Conference of Women, Baltimore, Maryland, April 20–30, 1922" (hereafter cited as Transcript), Series I, Boxes 64 and 65, LWV Papers, vol. 4, 10.

38. Transcript, vol. 4, 6.

39. Transcript, vol. 4, 16.

40. Transcript, vol. 6, 85.

41. Eleanor Flexner, "Carrie Chapman Catt," in *Notable American Women, 1607–1950: A Biographical Dictionary*, ed. Edward T. James and Janet Wilson James (Cambridge, Mass.: Harvard University Press, 1971), 309–13; Jacqueline Van Voris, *Carrie Chapman Catt: A Public Life* (New York: Feminist Press, 1987).

42. Rosalyn Terborg-Penn, *African American Women in the Struggle for the Vote, 1850–1920* (Bloomington: Indiana University Press, 1998), and Terborg-Penn, "Enfranchising Women of Color."

43. Transcript, vol. 6, 142.

44. Transcript, vol. 6, 148.

45. On suffrage movements in Latin America during this period, see Asunción Lavrin, "Suffrage in South America: Arguing a Difficult Case," in Daley and Nolan, *Suffrage and Beyond*, 184–209; Miller, *Search for Social Justice*.

46. Transcript, vol. 6, 168. Catt and Lutz had a particularly close personal relationship. See Hahner, *Emancipating the Female Sex*, 138–44; Mineke Bosch, ed., *Politics and Friendship: Letters from the International Woman Suffrage Alliance, 1902–1942* (Columbus: Ohio State University Press, 1990), 181.

47. Transcript, vol. 6, 186.

48. Transcript, vol. 6, 177.

49. Transcript, vol. 4, 126–28.

50. "Women Delegates Cheer for Wilson," *Philadelphia Inquirer*, April 29, 1922; "Cheers, Songs, and Sobs of 1,000 Women Greet Former President Wilson," *Baltimore Sun*, April 29, 1922; "En Fete for Women," *Washington Post*, April 29, 1922.

51. "Pan-American Women," *Washington Post*, April 29, 1922.

52. "Address of the Honorable Calvin Coolidge, Vice-President of the United States at the Planting of the Tree Commemorative of the Pan American Conference of Women, at the PAU," April 28, 1922, Series II, Box 15, LWV Papers.

53. Transcript, vol. 7, Part 5, 6.

54. Transcript, vol. 7, Part 5, 13–24.

55. Transcript, vol. 7, Part 5, 36–37.

56. Transcript, vol. 7, Part 5, 62.

57. Transcript, vol. 7, Part 5, 54.

58. Transcript, vol. 7, Part 5, 45.

59. Transcript, vol. 7, Part 5, 67–68.

60. Transcript, vol. 7, Part 3, 28–30.

61. Park to members of the publications committee, June 9, 1922, Series I, Box 29, LWV Papers; see also "Abridged Minutes," 48–49.

62. Catt to Park, December 9, 1921, Series II, Box 3, LWV Papers.

63. Catt to Cunningham, March 23, 1922, Series II, Box 3, LWV Papers.

64. "Minutes of the Meeting of the Latin American Delegates" [April 1922], Series I, Box 29, LWV Papers; Park to the Publications Committee, June 9, 1922, Series I, Box 29, LWV Papers.

65. "The Provisional Pan American Association for the Advancement of Women," Series I, Box 29, LWV Papers.

66. "Minutes of the Meeting of the Latin American Delegates."

67. "The Provisional Pan American Association for the Advancement of Women."

68. Married women's economic rights were still very much the concerns of other U.S. feminists. See Cott, *The Grounding of Modern Feminism*, 185–91.

69. Torres touched on the labor question when she spoke to the roundtable on women in industry, but those remarks centered on Mexican women's participation in labor unions, whereas her argument in the memo focused on the general exploitation of all Mexican workers. Transcript, vol. 5, 343–35.

70. Landázuri to Addams, April 3, 1922.

71. "Pan-American Conference to Hear Problems," *San Antonio Express*, April 16, 1922.

72. Torres, untitled memorandum, Reel 80, WILPF International Papers.

73. Torres, untitled memorandum. For more on U.S. mining companies in Guanajuato, see Hart, *Empire and Revolution*, 143–45; on labor practices in Mexico among U.S. businesses in general, see O'Brien, *The Revolutionary Mission*, 251–84.

74. Elena Landázuri, untitled memorandum, Reel 80, WILPF International Papers.

75. Torres, untitled memorandum.

76. Landázuri, untitled memorandum.

77. Quoted in Cott, *The Grounding of Modern Feminism*, 107. See also Kirsten Delegard, *Battling Miss Bolsheviki: The Origins of Female Conservatism in the United States* (Philadelphia: University of Pennsylvania Press, 2012), 32–38; Kim Nielsen. *Un-American Womanhood: Antiradicalism, Antifeminism, and the First Red Scare* (Columbus: Ohio State University Press, 2001); Joan M. Jensen, "All Pink Sisters: The War Department and the Feminist Movement in the 1920s," in *Decades of Discontent: The*

Women's Movement, 1920–1940, ed. Lois Scharf and Joan M. Jensen (Westport, Conn.: Greenwood Press, 1983), 199–222.

78. "Blockade of Mexico Proposed in Senate," *New York Times*, April 22, 1922.

79. See Rupp, *Worlds of Women*, 77; Alonso, *Peace as a Women's Issue*, 114.

80. Lavrin, "Suffrage in South America," 184; see also Pernet, "Chilean Feminists, the International Women's Movement, and Suffrage, 1915–1950."

Chapter 3. The Limits of Human Internationalism

1. Catt, "Anti-Feminism in South America," *Current History* (September 1923): 1033.

2. Catt to Park, March 31, 1923, Series II, Box 52, LWV Papers.

3. Cunningham to Torres, April 30, 1923, Series II, Box 17, LWV Papers.

4. "Pan American League of Women," Series I, Box 29, LWV Papers.

5. Sarah A. Buck, "The Meaning of the Women's Vote in Mexico, 1917–1953," in Mitchell and Schell, *The Women's Revolution in Mexico*, 77–78.

6. "Pan American League of Women."

7. See Weber, "Unveiling Scheherazade"; Margot Badran, "Competing Agenda: Feminists, Islam, and the State in Nineteenth- and Twentieth-Century Egypt," in *Global Feminisms Since 1945*, ed. Bonnie Smith (New York: Routledge, 2000), 13–44; Ellen L. Fleischmann, "The Other 'Awakening': The Emergence of Women's Movements in the Modern Middle East, 1900–1940," in Offen, *Globalizing Feminisms*, 170–92.

8. Edith Stanton, "Report Concerning the first convention of the Mexican section of the Pan-American League for the Advancement of Women," Reel 61, Microdex 4, YWCA Records; Jessie Daniel Ames, "Report of the First Congress of the North American Section of the Pan American League of Women," Series II, Box 15, LWV Papers.

9. *Primer congreso feminista de la Liga Pan-America de Mujeres: conclusiones y discurso de clausura* (Mexico City: Talleres Linotipográficos "El Modelo," 1923), 3–5.

10. *Primer congreso feminista de la Liga Pan-America de Mujeres*, 3.

11. Olcott, *Revolutionary Women in Postrevolutionary Mexico*, 39–40.

12. Ames, "Report."

13. *Primer congreso feminista de la Liga Pan-America de Mujeres*, 4–5.

14. "El Aquelarre Feminista," *Excelsior*, May 24, 1923, 3.

15. "En Defensa de Ellas," *Excelsior*, May 28, 1923, 3.

16. "Feminismo y Maternidad," *El Democrata*, May 23, 1923, 3.

17. Ames, "Report."

18. Zonia Baber to Lucy Biddle Lewis, June 23, 1923, Series C, Box 1, Folder 16, WILPF U.S. Records.

19. "La Situación de las Mujeres en la República," *El Universal*, May 29, 1923, 1. The image of the "greaser," for example, was one of many popular stereotypes of Mexicans in U.S. films. See Allen L. Woll, *The Latin Image in American Film* (Los Angeles: UCLA Latin American Center Publications, 1980).

20. Baber to Lewis and Amy Woods, September 29, 1923, Series C, Box 1, Folder 16, WILPF U.S. Records.

21. Ames, "Report."

22. Ames, "Report."

23. Ames, "Report."

24. Ames, "Report."

25. Jacquelyn Dowd Hall, *Revolt Against Chivalry: Jessie Daniel Ames and the Women's Campaign Against Lynching* (New York: Columbia University Press, 1993), 53–54.

26. Catt, "Busy Women in Brazil," *Woman Citizen*, March 24, 1923, 9.

27. Catt, "The Woman Question in Chile," *Woman Citizen*, April 21, 1923, 10.

28. Catt, "Summing Up South America," *Woman Citizen*, June 2, 1923, 8.

29. Catt, "Summing Up South America," 26.

30. Catt to Park, March 31, 1923, Series II, Box 52, LWV Papers; Catt, "Anti-Feminism in South America"; Jacqueline Van Voris, *Carrie Chapman Catt: A Public Life* (New York: Feminist Press at the City University of New York, 1987), 176–78.

31. Catt to Executive Committee of the League of Women Voters, April 23, 1924, Series II, Box 136, LWV Papers.

32. See Van Voris, *Carrie Chapman Catt*, 180–83.

33. Landázuri to Addams, April 3, 1922.

34. Landázuri to Addams, July 4, 1922, Series C, Box 1, Folder 5, WILPF U.S. Records; Landázuri to Balch, July 16, 1922, Reel 80, WILPF International Papers.

35. Balch to Addams, June 28, 1922, Reel 14, Frame 1626, Addams Papers.

36. Baber to Lucy Biddle Lewis, September 21, 1922, Series C, Box 1, Folder 16, WILPF U.S. Records.

37. Anna Graves to Baber, April 22, 1923, Series C, Box 1, WILPF U.S. Records. For more on Graves, see Melinda Plastas, *A Band of Noble Women: Racial Politics in the Women's Peace Movement* (Syracuse, N.Y.: Syracuse University Press, 2011), 119–28.

38. Graves to Balch, August 31, 1923, Series C, Box 1, WILPF U.S. Records.

39. Balch to Graves, September 15, 1923, Series C, Box 2, Folder 15, WILPF U.S. Records.

40. Pan American Round Table Resolution, Box 3, PAIWC Papers.

41. The Mexican government failed to make payment on its foreign debt in 1924 and had asked for a loan from the United States. Palacios to Swiggett, May 23, 1924, Box 5, PAIWC Papers.

42. Swiggett to Palacios, June 3, 1924, Box 5, PAIWC Papers.

43. *Proceedings and Report of the Columbus Day Conferences Held in Twelve American Countries on October 12, 1923* (New York: Inter-America Press, 1926).

44. "Sent to National Sections of the Women's Pan Am National Committee holding Columbus Day Conferences," October 12, 1923, Box 5, PAIWC Papers.

45. Palacios to Swiggett, March 11, 1923, Box 6, PAIWC Papers.

46. Executive Committee of the Second Pan American Congress of Women to Miles Poindexter, June 23, 1924, Box 6, PAIWC Papers.

47. Woods to Addams, January 12, 1925, Reel 17, Frame 79, Addams Papers.

48. Swiggett to Catt, April 2, 1925, Box 2, PAIWC Papers.

49. Annual Report, December 1924, Reel 61, Microdex 6, YWCA Records.

50. Caroline Duval Smith, "Report to the Foreign Division," Reel 61, Microdex 6, YWCA Records.

51. Elena Landázuri, "Report to the World's Committee of the Young Women's Christian Association and the Foreign Division," Reel 61, Microdex 5, YWCA Records.

52. Landázuri, "Report to World's Committee and the American National Board of the Young Women's Christian Association," Reel 61, Microdex 5, YWCA Records.

53. Carmen Gomez Siegler, "Report of the Mother's Club," Reel 61, Microdex 4, YWCA Records; Smith, "Report to the World's Committee and to the American National Board of the Young Women's Christian Association," Reel 61, Microdex 6, YWCA Records.

54. Graves to Balch, 31 August 1923, Series C, Box 1, WILPF U.S. Records.

55. John Dwyer, *The Agrarian Dispute: The Expropriation of American-Owned Rural Land in Postrevolutionary Mexico* (Durham, N.C.: Duke University Press, 2008), 37–38.

56. Graves to Balch, August 31, 1923.

57. Graves to Balch, August 31, 1923.

58. Rupp, *Worlds of Women*, 77–78.

59. Olcott, *Revolutionary Women in Postrevolutionary Mexico*, 12.

60. "Report of Carrie Chapman Catt on South American and European Trip, 1922–1923," Box 3, Carrie Chapman Catt Papers (Catt Papers), Manuscript Division, Library of Congress.

61. Catt to Park, March 31, 1923.

62. Catt to "American friends," March 6, 1923, Box 3, Catt Papers.

63. Catt to Mary Garrett Hay, January 28, 1923, Box 3, Catt Papers.

64. Brudena Mofoid to Harriet Taylor, July 1923, Reel 61, Microdex 5, YWCA Records.

65. Mary Wilhelmine Williams to Brinton, August 21, 1934, Series A4, Box 12, Folder 3, WILPF U.S. Records.

66. Balch to Elena Landázuri, April 13, 1922, Reel 80, WILPF International Papers.

67. See, among others, Reginald Horsman, *Race and Manifest Destiny: The Origins of American Racial Anglo-Saxonism* (Cambridge, Mass.: Harvard University Press, 1981); Matthew Frye Jacobson, *Whiteness of a Different Color: European Immigrants and the Alchemy of Race* (Cambridge, Mass.: Harvard University Press, 1998); Paul A. Kramer, "Empires, Exceptions, and Anglo-Saxons: Race and Rule Between the British and United States Empires, 1880–1910," *Journal of American History* 88, 4 (March 2002): 1315–53.

68. Terborg-Penn, *African American Women in the Struggle for the Vote*; Newman, *White Women's Rights*; Plastas, *A Band of Noble Women*; Robertson, *Christian Sisterhood, Race Relations, and the YWCA*.

69. Fredrick B. Pike, *The United States and Latin America: Myths and Stereotypes of Civilization and Nature* (Austin: University of Texas Press, 1992), 47–52.

70. Florence Terry Griswold, untitled address, May 1923, Box 16, Folder 36, Pan American Round Table of San Antonio Records (PART Records), 1909–1994, MS 3, UTSA Archives, Library, University of Texas at San Antonio.

71. "Report of Carrie Chapman Catt on South American and European Trip."

72. Williams to Brinton, June 29, 1934, Reel 92, WILPF International Papers.

73. Taylor and Smith, "Report to Foreign and Overseas Committee."

74. Thomas E. Skidmore, "Racial Ideas and Social Policy in Brazil, 1870–1940," in *The Idea of Race in Latin America, 1870–1940*, ed. Richard Graham (Austin: University of Texas Press, 1990), 21–23.

75. "Report of Carrie Chapman Catt on South American and European Trip." On *mestizaje* in Latin America in the early twentieth century, see José Vasconcelos, *The Cosmic Race: A Bilingual Edition*, trans. Didier Tisdel Jaén (Baltimore: Johns Hopkins University Press, 1997); Graham, *The Idea of Race in Latin America*; Marilyn Grace Miller, *Rise and Fall of the Cosmic Race: The Cult of Mestizaje in Latin America* (Austin: University of Texas Press, 2004).

76. "Elena Landázuri," from unknown periodical, 1922, Reel 61, Microdex 5, YWCA Records.

77. Jane Addams to Balch, October 26, 1920, Reel 14, Frame 548, Addams Papers.

78. Edith Stanton to Irene Sheppard, June 20, 1923, Reel 61, Microdex 4, YWCA Records.

79. Balch, "Statement on Behalf of the Women's International League for Peace and Freedom," May 1924, Series C, Box 1, Folder 17, WILPF U.S. Records.

80. Griswold, "Woman's Place and Sphere in Pan Americanism," November 1923, Box 13, Folder 6, PART Records.

81. Griswold, "Outline of Pan American Activities Under Direction of PART of SA, TX, 1916–1936," 1936, Box 1, Folder 3, PART Records; Griswold, untitled address delivered in Mexico City, October 7, 1938, Box 16, Folder 32, PART Records.

82. Alice Thacher Post, "Pan-American Conference," April 1922, Box 2, PAIWC Papers.

83. "Sent to National Sections of the Women's Pan Am National Committee holding Columbus Day Conferences Oct 12, 1923—it was read at all the Conferences," Box 5, PAIWC Papers.

84. *Proceedings and Report of the Columbus Day Conferences*.

85. Sheinin, "Rethinking Pan Americanism: An Introduction," in Sheinin, *Beyond the Ideal*, 1.

86. "Report of Discussions on Internationalism by City, Finance, Foreign and Education Staff Representatives," Box 305, Folder 8, YWCA Records.

87. "Report of Discussions on Internationalism."

88. Catt to Margaret Ashby, February 7, 1925, Reel 10, Papers of the National American Woman Suffrage Association, Manuscript Division, Library of Congress, Washington, D.C., quoted in Rupp, *Worlds of Women*, 78.

89. "Minutes of the Pan American Conference," April 29–May 2, 1925, Series II, Box 50, LWV Papers.

90. "Minutes of the Pan American Conference"

91. "Minutes of the Pan American Conference"

92. "Farewell Address of Mrs. Catt," Series II, Box 50, LWV Papers. It should be noted that the "minor question" Catt referred to was the Fifteenth Amendment, which granted suffrage to African American men and was one of the most divisive and emotional issues of the entire U.S. women's suffrage movement. See Ellen Carol DuBois, *Feminism and Suffrage: The Emergence of an Independent Women's Movement in America, 1848–1869* (Ithaca, N.Y.: Cornell University Press, 1978), 162–202.

93. Richard M. Whitney, *Peace at Any Old Price* (New York: Beckwith Press, 1923), 3.

94. Cott, *The Groundings of Modern Feminism*, 249–50; Nielsen, *Un-American Womanhood*, 76–77; Christy Jo Snider, "Patriots and Pacifists: The Rhetorical Debate About Peace, Patriotism, and Internationalism, 1914–1930," *Rhetoric & Public Affairs* 8, 1 (Spring 2005): 59–83.

95. On the ties between feminism and the Mexican Communist Party, see Olcott, *Revolutionary Women in Postrevolutionary Mexico*, 47–52.

96. Macías, *Against All Odds*, 131; Olcott, *Revolutionary Women in Postrevolutionary Mexico*, 109. See also James Horn, "U.S. Diplomacy and 'The Specter of Bolshevism' in Mexico (1924–1927)," *The Americas* 32, 1 (July 1975): 31–45.

97. "Minutes of the meeting of the board of officers of the IAUW, held at the Headquarters of the National LWV on May 4th, 1925," Series II, Box 50, LWV Papers.

98. Bertha Lutz to Belle Sherwin, October 13, 1925, Series II, Box 50, LWV Papers.

99. Esther de Calvo to Catt, November 25, 1925, Series II, Box 50, LWV Papers.

100. De Calvo to Catt, May 11, 1926, Box 3, PAIWC Papers.

Chapter 4. The "Peace with Mexico" Campaign

1. "What Americans Have at Stake in Mexico," *New York Times*, February 20, 1927, 16. See also Dwyer, *The Agrarian Dispute*, 37–43.

2. Vázquez and Meyer, *The United States and Mexico*, 129–31. On U.S.-Mexican relations during the 1920s, see Meyer, *Mexico and the United States in the Oil Controversy*; Spenser, *The Impossible Triangle*; Katz, *The Secret War in Mexico*; Hall, *Oil, Banks, and Politics*; Harrison, *Dollar Diplomat*; Horn, "U.S. Diplomacy and 'The Specter of Bolshevism' in Mexico"; Smith, *The United States and Revolutionary Nationalism in Mexico*; Moreno, *Yankee Don't Go Home!*.

3. Amy Woods, "America's Imperialism," *Bulletin of the United States Section* 5 (May 1923): Series E, WILPF U.S. Records

4. Vázquez and Meyer, *The United States and Mexico*, 135–36.

5. Frank B. Kellogg to James Sheffield, June 12, 1925, 711.12/546a, Record Group 59, U.S. State Department Papers, National Archives, Washington, D.C. (hereafter State Department papers will be cited by decimal file number only). See also L. Ethan Ellis, *Frank B. Kellogg and American Foreign Relations, 1925–1929* (New Brunswick, N.J.: Rutgers University Press, 1961).

6. "Memorandum for Use Before the Foreign Relations Committee," undated, *817.00/4852*. See also Jürgen Buchenau, *In the Shadow of the Giant: The Making of Mexico's Central America Policy, 1876–1930* (Tuscaloosa: University of Alabama Press, 1996); Richard V. Salisbury, *Anti-Imperialism and International Competition in Central America, 1920–1929* (Wilmington, Del.: SR Books, 1989).

7. "Mexico Torn Between Church and State," *New York Times*, August 1, 1926, 1. See also Jennie Purnell, *Popular Movements and State Formation in Revolutionary Mexico: The Agraristas and Cristeros of Michoacán* (Durham, N.C.: Duke University Press, 1999).

8. "Says We Have Duty in Mexican Trouble," *New York Times*, August 2, 1926, 2.

9. Knights of Columbus, *Red Mexico: The Facts* (New Haven, Conn.: Supreme Council, 1926), 2.

10. Spenser, *The Impossible Triangle*, 69–70.

11. Michael Krenn, *U.S. Policy Toward Economic Nationalism in Latin America, 1917–1929* (Wilmington, Del.: SR Books, 1990), 58–65; see also Lars Schoultz, *Beneath the United States: A History of U.S. Policy Toward Latin America* (Cambridge, Mass.: Harvard University Press, 1998), 277–78.

12. Francis White, "Cuba, Panama, and South America," Lectures to the Foreign Service School, Department of State, May 13, 14, 16, 18, 1925, quoted in Schoultz, *Beneath the United States*, 278.

13. Memorandum, Division of Latin American Affairs, August 22, 1922, 832.00/255.

14. James Rockwell Sheffield to Nicholas Murray Butler, November 17, 1925, Sheffield Papers, Yale University, quoted in Schoultz, *Beneath the United States*, 279.

15. Charles DeBenedetti, *The Peace Reform in American History* (Bloomington: Indiana University Press, 1980), 109.

16. Rosenberg, *Financial Missionaries to the World*, 123.

17. Among single-sex peace groups, the most notable absences here are the Women's Peace Union and the Women's Peace Society. Neither had the resources to contribute substantially to the Peace with Mexico campaign.

18. Charles DeBenedetti, *Origins of the Modern American Peace Movement, 1915–1929* (Millwood: KTO Press, 1978), 96–97.

19. For more on the CCCW, see Susan Zeiger, "Finding a Cure for War: Women's Politics and the Peace Movement in the 1920s," *Journal of Social History* 24, 1 (Autumn 1990): 69–86.

20. "Women Exclude Peace Societies," *New York Times*, December 11, 1924, 26.

21. "Attack on U.S. Stirs War Cure Congress," *New York Times*, December 10, 1926, 14.

22. Henry Lane Wilson to Catt, December 29, 1926, Carton 10, Committee on the Cause and Cure of War Records, 1923–1948 (CCCW Records), Schlesinger Library, Radcliffe Institute, Harvard University.

23. Catt to Nicholas Murray Butler, January 4, 1927, Carton 10, CCCW Records.

24. Catt to Josephine Schain, January 5, 1927, Carton 10, CCCW Records.

25. Joan M. Jensen, "All Pink Sisters: The War Department and the Feminist Movement in the 1920s," in *Decades of Discontent: The Women's Movement, 1920–1940*, ed. Lois Scharf and Joan M. Jensen (Westport, Conn.: Greenwood Press, 1983), 200, 216.

26. Jensen, "All Pink Sisters," 200; Alonso, *Peace as a Women's Issue*, 108–9.

27. "Mrs. Catt Hits Back on Peace Meeting," *New York Times*, December 2, 1926, 7.

28. Gladys K. G. McKenzie, "Historical Introduction," Records of National Council for Prevention of War (NCPW Records), DG 023, SCPC.

29. Harriet Hyman Alonso, *The Women's Peace Union and the Outlawry of War, 1921–1942* (Knoxville: University of Tennessee Press, 1989).

30. Frederick Libby, *To End War: The Story of the National Council for the Prevention of War* (Nyack, N.Y.: Fellowship Publications, 1969), 54.

31. [Untitled], 6 May 1930, Box 1, Folder 1, Laura Puffer Morgan and Ethel Puffer Howes Papers, 1862–1962 (Morgan and Howes Papers), Schlesinger Library, Radcliffe Institute, Harvard University; "Laura Puffer Morgan," 1941, Box 1, Folder 1, Morgan and Howes Papers.

32. "News Letter," May 1926, Series E, WILPF U.S. Records.

33. Harriet Hyman Alonso, "Dorothy Detzer," in *Notable American Women: A Biographical Dictionary Completing the Twentieth Century*, ed. Susan Ware (Cambridge, Mass.: Belknap Press of Harvard University Press, 2004), 169–71; Dorothy Detzer, *Appointment on the Hill* (New York: Henry Holt, 1948); Dorothy Detzer to Libby, April 5, 1924, Box 168, Folder 5, NCPW Records.

34. U.S. Senate Committee on Foreign Relations, *Foreign Loans*, February 25, 1925, quoted in Rosenberg, *Financial Missionaries to the World*, 139.

35. "Doherty Discusses Mexican Oil Laws," *New York Times*, June 21, 1926, 2; "Hands Off Mexico, Is Coolidge Policy," *New York Times*, August 7, 1926, 1; "America Protests Again to Mexico," *New York Times*, August 7, 1926, 2; "Stiff Note to Mexico on Oil Is Indicated," *New York Times*, October 28, 1926, 7; "Calles to Change Oil and Land Laws if Facts Justify It," *New York Times*, September 2, 1926, 1; Meyer, *Mexico and the United States in the Oil Controversy*, 122; "Sheffield to Stay as Envoy in Mexico," *New York Times*, August 20, 1926, 3.

36. "Nicaragua Installs Diaz," *New York Times*, November 15, 926, 4; "American Forces Ready to Compel Nicaraguan Peace," *New York Times*, November 19, 1926, 1;

"Nicaragua Charges Mexico is Preparing for Offensive War," *New York Times*, December 12, 1926, 1; "Sacasa Says Diaz Tried to Deceive U.S.," *New York Times*, December 15, 1926, 32.

37. "Kellogg Bars the Entry of Mme. Kollontai, Soviet Woman Envoy, on Her Way to Mexico," *New York Times*, November 5, 1926, 1; "Red Envoy in Mexico Denies Propaganda," *New York Times*, March 10, 1927, 5.

38. [Detzer], "News of the U.S. Section," *Pax International*, December 1926.

39. Report to the Executive Committee, December 14, 1926, Series A2, Box 5, Folder 18, WILPF U.S. Records.

40. Detzer to Madeleine Doty, December 23, 1926, Series C, Box 11, Folder 10, WILPF U.S. Records; [Detzer], "Let Us Have Peace with Mexico," *News of the U.S. Section*, December 1926, Series E, WILPF U.S. Records.

41. Libby to "Friend," December 31, 1926, Box 356, Folder 2, NCPW Records.

42. "Peace for Mexico Campaign," December 1926, Box 354, Folder 9, NCPW Records.

43. Laura Puffer Morgan to Sidney Gulick, December 21, 1926; Morgan to Catherine Gerwick, December 21, 1926; both Box 355, Folder 9, NCPW Records.

44. Morgan to Gerwick, December 21, 1926.

45. Libby to "Friend," December 31, 1926.

46. "Calles Gives Order to Enforce Oil Law," *New York Times*, January 5, 1927, 3.

47. "Coolidge Is Assailed in Both Houses for Policy in Mexico and Nicaragua," *New York Times*, January 9, 1927, 1.

48. Meyer, *Mexico and the United States in the Oil Controversy*, 127–28.

49. "Kellogg Offers Evidence of Red Plots in Nicaragua and Aid from Calles," *New York Times*, January 13, 1927, 1.

50. "Minutes of second meeting of Committee on Peace with Latin America," January 12, 1927, Box 354, Folder 8, NCPW Records.

51. "Statements of Support," January 1927, Box 354, Folder 8, NCPW Records.

52. Minutes of CPLA Meeting, January 16, 1927, Box 354, Folder 8, NCPW Records.

53. Untitled Report of the Peace with Latin America Meeting, January 16, 1927, Box 354, Folder 8, NCPW Records.

54. Johnson, *The Peace Progressives and American Foreign Relations*, 125.

55. "The Situation in Mexico and Nicaragua," January 14, 1927, Box 356, Folder 2, NCPW Records.

56. Johnson, *The Peace Progressives and American Foreign Relations*, 124.

57. Detzer to Doty, February 23, 1927, Series C, Box 11, Folder 10, WILPF U.S. Records.

58. Johnson, *The Peace Progressives and American Foreign Relations*, 231–32.

59. Clara Mortenson Beyer to "Friend," January 28, 1927, Box 354, Folder 8, NCPW Records.

60. Beyer to "Editor," February 25, 1927, Box 354, Folder 8, NCPW Records.

61. Beyer to Ruth Morgan, February 4, 1927, Series II, Box 107, LWV Papers.

62. *NCPW News Bulletin* 6, 3 (1 March 1927), Box 355, Folder 5, NCPW Records; Libby to "Friend," March 8, 1927, Box 354, Folder 9, NCPW Records; Beyer to "Editor," March 15, 1927, Box 354, Folder 8, NCPW Records; Beyer to "Friend," 25 March 1927, Box 354, Folder 8, NCPW Records; Meyer, *Mexico and the United States in the Oil Controversy*, 128.

63. Press release, March 16, 1927, Box 355, Folder 4, NCPW Records.

64. Press release, March 17, 1927, Box 356, Folder 2, NCPW Records.

65. CPLA to "Friend," March 18, 1927, Box 356, Folder 2, NCPW Records.

66. Beyer to Julia Lathrop, March 23, 1927, Box 355, Folder 4, NCPW Records.

67. Meyer, *Mexico and the United States in the Oil Controversy*, 129–37; James J. Horn, "Did the United States Plan an Invasion of Mexico in 1927?," *Journal of Inter-American Studies and World Affairs* 15, 4 (November 1973): 454–71; Richard V. Salisbury, "Mexico, the United States, and the 1926–1927 Nicaraguan Crisis," *Hispanic American Historical Review* 66, 2 (May 1986): 319–39; Jürgen Buchenau, *Plutarco Elías Calles and the Mexican Revolution* (Lanham, Md.: Rowman and Littlefield, 2007), 130–35.

68. "Red Envoy in Mexico Linked to Our Note," *New York Times*, March 13, 1927, 24; "Mme. Kollontai Sails," *New York Times*, June 6, 1927, 12.

69. "Coolidge Defines Our World Policies," *New York Times*, April 26, 1927, 1.

70. "Sheffield Resigns; Coolidge Praises His Work in Mexico," *New York Times*, July 9, 1927, 1.

71. Meyer, *Mexico and the United States in the Oil Controversy*, 130.

72. Meyer, *Mexico and the United States in the Oil Controversy*, 135.

73. Morgan, "Public Opinion and Our Foreign Policy," April 30, 1927, Box 2, Folder 41, Morgan and Howes Papers.

74. Annual Report of Executive Secretary, 1927, Series A2, Box 5, Folder 22, WILPF U.S. Records.

75. "Mexican Women for Peace," *New York Times*, January 21, 1927, 4.

76. Alonso, *Peace as a Women's Issue*, 114.

Chapter 5. Politicizing Internationalism

1. Doris Stevens, "International Feminism is Born," *Time and Tide* 9, 15 (April 13, 1928): 354–55.

2. Doris Stevens, "Address before a special plenary session of 6th Pan American Conference, 1928," February 7, 1928, MC 546, Folder 94.4, Doris Stevens Papers (Stevens Papers), Schlesinger Library, Radcliffe Institute, Harvard University.

3. The international campaign for "equal nationality" sought to reform laws that limited or stripped a woman of citizenship in the country of her birth when she married a foreign national.

4. Stoner, *From the House to the Streets*, 187.

5. Stoner, "In Four Languages But with One Voice," 85.

6. Stoner, "In Four Languages But with One Voice," 86–87.

7. Doris Stevens, "Address Before a Special Plenary session of 6th Pan American Conference, 1928."

8. "Sixth International Conference of American States," *Pan American Union Bulletin*, April 1928, 1.

9. Stevens, "International Feminism Is Born," 354–55.

10. Stevens, "International Feminism Is Born," 355.

11. "Report of work done from April 1928 to April 1929 by the IACW," II: 241, National Woman's Party Records (NWP Records), Manuscript Division, Library of Congress.

12. Stevens, unpublished manuscript, Folder 126.7, Stevens Papers. For more on this aspect of the IACW approach, see Beatrice McKenzie, "The Power of International Positioning: The National Woman's Party, International Law and Diplomacy, 1928–1934," *Gender & History* 23, 1 (April 2011): 130–46.

13. For more on Stevens's life and career, see Leila Rupp, "Feminism and the Sexual Revolution in the Early Twentieth Century: The Case of Doris Stevens," *Feminist Studies* 15, 2 (Summer 1989): 289–309; Mary Trigg, "'To Work Together for Ends Larger Than Self': The Feminist Struggles of Mary Beard and Doris Stevens in the 1930s," *Journal of Women's History* 7, 2 (Summer 1995): 52–85.

14. Stevens, unpublished manuscript, Folder 126.7, Stevens Papers.

15. For more on this debate, see Susan Becker, "International Feminism Between the Wars: The National Woman's Party Versus the League of Women Voters," in *Decades of Discontent: The Women's Movement, 1920–1940*, ed. Lois Scharf and Joan M. Jensen (Westport, Conn.: Greenwood Press, 1983), 223–42; Susan Becker, *The Origins of the Equal Rights Amendment: American Feminism Between the Wars* (Westport, Conn.: Greenwood Press, 1981); Cott, *Grounding of Modern Feminism*; Candice Lewis Bredbenner, *A Nationality of Her Own: Women, Marriage, and the Law of Citizenship* (Berkeley: University of California Press, 1998); Naomi Black, *Social Feminism* (Ithaca, N.Y.: Cornell University Press, 1989).

16. Lavrin, *Women, Feminism, and Social Change*, 14. See also Lavrin, "Suffrage in South America."

17. "Foreign Policy—1926–1927," Box 305, Folder 8, YWCA Records.

18. "Recommendations from Miss Leona Scott, Mexico City," Reel 61, Microdex 6, YWCA Records.

19. Elizabeth Curtiss, "The Y.W.C.A. in Mexico," Reel 61, Microdex 5, YWCA Records.

20. Curtiss to Sarah Lyon, January 1928, Reel 61, Microdex 5, YWCA Records.

21. "Report of Elizabeth H. Curtiss to the General Meeting of the YWCA, Mexico City" Reel 61, Microdex 5, YWCA Records; Curtiss, "The Y.W.C.A. in Mexico."

22. Curtiss, "Health Needs of Mexican Women Being Met by Y.W.C.A.," Reel 61, Microdex 5, YWCA Records.

23. Myra Smith, "Report on Mexico Visit," Reel 61, Microdex 6, YWCA Records.

24. Smith, "Report on Mexico Visit."

25. "Recommendations from Miss Leona Scott"; Scott to Lyon, July 12, 1927, Reel 61, Microdex 6, YWCA Records.

26. "Recommendations from Miss Leona Scott."

27. Smith, "Report on Mexico Visit."

28. Smith, "Report on Mexico Visit."

29. Margaret K. Strong and C. E. Silcox, "Area Report on Latin America," 95, Box 328, Folders 4 and 5, YWCA Records, 148.

30. Strong and Silcox, "Area Report on Latin America," 157–58.

31. Perry, "An Open Letter from Mexico," April 17, 1931, Reel 61, Microdex 6, YWCA Records.

32. Mildred Scott Olmsted, "A Mexican Section Begins," *News of the U.S. Section* (September 1928): 3, Series E, WILPF U.S. Records. On Olmsted, see also Margaret Hope Bacon, *One Woman's Passion for Peace and Freedom: The Life of Mildred Scott Olmsted* (Syracuse, N.Y.: Syracuse University Press, 1993).

33. Minutes of the National Board Meeting, October 14 and 15, 1928, Series A2, Box 2, Folder 1, WILPF U.S. Records.

34. Olmsted, "A Mexican Section Begins," 3.

35. Minutes of the National Board Meeting, December 5, 1928, Series A2, Box 6, Folder 1, WILPF U.S. Records.

36. Balch to Sybil Jane Moore, March 26, 1929, Series C, Box 12, Folder 24, WILPF U.S. Records.

37. Dorothy Detzer to Mexican Ambassador, March 27, 1929, Series C, Box 12, Folder 24, WILPF U.S. Records.

38. Moore to Detzer, May 29, 1929, Series C, Box 12, Folder 24, WILPF U.S. Records.

39. Moore to Detzer, May 29, 1929.

40. Minutes of the National Board Meeting, November 2, 1929, Series A2, Box 6, Folder 4, WILPF U.S. Records.

41. Lowrie to Balch, March 24, 1930, Series C, Box 12, Folder 14, WILPF U.S. Records; Lowrie to Detzer, March 29, 1930, Series C, Box 12, Folder 14, WILPF U.S. Records.

42. Clemencia de Kiel to Mary Sheepshanks, May 18, 1930, Reel 80, WILPF International Papers.

43. Kiel to Sheepshanks, June 5, 1930, Reel 80, WILPF International Papers.

44. Minutes of National Board meeting, April 8, 1930, Series A2, Box 2, Folder 7, WILPF U.S. Records.

45. "Brief Summary, Inter American Conference, Mexico City, July 9, 10, 11, 12, 15," Reel 80, WILPF International Papers.

46. "Brief Summary, Inter American Conference, Mexico City."

47. Minutes of National Board Meeting, October 21, 1930, Series A2, Box 6, Folder 7, WILPF U.S. Records.

48. "Confidential Information Prepared for the International Survey in Mexico," Reel 62, Microdex 1, YWCA Records.

49. Moore to Balch, April 28, 1929, Series C, Box 12, Folder 24, WILPF U.S. Records.

50. Sybil Jane Moore to Detzer, April 21, 1929, Series C, Box 12, Folder 24, WILPF U.S. Records; Emily Greene Balch to Ellen Starr Brinton, 16 July 1934, Reel 92, WILPF International Papers.

51. Balch to Elena Landázuri, 13 April 1922, Reel 80, WILPF International Papers.

52. Smith, "Report on Mexico Visit."

53. Joanne Hershfield, *Imagining La Chica Moderna: Woman, Nation, and Visual Culture in Mexico, 1917–1936* (Durham, N.C.: Duke University Press, 2008).

54. "Annual Report to the Foreign Division [1933–1934]," Reel 61, Microdex 4, YWCA Records.

55. Dorothy Detzer, "Report of the Executive Secretary," 1931, Series A2, Box 6, Folder 12, WILPF U.S. Records.

56. Moore to Balch, 28 April 1929, Series C, Box 12, Folder 24, WILPF U.S. Records.

57. Brinton, "Co-operation Between U.S. and Mexican W.I.L."

58. Alonso, *Peace as a Women's Issue*, 102.

59. Moore to Balch, April 28, 1929.

60. Walter Nugent, *Into the West: The Story of Its People* (New York: Knopf, 1999), 234–38; Francisco E. Balderrama and Raymond Rodríguez, *Decade of Betrayal: Mexican Repatriation in the 1930s* (Albuquerque: University of New Mexico Press, 2006), 118–19; Camille Guerin-Gonzales, *Mexican Workers and American Dreams: Immigration, Repatriation, and California Farm Labor, 1900–1939* (New Brunswick, N.J.: Rutgers University Press, 1994), 78–79.

61. Nellie Foster to Detzer, October 30, 1931, Series C, Box 12, Folder 24, WILPF U.S. Records.

62. Ellen Carol DuBois, "Internationalizing Married Women's Nationality: The Hague Campaign of 1930," in Offen, *Globalizing Feminisms*, 214.

63. DuBois, "Internationalizing Married Women's Nationality"; McKenzie, "The Power of International Positioning"; Garner, *Shaping a Global Women's Agenda*; Rupp, *Worlds of Women*; Paula Pfeffer, "'A Whisper in the Assembly of Nations': United States' Participation in the International Movement for Women's Rights from the League of Nations to the United Nations," *Women's Studies International Forum* 8, 5 (1985): 459–71; Becker, "International Feminism Between the Wars," in Scharf and Jensen, *Decades of Discontent*, 223–42; Bredbenner, *A Nationality of Her Own*; Warren F. Kuehl and Lynne K. Dunn, *Keeping the Covenant: American Internationalists and the League of Nations, 1920–1939* (Kent, Ohio: Kent State University Press, 1997).

64. Margarita Robles de Mendoza to Stevens, May 2, 1929, Folder 76.24, Stevens Papers. See also Lau Jaiven, "Entre ambas fronteras."

65. "Memorandum concerniente al nombramiento de la Senora MRM en la CIM," Folder 77.6, Stevens Papers.

66. Jaiven, "Entre ambas fronteras," 237.

67. Robles de Mendoza to Plutarco Elias Calles, 6 March 1932, Folder 77.7, Stevens Papers (emphasis in original). See also Buck, "The Meaning of the Women's Vote in Mexico," 82–86.

68. Buck, "The Meaning of the Women's Vote in Mexico," 78–83, emphasis in original.

69. Robles de Mendoza declared herself committed to the equal rights platform, although it is difficult to tell where her commitment originated, or how fully she understood it. In 1931 she argued that feminism encompassed women's political, economic, social, and personal rights; feminists could be focused on "economic or social aspects of the movement" without "meddling in political affairs." No member of the NWP would have agreed with such an assertion. See Robles de Mendoza, *La evolución de la mujer en México* (Mexico City: Imprente Galas, 1931), 97–98, 100.

70. See Jaiven, "Entre ambas fronteras," 251.

71. Robles de Mendoza to Stevens, June 27, 1930, Folder 77.6, Stevens Papers.

72. "Ladies in Politics," *Washington Post*, January 30, 1932, 24; Robles de Mendoza to *Chicago Tribune*, February 8, 1932, Folder 77.6, Stevens Papers.

73. Robles de Mendoza to Stevens, June 14, 1931, Folder 77.6, Stevens Papers.

74. It is worth noting that Ana Lau Jaiven's portrayal of Robles de Mendoza's role on the commission is much more flattering, though it is based entirely on books and sources produced by Robles de Mendoza herself. Jaiven, "Entre ambas fronteras."

75. James Brown Scott, ed., *The Inter-American Commission of Women: Documents Concerning Its Creation and Organization* (Washington, D.C.: Pan American Union, 1935), 36, 35.

76. "The Inter-American Commission of Women: Documents Concerning Its Creation and Organization," Series II, Box 239, NWP Papers.

77. *Seventh International Conference of American States, Montevideo, Uruguay, December 2–26, 1933: Final Act* (Montevideo: J. Florensa Cerrito, 1934), 42.

78. *Final Act*, 145.

79. Scott, *The Inter-American Commission of Women*, 27.

80. Stoner, "In Four Languages But with One Voice," 91.

81. Becker, "International Feminism Between the Wars," 230.

82. "Strictly confidential memorandum Re Attitude and Conduct of IACW," [n.d.], Folder 127.9, Stevens Papers.

83. "Factors Surrounding the Conference Contributing to Our Success," [n.d.], Folder 127.8, Stevens Papers.

Chapter 6. Not Such Good Neighbors

1. Franklin Roosevelt, "First Inaugural Address," March 4, 1933, Avalon Project at Yale Law School.

2. Fredrick B. Pike, *FDR's Good Neighbor Policy: Sixty Years of Generally Gentle Chaos* (Austin: University of Texas Press, 1995); David Green, *The Containment of Latin America: A History of the Myths and Realities of the Good Neighbor Policy* (Chicago: Quadrangle, 1971); Irwin F. Gellman, *Good Neighbor Diplomacy: United States Policies in Latin America, 1933–1945* (Baltimore: Johns Hopkins University Press, 1979). From the Mexican perspective, see Friedrich Engelbert Schuler, *Mexico Between Hitler and Roosevelt: Mexican Foreign Relations in the Age of Lázaro Cárdenas, 1934–1940* (Albuquerque: University of New Mexico Press, 1998).

3. Mary Kay Vaughan, *Cultural Politics in Revolution: Teachers, Peasants, and Schools in Mexico, 1930–1940* (Tucson: University of Arizona Press, 1997), 7–8; Alan Knight, "Cardenismo: Juggernaut or Jalopy?" *Journal of Latin American Studies* 26, 1 (February 1994): 73–107.

4. Knight, "Cardenismo."

5. Brinton, "Report of Committee on Latin American Contacts," Series A4, Box 1a, Folder 1, WILPF U.S. Records.

6. Brinton to Crooks, 21 December 1934, Series A4, Box 17, Folder 2, WILPF U.S. Records.

7. Crooks to Hull, 9 June 1935, Series C, Box 18, WILPF U.S. Records.

8. Hull to International office, [n.d.], reel 92, WILPF International Papers.

9. Anne Yoder, *Papers of Heloise Brainerd*, CDG-A, SCPC.

10. Brainerd, "Inter-American Committee Report," January 1936, Series A4, Box 1a, folder 1, WILPF U.S. Records.

11. Brainerd, "Inter-American Committee Report," January 1936.

12. Brainerd, "Report on Work in Mexico for WILPF and People's Mandate Committee," March 2, 1936, Series A4, Box 1a, Folder 1, WILPF U.S. Records; Brainerd to Detzer, March 15, 1936, Series C, Box 17, Folder 16, WILPF U.S. Records; Detzer to Gertrude Baer, May 27, 1936, Series C, Box 17, Folder 7, WILPF U.S. Records.

13. Brainerd, "Report of the Inter-American Committee," October 15, 1936, Series A4, Box 1a, Folder 1, WILPF U.S. Records.

14. Brainerd, "Report of the Inter-American Committee."

15. Brainerd, "Report on Work in Mexico"; Brainerd to Detzer, March 15, 1936.

16. Brainerd, "Carta Circular #1," June 22, 1936, Reel 92, WILPF International Papers.

17. Kiel to Baer, 24 March 1936, Reel 80, WILPF International Papers.

18. "World Cooperation of the Young Women's Christian Associations of the United States of America: A Record of the Foreign Work of the American Associations, 1936–1941," comp. Alison H. Currie, Box 305, Folder 2, YWCA Records.

19. Margaret E. Forsyth, "Confidential Report of Visit to Mexico City," Reel 61, Microdex 4, YWCA Records; Katharine Briggs, "Suggested Outline of Data: Mexico," Reel 61, Microdex 5, YWCA Records.

20. "Memorandum in Regard to the Work of the Foreign Division Within the United States," Box 305, Folder 8, YWCA Records (emphasis in original).

21. Quoted in "Memorandum in Regard to the Work of the Foreign Division."

22. "Paragraph on Mexico prepared by Miss Myra Smith following her visit in the summer of 1934," Reel 61, Microdex 4, YWCA Records; Forsyth, "Confidential Report"; Minutes of the Foreign Division, June 7, 1938, Box 308A, Folder 21, YWCA Records.

23. Forsyth, "Confidential Report."

24. Perry to Miss Lanham, February 24, 1936, Reel 61, Microdex 6, YWCA Records.

25. Perry to Sarah Lyon, February 22, 1935, Reel 61, Microdex 6, YWCA Records; Matthew Redinger, *American Catholics and the Mexican Revolution, 1924–1936* (Notre Dame, Ind.: University of Notre Dame Press, 2005), 95.

26. Forsyth, "Confidential Report."

27. Briggs to Moore, January 29, 1936, Reel 61, Microdex 5, YWCA Records.

28. Forsyth, "Confidential Report."

29. Forsyth, "Confidential Report."

30. Guadalupe Ramirez, "The Education and Problems of the Mexican Woman," Reel 61, Microdex 6, YWCA Records.

31. Olcott, *Revolutionary Women in Postrevolutionary Mexico*, 4.

32. *Seventh International Conference of American States, Montevideo, Uruguay, December 2–26, 1933: Final Act* (Montevideo: J. Florensa Cerrito, 1934), 43.

33. Press release, May 7, 1934, Series II, Box 241, NWP Papers.

34. "The First Treaty Giving Complete Equality to Women in the History of the World Signed at Montevideo," *Equal Rights* (July 7, 1934): 179.

35. Bredbenner, *A Nationality of Her Own*, 243.

36. Olcott, *Revolutionary Women in Postrevolutionary Mexico*, 162.

37. Macías, *Against All Odds*, 132.

38. Press release, February 19, 1935, Series II, Box 241, NWP Papers.

39. Brainerd to Frances Benedict Stewart, 27 June 1937, Series A4, Box 17, Folder 7, WILPF U.S. Records.

40. Samuel Guy Inman, *Inter-American Conferences, 1826–1954: History and Problems* (Washington: University Press, 1965), 160–61.

41. Franklin D. Roosevelt, "Address Before the Inter-American Conference for the Maintenance of Peace, Buenos Aires, Argentina," December 1, 1936, American Presidency Project, online by Gerhard Peters and John T. Woolley.

42. Gellman, *Good Neighbor Diplomacy*, 61–67; Inman, *Inter-American Conferences*, 160–80.

43. Brainerd, "Annual Report of the Inter American Committee," May 3, 1937, Series A4, Box 1a, Folder 1, WILPF U.S. Records.

44. Stevens to Detzer, July 2, 1936, Folder 62.14, Stevens Papers.

45. IACW to Tulio M. Cestero, December 15, 1936, Series B, Box 11, Records of the People's Mandate Committee, SCPC.

46. Hannah Clothier Hull to Cordell Hull, July 4, 1936, Folder 62.14, Stevens Papers.

47. "Text of Resolution on Women's Rights Adopted by the People's Conference for the Peace of America, Buenos Aires, November 22–25, 1936," Series II, Box 241, NWP Papers.

48. Doris Stevens, "The Rights of Women in Inter-American Relations," Folder 91.7, Stevens Papers.

49. Stevens to Robles de Mendoza, 24 May 1937, Folder 77.8, Stevens Papers.

50. Hazel Moore to Stevens, August 12, 1937, Folder 67.2, Stevens Papers.

51. Robles de Mendoza to Fanny Sevastos, August 25, 1937, Folder 77.8, Stevens Papers; Moore to Stevens, 29 August 1937, Folder 67.2, Stevens Papers; Stevens to Moore, September 14, 1937, Folder 67.2, Stevens Papers.

52. Anna Kelton Wiley to Stevens, 26 May 1937, Folder 93.4, Stevens Papers; "Speech of Mrs. Harvey W. Wiley before the Frente Único Pro-Derechos de la Mujer," May 26, 1937, Folder 93.4, Stevens Papers.

53. "Message of Cuca Garcia to the Women of North America," May 10, 1937, Folder 93.4, Stevens Papers.

54. Lotti Birch to Kiel, 21 August 1937, Reel 80, WILPF International Papers; Baer to Brainerd, 12 October 1937, Series A4, Box 13, Folder 4, WILPF U.S. Records; Baer to Marta B. de Mues, 12 October 1937, Reel 80, WILPF International Papers.

55. Stewart to Brainerd, September 7, 1937, Series A4, Box 17, Folder 7, WILPF U.S. Records.

56. Crooks to Brainerd, September 3, 1937, Series A4, Box 17, Folder 2, WILPF U.S. Records; Stewart to Brainerd, September 7, 1937, Series A4, Box 17, Folder 7, WILPF U.S. Records; Sue Perry to Brainerd, September 3, 1937, Series A4, Box 28, Folder 1, WILPF U.S. Records; Kiel to Brainerd, October 28, 1937, Series A4, Box 28, Folder 2, WILPF U.S. Records.

57. Stewart to Brainerd, September 7, 1937.

58. Brainerd to Baer, September 10, 1937, Series A4, Box 13, Folder 4, WILPF U.S. Records.

59. Mues to Brainerd, May 11, 1938, Series A4, Box 28, Folder 2, WILPF U.S. Records.

60. See Meyer, *Mexico and the United States in the Oil Controversy*, 157–72; George W. Grayson, *Oil and Mexican Foreign Policy* (Pittsburgh: University of Pittsburgh Press, 1988); Catherine E. Jayne, *Oil, War, and Anglo-American Relations: American and British Reactions to Mexico's Expropriation of Foreign Oil Properties, 1937–1941* (Westport, Conn.: Greenwood Press, 2001); Clayton R. Koppes, "The Good Neighbor Policy and the Nationalization of Mexican Oil: A Reinterpretation," *Journal of American History* 69, 1 (June 1982): 62–81.

61. Meyer, *Mexico and the United States in the Oil Controversy*, 171.

62. Bernard Baruch to Franklin Delano Roosevelt, October 11, 1938, Bernard Baruch Papers, Seeley Mudd Manuscript Library, Princeton University, quoted in Schoultz, *Beneath the United States*, 306.

63. María Refugio García to Stevens, April 21, 1938, Folder 77.3, Stevens Papers; Stevens to García, May 2, 1938, Folder 77.3, Stevens Papers.

64. Briggs to Cotton, March 25, 1938, Reel 61, Microdex 5, YWCA Records.

65. Detzer, "Annual Report of the Executive Secretary," April 29, 1938, Series A2, Box 9, Folder 6, WILPF U.S. Records.

66. Branch Letter 66, October 28, 1938, Series E, Box 2, WILPF U.S. Records.

67. Brainerd, "Annual Report of the Committee for the Americas," April 1938, Series A4, Box 1a, Folder 2, WILPF U.S. Records.

68. Brainerd, "The Peace Outlook on the Latin American Front," Series A2, Box 9, Folder 4, WILPF U.S. Records.

69. Blanca Saunders, "Mexico and Her Good Neighbor," December 10, 1938, Series A4, Box 1a, Folder 2, WILPF U.S. Records.

70. Meyer, *Mexico and the United States in the Oil Controversy*, 192.

71. Crooks, "The People's Mandate to End War at the Lima Conference," February 15, 1939, Box 3, Folder 9, PART Papers.

72. Cordell Hull, *Report of the delegation of the United States of America to the Eighth International Conference of American States, Lima, Peru, December 9–27, 1938* (Washington, D.C.: Government Printing Office, 1938), 8.

73. Carnegie Endowment for International Peace, *International Conferences of American States: First Supplement, 1933–1940* (Washington, D.C.: Carnegie Endowment for International Peace), 250–51.

74. "Equal Rights Plan of Women Revised," *New York Times*, December 17, 1938, 9.

75. In making the commission permanent, the delegates agreed that nations that had not yet appointed official representatives had to do so as soon as possible. While the Pan American Union had appointed Stevens chair of the commission in 1928, she had never been formally named U.S. representative to it. The agreement was thus a backhanded way to destabilize Stevens's status and allow the United States to name a different woman as its commissioner.

76. Alonso, *Peace as a Women's Issue*, 136–46.

77. Vázquez and Meyer, *The United States and Mexico*, 148–52.

78. "Memorandum on Adoption of New Policy by the Foreign Division, 1940," Box 305, Folder 8, YWCA Records.

79. Stevens to Florence Bayard Hilles, March 6, 1939, Folder 31.9, Stevens Papers.

80. Elinor Byrns to Stevens, February 17, 1939, Folder 62.2, Stevens Papers.

81. Eleanor Roosevelt to Una Winter, February 28, 1939, Folder 125.1, Stevens Papers.

82. Robles de Mendoza to Stevens, February 25, 1939, Folder 77.8, Stevens Papers.

83. The IACW headquarters moved back to Washington in 1943, where it remains to this day.

84. Macías, *Against All Odds*, 112–13.

85. Olcott, *Revolutionary Women in Postrevolutionary Mexico*, 183.

86. Olcott, *Revolutionary Women in Postrevolutionary Mexico*, 184–85; for more on the long suffrage battle in Mexico, see Gabriela Cano, "Una ciudadanía igualitaria: El presidente Lázaro Cárdenas y el sufragio feminino," *Desdeldiez* (1995): 69–116; Ward Morton, *Woman Suffrage in Mexico* (Gainesville: University Press of Florida, 1962); Carmen Ramos Escandón, "La participacion politica de la mujer en Mexico: del fusil al voto 1915–1955," *Boletin Americanista* 44 (1994): 155–69; Enriqueta Tuñón, *Por fin . . . ya podemos elegir y ser electas! El sufragio femenino en México, 1935–1953* (Mexico, D.F.: Instituto Nacional de Antropología y Historia, 2002).

Epilogue

1. Diego Rivera, *My Art, My Life: An Autobiography* (New York: Citadel Press, 1960), 244.

2. Delpar, *The Enormous Vogue of Things Mexican*; see also Corinne Pernet, "'For the Genuine Culture of the Americas': Musical Folklore, Popular Arts, and the Cultural Politics of Pan Americanism, 1933–1950," in *Decentering America*, ed. Jessica C. E. Gienow-Hecht (New York: Berghahn, 2007), 132–68.

3. Van Voris, *Carrie Chapman Catt*, 217–18.

4. Libby, *To End War*, 177–83.

5. Helen Laville, *Cold War Women: The International Activities of American Women's Organisations* (Manchester: Manchester University Press, 2002), 68–91.

6. Mire Koikari, "Exporting Democracy? American Women, Feminist Reforms, and the Politics of Imperialism in the U.S. Occupation of Japan, 1945–1952," *Frontiers: A Journal of Women's Studies* 23, 1 (2002): 29.

7. Laville, *Cold War Women*; Alonso, *Peace as a Women's Issue*. On the work of the IACW for the rest of the twentieth century, see Inter-American Commission of Women, *History of the Inter-American Commission of Women (CIM), 1928–1997* (Washington, D.C.: CIM/OEA, 1999).

8. Margaret Snyder, "Unlikely Godmother: The UN and the Global Women's Movement," in *Global Feminism: Transnational Women's Activism, Organizing, and Human Rights*, ed. Myra Marx Ferree and Aili Mari Tripp (New York: New York University Press, 2006), 24–50; see also Arvonne S. Fraser, *The U.N. Decade for Women: Documents and Dialogue* (Boulder, Colo.: Westview, 1987); Judith P. Zinsser, "From Mexico to Copenhagen to Nairobi: The United Nations Decade for Women, 1975–1985," *Journal of World History* 13, 1 (Spring 2002): 139–68.

9. For a general introduction to the conflicts between "First World" and "Third World" feminists since 1975, see Wendy S. Hesford and Wendy Kozol, eds., *Just Advocacy? Women's Human Rights, Transnational Feminisms, and the Politics of Representation* (New Brunswick, N.J.: Rutgers University Press, 2005); Cynthia Enloe, *The Curious Feminist: Searching for Women in a New Age of Empire* (Berkeley: University of California Press, 2004); Bonnie G. Smith, "Introduction," in Smith, *Global Feminisms Since 1945*, 1–10.

Index

Acknowledgments

I have received inestimable guidance and support since I began this book more than ten years ago. The bulk of my research was accomplished thanks to grants and fellowships from the History Department and the Graduate College at the University of Iowa, the National Society of the Colonial Dames in the State of Iowa, the Schlesinger Library at the Radcliffe Institute in Cambridge, Massachusetts, the Ohio Academy of History, the Society for Historians of American Foreign Relations, and Denison University. Several friends and family members further subsidized my research by providing food and shelter, including Laurisa Sellers and Arnie Shore in Boston, and Geneva Overholser, David Westphal, and Cindy Threlkeld in Washington, D.C. Members of the staff at the Library of Congress Manuscript Reading Room, the Swarthmore College Peace Collection, the Schlesinger Library, and the Sophia Smith Collection at Smith College offered helpful and cheerful assistance. A semester's leave from Denison University was crucial to finishing the manuscript.

Colleagues and friends at the University of Iowa helped launch the project that became this book. In particular I want to thank Michel Gobat, Claire Fox, Colin Gordon, Michaela Hoenicke-Moore, Erica Hannickel, Dana Quartana, Sharon Romeo, Christy Clark-Pujara, and Charissa Threat. I owe a special debt of gratitude to Linda Kerber, whose counsel and example I appreciate more with each passing year.

The welcoming and stimulating scholarly community I found at Denison University has further enriched this book. Along with their friendship and plenty of good food, members of my department have offered useful comments on portions of the book: Lauren Araiza, Adam Davis, Cathy Dollard, Barry Keenan, Marlee Meriwether, Trey Proctor, Don Schilling, Mitchell Snay, and Karen Spierling. I am also grateful to my students for their insights and enthusiasm, and for reminding me of the interconnections between my research and teaching. Special thanks go to Brittani Ferguson, Michaela Grenier, Natalie Gross, Meghan Hillman Lynch, and Hannah Miller.

I am fortunate to have found support in my larger scholarly communities as well. Dirk Bönker, Jennifer Morris, Jonathan Winkler, and Molly Wood provided helpful feedback on pieces of the manuscript. Frank Costigliola, Kristin Hoganson, and Kathryn Kish Sklar offered encouragement at key moments. Kim Jensen and Erika Kuhlman did both, repeatedly; I am so thankful for their input and assurances over the last several years.

My experience with the University of Pennsylvania Press has been very rewarding. Thank you especially to Bob Lockhart, whose guidance and enthusiasm have sustained me over the last few years. The feedback I received from the two anonymous readers and from series editor Glenda Gilmore helped make this book much stronger.

I am grateful to Republic of Letters Publishing for permission to reproduce portions of "How to 'Make This Pan American Thing Go?' Interwar Debates on U.S. Women's Activism in the Western Hemisphere," originally published in Women and Transnational Activism in Historical Perspective, ed. Kimberly Jensen and Erika Kuhlman (Dordrecht: Republic of Letters, 2010), and to Wiley-Blackwell and the Society for Historians of American Foreign Relations for permission to reproduce portions of "The Pan American Conference of Women, 1922: Successful Suffragists Turn to International Relations," Diplomatic History 31, 5 (November 2007): 801–28.

The process of securing permission to reproduce the image on the cover of this book was long and complicated, and could not have been accomplished without Hannah Rhadigan at the Artist Rights Society and Will Maynez at the City College of San Francisco. Will's dedication to the Diego Rivera Mural Project at CCSF is truly extraordinary.

My deepest thanks go to my friends and family. From Iowa to Minnesota to Wisconsin to Massachusetts to Ohio and beyond, I am blessed to have so many enduring, sustaining relationships. Sarah Hunt, Courtney Gerber, and their families have enriched my life for almost twenty years. Life in Granville wouldn't be nearly so much fun without Marlaine Browning, Amanda Gunn, Anna Nekola, and Heather and Adam Rhodes.

Finally, I want to acknowledge the loving support I have received over the years from my entire extended, blended family. Thank you especially to my stepdaughter, Taylor Proctor; to my siblings, Phoebe Becker, Breck Burns, and Brian Threlkeld; and to all my parents: Wes Burns, Jill Palmer, Ann Proctor, Frank Proctor, Arnie Shore, and especially Laurisa Sellers and Mark Threlkeld. This book is dedicated to my husband, Trey Proctor, who makes me laugh, makes me think, makes me dinner, and makes everything worthwhile.